MODERN CHESS
MINIATURES

by

LEONARD BARDEN
British Champion (1954)

and

WOLFGANG HEIDENFELD
Eight times S. African Champion (1939-60)
Irish Champion (1958)

DOVER PUBLICATIONS, INC.
NEW YORK

Published in Canada by General Publishing Com-
pany, Ltd., 30 Lesmill Road, Don Mills, Toronto,
Ontario.
Published in the United Kingdom by Constable
and Company, Ltd., 10 Orange Street, London
WC2H 7EG.

This Dover edition, first published in 1977, is an
unabridged and unaltered republication of the work
first published by Routledge & Kegan Paul, London, in 1960.

International Standard Book Number: 0-486-23541-6
Library of Congress Catalog Card Number: 77-78590

Manufactured in the United States of America
Dover Publications, Inc.
180 Varick Street
New York, N.Y. 10014

CONTENTS

Preface   *page* xi

1 THE GIUOCO PIANO
  1 Corte-Bolbochan. Mar del Plata, 1946   1
  2 Heidenfeld-Zietemann. Berlin, 1929   1

2 TWO KNIGHTS' DEFENCE
  3 Durao-Prins. Malaga, 1954   2
  4 Wirtz-Fahnenschmidt. Marburg, 1955   3
  4a Foltys-Rossolimo. Amsterdam, 1950   3
  5 Alexander-Euwe. Utrecht, 1949   4
  5a Kinzel-Dückstein. Vienna 1958   4

3 RUY LOPEZ
  6 Incutto-Keres. Mar del Plata, 1957   5
  6a Spassky-Fuderer. Vienna, 1957   5
  7 Honan-Mardle. Correspondence, 1958   6
  7a Zaitsev-Rochlin. Yaroslavl, 1954   6
  8 Karaklaic-Rellstab. West Germany *v*. Yugoslavia, 1956   7
  8a Soultanbéieff-X. Liège, 1923   7
  9 Schmid-Herzog. Dresden, 1943   8
  9a Eriksen-Dreyer. Johannesburg, 1956   8
  10 Tal-Teschner. Vienna, 1957   8
  11 Farré-Pomar. Spain, 1958   9
  12 Madame Zvorykina-Gladkov. White Russia, 1958   10
  13 Schmid-Enevoldsen. Travemünde, 1951   11
  14 Bisguier-Toran. Munich, 1958   12
  14a Varain-X. Leipzig, 1890   12
  15 Matanovic-Janosevic. Yugoslavia, 1953   13
  16 Zaitsev-Timchenko. Moscow, 1956   13
  17 Schmid-Welz. Radebeul, 1945   14

4 FOUR KNIGHTS' GAME
  18 Posch-Dorrer. Vienna, 1957 (?)   15

5 PETROFF'S DEFENCE
  19 Sanguinetti-Puiggros. Mar del Plata, 1957   16
  20 Keres-Alexander. Hastings, 1954/55   17

6 EVANS GAMBIT
  21 Ciocaltea-Brzozka. Polanica, 1958   18
  21a Tchigorin-X.   18
  22 Clemenz-Eisenschmidt. Dorpat, 1862   19

v

CONTENTS

7   SCOTCH GAME AND SCOTCH GAMBIT
    23 Penrose-Blau. Hastings, 1957/58   *Page* 20
    23a Martin-Pompei. Rapperswil, 1955   20
    24 Lepichin-Tarasov. Novosibirsk, 1958   21

8   DANISH GAMBIT
    25 Wysowski-Rozman. Correspondence, 1951   22

9   KING'S GAMBIT
    26 Stoltz-Sämisch. Swinemünde, 1932   23
    27 Horseman-Horne. Hastings, 1955/56   24
    28 Podgorny-Stulik. Czechoslovakia, 1956   25
    29 Schuster-Karl. Heilbronn, 1957   26

10 FALKBEER COUNTER GAMBIT
    30 Marshall-Von Soldatenkov. New York, 1926 (?)   27

11 VIENNA GAMBIT
    31 Milner-Barry-Hanninen. Moscow, 1956   28
    31a Honfi-Kluger. Budapest, 1958   28

12 PHILIDOR'S DEFENCE
    32 Adams-Torre. New Orleans, 1920   29
    33 Heidenfeld-Wolpert. Johannesburg, 1955   30

13 FRENCH DEFENCE
    34 Rossetto-Stahlberg. Vina del Mar, 1947   31
    35 Keres-Wade. Anglo-Soviet Match, 1954   32
    36 Giusti-Cipriani. Correspondence, 1954/55   33
    37 Oxford University-Canisius College. Correspondence, 1958   34
    38 Schmeil-Mertins. Berlin, 1957   35
    39 Barendregt-Van Oosterwijk Bruin. Holland, 1951   36
    40 Kunin-Ochsengoit. Moscow, 1958   36
    41 Fichtl-Winiwarter. Salzbrunn, 1957   37
    42 Bonsdorff-Liipola. Helsinki, 1957   38
    43 Janosevic-Ugrinovic. Belgrade, 1958   39
    44 Perfors-van Seters. Wageningen, 1955   39
    45 Rabar-Matulovic. Sombor, 1957   40
    46 Foulds-Lang. New Zealand, 1956   41
    46a Herter-Nievergelt. Stuttgart, 1957   41
    47 Diemer-Illig. Correspondence, 1954   42

14 SICILIAN DEFENCE
    48 Farré-Gudmundsson. Munich, 1958   43
    48a Rubenchik-Kanayan. White Russia, 1957   43
    48b Joppen-Schneider. West Germany, 1958   43
    48c Rhodin-Siegel. Landau, 1958   44
    48d Rhodin-Behrenbruch. Hamburg, 1957   44
    49 Galula-Leone. Paris, 1955   44

CONTENTS

50 Moran-Franco. Gijon, 1955   *Page* 45
50a Kondratjev-Rovner. Leningrad, 1956   45
51 Sterner-Boleslavsky. Russia *v.* Sweden, 1954   46
51a Kalkstein-Gligoric. Montevideo, 1953   47
52 Söderborg-Olafsson. Reykjavik, 1957   48
53 Sherbakov-Taimanov. Russian Championship Semi-Finals, 1954   48
54 Geller-Vatnikov. Kiev, 1950   49
55 Perez-Toran. Gijon, 1956   50
56 Hearst-Franklin. Correspondence, 1955   51
56a Lepikhin-Alekseev. White Russia, 1955   51
57 Boey-O'Kelly. Belgium, 1957   52
58 Keres-Sajtar. Amsterdam, 1954   53
58a Goldin-Ambarian. Armenia, 1955   53
59 Kluger-Nagy. Budapest, 1942   54
60 Rossetto-Behrensen. Mar del Plata, 1958   54
61 Jezek-Boleslavsky. Vienna, 1957   55
61a Wade-Boxall. Bognor Regis, 1953   55
62 Junge-Sahlmann, Hamburg, 1944   56
62a Olafsson-Gudmundsson. Reykjavik, 1953   56
63 Klovan-Pukudruva. Latvia, 1955   57
63a Dubinin-Suetin. Moscow, 1953   57
64 Olafsson-Pilnik. Reykjavik, 1957   58
65 O'Kelly-Ahlbach. Correspondence, 1938   59
66 Canal-Scafarelli. San Benedetto del Tronto, 1957   59
66a Horowitz-X. Chicago, 1958   59
67 Haag-Koranyi. Budapest, 1953   60
67a Roiter-Boleslavsky. Kiev, 1958   60
68 Fichtl-Gereben. Warsaw, 1956   61
69 Thal-Granitzky. East Germany, 1958   62
69a Tartakower-Andor. Paris, 1952   62

15 CARO-KANN DEFENCE
70 Bilek-Bronstein. Budapest, 1955   63
71 Harnik-Mieses. Vienna, 1936   64
72 Mora-Lange. Luxemburg, 1955   65
73 Espeli-Andersen. Oslo, 1952   66

16 CENTRE COUNTER GAME
74 Karakhan-Kakabadze. Leningrad, 1957   66

17 ALEKHINE'S DEFENCE
75 Scholtens-van Oosterwijk Bruin. Holland, 1944   68
76 Bogolyubov-Barnstedt. South Baden, 1950   69

18 NIMZOVITCH'S DEFENCE
77 Rojahn-Czerniak. Buenos Aires, 1939   69

19 PIRC DEFENCE
78 Balogh-Sandor. Budapest, 1956   71
78a Pedersen-Keller. Helsinki, 1952   71
79 Radulescu-Pirc. Balkan Team Tournament, 1956   72

CONTENTS

20 ROBATSCH DEFENCE

80	Kilyin-Gurgenidze. Rostov, 1958	*Page* 72
81	Karaklaic-Robatsch. Smederevska Palanka, 1956	73

21 QUEEN'S GAMBIT

82	Casas-Piazzini. Buenos Aires, 1952	74
83	Gereben-Komarov. Leningrad, 1949	74
84	Ahman-Malmgren. Correspondence, 1947	75
85	Borisenko-Keres. U.S.S.R. Championship, 1955	76
86	Borisenko-Jaroslavtsev. U.S.S.R. Championship, 1957	77
86a	Borisenko-Gorfinkel. U.S.S.R., 1955	77
87	Bolbochan-Pachman. Moscow, 1956	77
88	Christoffersen-Harksen. Correspondence, 1915	78
89	Tal-Milev. Munich, 1958	79
90	Miroshnichenko-Anokhin. Kirgisia, 1957	80
91	Tolush-Furman. Moscow, 1957	80
92	Szekely-Canal. Budapest, 1933	81
93	Vidmar-Christoffel. Basle, 1952	82
94	Panno-Keller. Moscow, 1956	83
95	Vera Menchik-Sonja Graf. Semmering, 1937	84
96	Johansson-Nilsson. Amsterdam, 1954	85
96a	Rosenberg-Tartakower. Paris, 1954	85
97	Reti-Grau. London, 1927	85

22 ALBIN COUNTER GAMBIT

98	Woolverton-Pritchard. London, 1959	87
99	Sämisch-Medina. Madrid, 1943	87

23 BLACKMAR GAMBIT

100	Bartsch-Jennen. Essen, 1948	88
101	Diemer-Fuller. Hastings, 1957/58	89
101a	Diemer-Kloss. Correspondence, 1958	89

24 STAUNTON GAMBIT

102	Barda-Rossolimo. Hastings, 1949/50	90
102a	Toran-Canal. Venice, 1953	90
103	Edgar-Lott. Correspondence, 1955	91

25 OLD INDIAN DEFENCE

104	Korchnoi-Zilber. Russian Team Championship, 1958	92
104a	Meyer-Schmid. Correspondence, 1948	92

26 KING'S INDIAN DEFENCE

105	Donner-Euwe. Match, 1955	93
105a	Smyslov-Plater. Moscow, 1947	93
106	Ravinsky-Bronstein. Moscow, 1953	94
107	Oren-Dyner. Tel Aviv, 1952	94
108	Wallis-Horseman. Nottingham, 1954	95
109	Tarasov-Buslaev. Tiflis, 1956	96
109a	Rabar-Znosko-Borovsky. Lucerne, 1949	96

CONTENTS

110 Szukszta-Tal. Uppsala, 1956   *Page* 97
111 Smollny-Asafov. Leningrad, 1956   97
111a Bisguier-Baker. New York, 1958   97
112 Darga-Toran. Luxemburg, 1955   98
112a Keres-Geller. Russia, 1952   98
113 Darga-Wade. Moscow, 1956   99
114 Freeman-Mednis. New York 1955   100
114a Mühlberg-Averbakh. Dresden, 1956   100
115 Rojahn-Angos. Munich, 1958   100

27 GRÜNFELD DEFENCE

116 Gruber-Bozic. Skopje, 1950   101
116a Smyslov-Botvinnik. Match, 1958   101
117 Kiarner-Rozhdestvensky. Estonia, 1958   102
117a Padevsky-Korchnoi. Uppsala, 1956   102
118 Szabo-Olafsson. Dallas, 1957   103
118a Feuerstein-Bennett. New York, 1955   103
119 Tartakower-Stumpers. Baarn, 1947   104

28 BENONI DEFENCE

120 Naylor-Wade. Whitby, 1958   105
120a Smyslov-Schmid. Helsinki, 1952   105
121 Averbakh-Tolush. Training Game, 1952   106
121a Bolotsov-Mühlberg. Varna, 1957   106
122 Shaposhnikov-Bastrikov. White Russia, 1954   107
122a Matchett-O'Kelly. Bognor Regis, 1956   107
122b Van Scheltinga-Opocensky. Buenos Aires, 1939   107

29 QUEEN'S INDIAN DEFENCE

123 Uhlmann-Balanel. Erfurt, 1955   108
124 Uhlmann-Smyslov. Moscow, 1956   109
125 Soultanbéieff-Dubyna. Liège, 1953   110

30 NIMZO-INDIAN DEFENCE

126 Dyckhoff-Koch. Correspondence, 1948   110
127 Geller-Golombek. Budapest, 1952   111
128 Uhlmann-Botvinnik. Munich, 1958   112
129 Gonzalez-Perrine. Correspondence, 1943   113
130 Makarczyk-Sliwa. Warsaw, 1952   114
130a Gerusel-Lombardy. Toronto, 1957   114
131 Navarovszky-Florian. Budapest, 1955   115
132 Feigin-Monticelli. Munich, 1936   116
133 Toth-Najdorf. Mar del Plata, 1956   117
134 Korchnoi-Durasevic. Belgrade, 1956   118

31 BUDAPEST DEFENCE

135 Deutgen-Schmid. Celle, 1948   119

32 ENGLISH OPENING

136 Schmid-Muth. Bamberg, 1949   119
137 Filip-Beni. Prague, 1956   120

CONTENTS

137a Najdorf-Botvinnik. Moscow, 1956 *Page* 120
138 Ney-Shamkovitch. Russian Team Championship, 1956 121
138a Shaposnikov-Shamkovitch. Correspondence, 1953 121
139 Barshauskas-Chesnauskas. Lithuania, 1955 122
139a Sokolsky-Roizman. Minsk, 1958 122
140 Botvinnik-Sherbakov. Russian Championship, 1955 123

33 PETROSIAN SYSTEM
141 Perez-Bouwmeester. Vevey, 1958 124
141a Ufimtsev-Grushevsky. Alma Ata, 1958 124
142 Fischer-Lapiken. Oklahoma, 1956 125

34 CATALAN OPENING
143 Olafsson-Van Scheltinga. Beverwijk, 1959 126

35 KING'S FIANCHETTO OPENING
144 Larsen-Olafsson. Beverwijk, 1959 127

36 RETI OPENING
145 Braun-Fuchs. Kienbaum, 1958 127
146 Hanninen-Szabo. Wageningen, 1957 128

37 RETI DUTCH and RETI STAUNTON GAMBIT
147 Zimmermann-Walther. Zurich, 1955 129
148 Robatsch-Weghofer. Kapfenberg, 1955 130

38 BIRD'S OPENING
149 Laaber-Högborg. Correspondence, 1954/55 131

39 ORANG OUTANG OPENING
150 Sokolsky-Strugatsch. White Russia, 1958 132

APPENDIX
151 Wade-Mardle. Bognor, 1960 (Ruy Lopez) 133
152 Becher-Achenbach. Heidelberg, 1960 (Ruy Lopez) 133
153 Gipslis-Spassky. Riga, 1959 (Ruy Lopez) 134
154 Milner-Barry-Haygarth. York, 1959 (King's Gambit) 136
154a Spassky-Sakharov. Russian Championship, 1960 (King's Gambit) 136
155 Spassky-Bronstein. Russian Championship, 1960 (King's Gambit) 137
156 Pietzsch-O'Kelly. Madrid, 1960 (Sicilian Defence) 138
157 Tal-Smyslov. Bled, 1959 (Caro-Kann Defence) 139
158 Taimanov-Polugaevsky. Russian Championship, 1960 (Queen's Gambit Accepted) 141
159 Spassky-Mikenas. Riga, 1959 (Albin Counter Gambit) 142
160 Gligoric-Uhlmann. Hastings, 1959-60 (Grünfeld Defence) 143
161 Giustolisi-Zichichi. Lerici, 1959 (Anglo-Dutch Opening) 144

INDEX OF PLAYERS 145

PREFACE

WHEN the unforgotten and unforgettable Mr. du Mont, in whose footsteps we follow in presenting this third volume of miniature games, prefaced the second volume, he gave expression to his surprise that in these days of advanced chess theory and technique so many short games should still be played.

This was in 1953. Since then we have learnt that more miniature games are produced today than at any other period of competitive chess. Nor is this surprising. On the one hand, chess has reached so many outposts of civilization—outposts that are in constant and fertile touch with the established centres of tournament play so that players of very different calibre meet one another in international combat—that the numerical output of interesting though by no means grandmasterly games has risen tremendously and is still rising. On the other hand, the development of modern chess (reaching its zenith in the phenomenon of Tal) is towards ever sharper and more aggressive lines of play, in contrast to the quiet scientific style preferred by the grandmasters of the thirties and early forties. Both these factors have combined in contributing to the enormous growth in the number of miniature games.

Thus, our main task in the present volume was to discard, rather than to scratch for, material. On the whole we have discarded the stereotype and common-place—we can see no particular merit in giving our readers the 455th example of a bishop sacrifice on KR7 or the 39th specimen of a double rook sacrifice. The emphasis throughout is on the complex, the profound (which has invaded the field of the miniature to a remarkable extent) and the original. This is brought home especially in the many games from the U.S.S.R. (for which we wish to record our special thanks to such invaluable source material as Peter Clarke's series of *Soviet Miniatures* in the British Chess Magazine).

It is largely because of the complexity of these and other games that the reader will find the notes a little more voluminous than in the preceding collections—many of these modern games would be incomprehensible without detailed annotation. It is only for this reason—and not for lack of material—that we had to curtail the number of games so as not to burst the format to which readers of the series have become accustomed.

At the same time we have included a number of older games which for one reason or another had so far escaped the net. This applies especially to such *positional* masterpieces as Nos. 26 and 97; to such very famous and widely known games as No. 32, which we felt should not be permanently absent from a collection of games purporting to be a definitive anthology in the English language; and, on the contrary, to such almost unknown games as we felt worthy of rescuing from the obscurity of magazine and newspaper files (No. 30 comes to mind as an excellent example). It hardly needs saying that the overwhelming majority of the games are from the output of the past few years.

There only remains a word to be said about the allocation of labour as between the two of us. We have given each other a free hand in matters of selection, treatment, style, etc., and we hope that the resultant impression of two minds at work rather than one will be welcomed by the reader as contributing to the variety and readability of the book. To enable the reader who might not be able to do so otherwise, to distinguish between the voice of Barden and the hand of Heidenfeld (or vice versa, if you wish), the plan we have followed is roughly this:

Barden is in charge of the Ruy Lopez, the Evans Gambit, and the Scotch Game and Gambit; and further of all those lines that are essentially based on the King's fianchetto and the move P—QB4, whether for White or Black—the Reti and English Openings, the King's Indian (including the old Indian) Defence, the Benoni Formation, the Sicilian Defence, and the Pirc and Robatsch Defences.

Heidenfeld's responsibility comprises all open games except the three singled out above; all half-open defences bar the Sicilian, Pirc and Robatsch; such Queen's Pawn Openings as the various forms of the Queen's Gambit, the Queen's and Nimzo-Indian Defences, the Dutch Defence (also in the form of the Reti-Dutch and the Anglo-Dutch), and various odds and ends such as the Bird's and the Orang Outang.

We feel that, beside neatly splitting the material in two, this method has worked very well indeed; whether you share this complacent feeling is of course up to you. But whatever complaints or criticisms may reach us, we can no longer seek shelter one behind the other's back, as so often happens in joint publications.

L.W.B.
W.H.

1. THE GIUOCO PIANO

1 WHITE: CORTE—BLACK:
JAC. BOLBOCHAN

Mar del Plata, 1946

1 P—K4	P—K4
2 Kt—KB3	Kt—QB3
3 B—B4	B—B4
4 P—B3	Kt—B3
5 P—Q4	P×P
6 P×P	B—Kt5 ch.
7 Kt—B3	Kt×KP
8 Castles	Kt×Kt
9 P×Kt	B×P
10 B—R3	

Partly as a result of the present game, this is today regarded as even stronger than the traditional continuation 10. Q—Kt3 P—Q4! 11. B×P Castles.

10 ...	P—Q4!
11 B—Kt5	B×R
12 R—K1 ch.	B—K3
13 Q—R4	

13 ...   R—QKt1?

Black assumes that he can protect his QB3 no further because 13... Q—Q2! would have been followed by 14. Kt—K5. However, after 14... Kt×Kt! 15. B×Q ch. Kt×B 16. R×B (if 16. Q—Kt4 Castles 17. R—Kt1 Kt—Kt3) K—Q1! White would have a far from easy task. The obvious attack by 17.

Q—Kt4 Kt—Kt3 18. Q—K7 ch. K—B1 19. R—QB1 would be refuted by 19... Kt—B5, permanently blocking the QB-file. White might have retained winning chances by playing his bishop via B1 to B4; after the text, on the other hand, he crashes through.

14 Kt—K5!	Q—B1
15 B×Kt ch.	P×B
16 Q×P ch.	K—Q1
17 Kt×P ch.	B×Kt
18 B—K7 mate.	

2 WHITE: HEIDENFELD—BLACK:
ZIETEMANN

Berlin, 1929

1 P—K4	P—K4
2 Kt—KB3	Kt—QB3
3 B—B4	B—B4
4 Castles	Kt—B3
5 P—Q4	B×P

Black avoids the torrential waters of the Max Lange Attack proper, which continues with P×P 6. P—K5 P—Q4 7. P×Kt P×B 8. R—K1 ch. B—K3 9. Kt—Kt5 Q—Q4 10. Kt—QB3 Q—B4 11. QKt—K4. He soon loses his way, however.

6 Kt×B	Kt×Kt
7 P—B4	Kt—B3?
8 B×P ch.!	K—B1

If 8... K×B 9. P×P Kt×P 10. Q—R5 ch. Kt—Kt3 11. P—K5. This goes back to Mackenzie-Boden, 1863!

9 P×P	QKt×P
10 B—Kt3	P—Q3
11 B—Kt5	B—Kt5?

It would have been better to aim at neutralizing the white-squared bishop and play 11... Q—K2 12. Kt—B3 P—B3, followed by 13... B—K3. In reply to the text, the white queen moves away with a strong threat.

1

1. THE GIUOCO PIANO

12 Q—Q2	K—K2
13 Q—B4	R—KB1
14 P—KR3	B—Q2

He has no great choice. If 14... B—K3 15. B×B K×B 16. Q—B5 ch. any 17. Q×P.

15 Kt—B3	P—B3

If 15... B—B3 16. Q—B5 threatening both mate on K6 and Q×RP.

16 QR—Q1!

Preparing for the following orgy of sacrifices.

16 ...	P—KR3
17 R×P!	

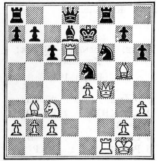

The position is ripe for the final assault. If now 17... K×R 18. Q×Kt (K5) ch. K×Q 19. B—B4 ch. K—Q5

20. R—Q1 ch. K—B4 21. B—K3 ch. K—Kt5 22. R—Q4 ch. K—B4 23. R—Q5 db. ch. K—Kt5 24. P—R3 mate. This type of king hunt has been seen before, especially in 19th century games, but here it is blended with a second sacrifice of the queen after 17... Kt—Kt3! 18. R×Kt! Kt×Q 19. R—K6 db. ch. K—B2 20. R×Kt ch. K—Kt1 21. R×RP ch. and mate in two.

Black's best defence was to interpolate 18... Q—Kt3 ch. after 17... Kt—Kt3 18. R×Kt. If then 19. K—R1 Kt×Q! because in reply to R×RP ch. in the above variation Black could play Q×B! The game would then continue 19. Q—B2! P×R 20. Q×Q P×Q 21. B×P followed by 22. B—Kt7, winning three pawns for the exchange.

17...	Q—Kt3 ch.
18 K—R1	K×R

If now 18... Kt—Kt3 19. B×Kt ch. R×B 20. R×B ch. K×R 21. Q—Kt4 ch. K—K2 22. R×R K×R 23. Q—K6 ch. K—Kt4 24. Q—B5 ch. and mate next move.

19 Q×Kt (K5) ch.!	K×Q
20 B—B4 ch.	K—Q5
21 R—Q1 ch.	K—B4
22 B—Q6 mate.	

2. TWO KNIGHTS' DEFENCE

3 WHITE: DURAO—BLACK: PRINS
Malaga, 1954

1 P—K4	P—K4
2 Kt—KB3	Kt—QB3
3 B—B4	Kt—B3
4 Kt—Kt5	P—Q4
5 P×P	Kt—QR4

The main line of the Two Knights' Defence. 5... Kt×P? 6. P—Q4! B—Kt5 ch. 7. P—B3 B—K2 8. Kt× BP! K×Kt 9. Q—B3 ch. K—K3 went out of fashion when Barden, against Adams (Hastings, 1950/51) found 10. Q—K4! with a winning advantage,

instead of the previously accepted 10. Castles.

6 B—Kt5 ch.	P—B3
7 P×P	P×P
8 Q—B3	P×B

This sacrifice of the exchange is insufficient, though White must play very sharply to prove it. After many trials and errors, the sarcifice of a second pawn by 8... R—QKt1 is preferred today; after 9. B×P ch. Kt×B 10. Q×Kt ch. Kt—Q2 Black gets an attack fully worth the sacrificed material.

9 Q×R	Q—Q2
10 P—QKt4!	

2

2. TWO KNIGHTS' DEFENCE

First played by Bogolyubov *v.* Euwe (match 1941) in a similar, though not the identical position. White offers to return some of the material he has gained for the sake of developing quickly: this, curiously enough, can best be done via the QR file. If now 10... B×P 11. P—QR4! and Black cannot advance the KtP and must submit to a decisive opening of files. The following play all revolves round this theme.

```
10 ...          Kt—B3
11 P—QR4        Kt×P
12 Castles      Kt×P
13 B—Kt2!       P—Kt5
```

For if 13... Kt×R 14. R—B1 K—Q1 15. Kt×P ch.

```
14 R—B1         P—Kt6
15 Q—Kt8        Q—Kt2
```

Clearly Black cannot give the KtP. Note that as a result of White's sharp play Black has not been able to make a single developing move in the previous six moves.

```
16 Q×P ch.      B—K2
17 Kt—QR3!      Castles
```

The threat of 18. R—B7 keeps the knight pinned.

```
18 Kt×Kt        P×Kt
19 R×P          B—Q1
20 Kt—K4        Q—R1
```

If 20... Q×Kt 21. Q×Q Kt×Q 22. R×B. Black ineffectually tries to bring the bishop to bear on his K5 as well.

```
21 R—R3!
```

```
21 ...          B—Kt2
```

If 21... Kt—K1 22. Kt—Q6 B—B3 23. R×B, etc.

```
22 Kt×Kt ch.    B×Kt
23 Q×B!         Resigns.
```

If 23... P×Q 24. R—Kt3 ch. followed by 25. B×P mate.

4 WHITE: WIRTZ—BLACK: FAHNEN·SCHMIDT

Marburg, 1955

```
1 P—K4          P—K4
2 Kt—KB3        Kt—QB3
3 B—B4          Kt—B3
4 Kt—Kt5        B—B4
```

The Traxler variation—a line so complicated that it would be presumptuous to try a final assessment within the scope of this book. Present opinion favours 5. P—Q4 as a reply.

```
5 Kt×BP         B×P ch.
6 K×B           Kt×P ch.
7 K—K3
```

A rarely-played, audacious move. The usual continuation is 7. K—Kt1, after which a game *Foltys-Rossolimo, Amsterdam, 1950*, went: 7... Q—R5 8. P—KKt3 Kt×Kt Q×Kt 9. P×Kt Q×P ch. 10. K—B1 R—B1 11. Q—R5 P—Q3 12. Kt—B3 B—Kt5 13. Q—R2 Q—B6 ch. 14. K—Kt1 Kt—Q5 15. B—Q5, Kt—K7 ch. 16. Q×Kt (if 16. Kt×Kt Q×B 17. Kt—Kt5 Q—B4 ch. 18. P—Q4 Q×BP would recover the piece with a winning attack), Q—Kt6 ch. 17. Q—Kt2 Q—K8 ch. and drew by perpetual check.

```
7 ...           Q—K2
8 K×Kt
```

The wrong piece. After 8. Kt×R, which looks even riskier, it is doubtful whether Black gets enough. Brinckmann, in a theoretical note in *Schachecho (1955)*, gives 8... Q—Kt4 ch. 9. K×Kt P—Q4 ch. 10. B×P Q—B5 ch., but after 11. K—Q3 the white king works back to K2 and K1. Nor is the "win of the queen" by 10... B—B4 ch. 11. K—B3 B—Kt5 ch. 12. K—B2 B×Q 13. B×Kt ch. P×B 14. R×B sufficient:

3

White retains too much material. After the text move the win is forced—and very pretty.

8 ...	P—Q4 ch.
9 B×P	Q—R5 ch.
10 P—Kt4	B×P
11 B×Kt ch	

11 ...	B—Q2 ch!
12 K—K3	Q—Q5 ch.
13 K—K2	P×B
14 R—Kt1	B—Kt5 ch.
15 R×B	Q×R ch.
16 K—K1	Q—R5 ch.
17 K—B1	Castles!

An enchanting decision!

18 Q—K2	R×Kt ch.
19 K—Kt1	QR—KB1
20 P—Q3	R—B7
Resigns.	

5 WHITE: ALEXANDER—BLACK: EUWE

Utrecht, 1949

1 P—K4	P—K4
2 Kt—KB3	Kt—QB3
3 B—B4	Kt—B3
4 P—Q4	

Less complicated and (therefore?) less popular than the main line 4. Kt—Kt5.

4 ...	P×P
5 Castles	Kt×P
6 R—K1	P—Q4
7 B×P	Q×B
8 Kt—B3	Q—QR4
9 Kt×Kt	B—K3
10 B—Q2	

So far all book. Here, however, 10. Kt(K4)—Kt5 is the usual continuation. The text could well be answered with the return, 10... Q—Q4! unless Black prefers to strive for complications with his next move.

10 ...	B—QKt5
11 B×B?	

After this move White will have no compensation for the combined pressure against his K1 and QKt2. 11. Kt×P! a pseudo-sacrifice emanating from Yugoslav masters, is the accepted follow-up of White's 10th move. A game *Kinzel-Dückstein, Vienna, 1958,* continued: 11... Kt×Kt 12. P—QB3 Q—Q4 13. P×B Castles (K) 14. R—QB1 QR—Q1 15. R—B5 Q×P? 16. B—B3 Kt—Kt4 17. Kt—B6 ch.! P×Kt 18. B×P! R—Q4 19. Q—Q2! Resigns.

11 ...	Q×B
12 Kt(K4)—Kt5	Castles (Q)
13 Kt×B	P×Kt
14 Kt—Kt5	

To plant the knight on K6 is the point of the whole variation. In this particular line, however, it cannot be done with impunity because of Black's pressure against K1. The finish is very instructive.

14 ...	R—Q2!

Stopping Kt—B7, blocking the QB1—KKt5 diagonal, and preparing an eventual doubling on the K-file.

15 Kt×KP	R—K1
16 Q—Kt4	

2. TWO KNIGHTS' DEFENCE

On any other move Black could simply capture the KtP, while if 16. P—QKt3? R(2)—K2 17. Q—Kt4 K—Kt1 18. R—K4, Kt—Q1 19. R×P Q—B6 20. R(1)—Q1 Kt×Kt 21. Q×Kt Q×R! (or 19. R(1)—K1 R×Kt 20. R×R Q×R ch.).

| 16 ... | P—Q6! |
| 17 Q×Q | |

If White obstructs the horizontal by 17. R—K4, there would follow 17... Q×P 18. R—KB1 Kt—K4! 19. Q—B5 P—KKt3 20. Q×Kt Q×Q 21. R×Q P×P and wins; if by 17. P—QB4 Kt—Q5 wins. The text continuation looks like a way out, but Euwe concludes with a pretty finesse.

17 ...	Kt×Q
18 Kt—B5	R×R ch.
19 R×R	P×P!

And not 19... P—Q7? 20. R—Q1 R—K2 21. K—B1 Kt×BP 22. Kt—Q3 when White would regain his pawn and hold the position.

| 20 Kt×R | Kt—Q6! |
| Resigns. | |

For if the rook moves, there follows 21... K×Kt, and afterwards the passed pawn costs the rook.

3. RUY LOPEZ

6 WHITE: INCUTTO—BLACK: KERES

Mar del Plata, 1957

1 P—K4	P—K4
2 Kt—KB3	Kt—QB3
3 B—Kt5	P—QR3
4 B—R4	Kt—B3
5 Castles	B—K2
6 R—K1	P—QKt4
7 B—Kt3	P—Q3
8 P—B3	Castles
9 P—KR3	P—QR4

This Russian idea is one of a number of attempts made to avoid the hackneyed 9... Kt—QR4. A game *Spassky-Fuderer, Vienna, 1957*, continued 9... Kt—Q2 10. P—Q4 B—B3 11. P—QR4 R—Kt1 12. P×KtP P×KtP 13. B—K3 Kt—K2 14. Kt—Kt5 Kt—KKt3 15. Kt×RP K×Kt 16. Q—R5 ch. K—Kt1 17. Q×Kt P—Kt5 18. B—QB4 Kt—Kt3 19. B—Kt3 Kt—Q2 20. B—QB4, when both sides have nothing better than the draw by repetition of moves, Black because of his pawn minus and White because of the attack on his KB.

| 10 P—Q4 | P×P |
| 11 Kt×P | |

An interesting alternative is 11. P×P P—R5 12. B—B2 Kt—QKt5 13. P—Q5 B—Q2 14. Kt—Q4, Q—B1 15. Kt—QB3, Kt×B 16. Kt×Kt Q—Kt2 17. Kt—Kt4 (*Vasilchik-Neystadt, Moscow, 1956*), when Black's advance of the queen's side pawns has created holes for the white knights. A possible improvement is an immediate 13... Kt×B 14. Q×Kt B—Q2 15. Kt—Q4 R—R3.

| 11 ... | Kt×Kt |
| 12 Q×Kt | |

Now Black quickly gets on top. A more critical variation, not yet fully analysed, is 12. P×Kt B—Kt2 13. Q—Q3 Q—Q2.

12 ...	B—Kt2
13 B—B2	R—K1
14 Q—Q1	

As so often when a player meets an opponent with a greatly superior reputation, White begins to play as if hypnotized. Better is 14. Kt—Q2 B—KB1 15. Kt—B3.

14 ...	B—KB1
15 B—Kt5	P—R3
16 B×Kt	Q×B
17 Kt—Q2	P—Kt5

Keres is not the man to whom to present the two bishops on a plate.

18 Q—B3	Q—Kt3
19 Q—Kt4	Q—B3
20 Q—B3	Q—Kt4

3. RUY LOPEZ

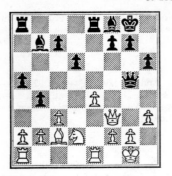

21 Kt—B1	R—K4
22 P×P	P×P
23 R—K3	

If 23. QR—Q1 QR—K1 and White lacks a good defence to the threatened 24... P—Q4.

23 ...	P—Q4
24 P×P	B×P
25 B—K4?	

This blunder loses immediately, but White's alternative is a lost ending after 25. Q—Kt4 Q×Q 26. P×Q R×R 27. Kt×R B—K3 28. P—QKt3 (otherwise 28... P—Kt6), B—K2, with the decisive threat of 29... B—KB3.

25 ...	R×B
26 Resigns.	

If 26. R×R P—KB4 27. R—Kt4 P×R wins a piece.

The following two games have combined the most remarkable feature, which is still exceptional in chess apart from very short opening traps, that they are identical for the first 16 moves. In this case, unlike the game a couple of years ago in a Swiss junior tournament in which the young hopefuls deliberately reproduced a ninety-year-old brilliancy between Hamppe and Meitner (which is itself of dubious authenticity), collusion is not suspected.

7 WHITE: HONAN / ZAITSEV   BLACK: MARDLE / ROCHLIN

The first game was played in the Infantile Paralysis Fellowship Corre-

spondence Championship in 1958, the second at Yaroslavl in 1954.

1 P—K4	P—K4
2 Kt—KB3	Kt—QB3
3 B—Kt5	P—QR3
4 B—R4	Kt—B3
5 Castles	Kt×P
6 P—Q4	P—QKt4
7 B—Kt3	P—Q4
8 Kt×P	

The usual move is 8. P×P, but the capture with the knight gives White rather more chance of developing a king's side pawn roller.

8 ...	Kt×Kt
9 P×Kt	B—Kt2

Another safe line is 9... P—QB3 10. P—QB3 B—K2 11. B—K3 Castles 12. Kt—Q2 Kt×Kt 13. Q×Kt B—KB4

10 B—K3	B—B4
11 Q—Kt4?	

The pawn hunt is brilliantly refuted. Positionally correct is 11. B×B Kt×B 12. Kt—Q2, followed by P—KB4.

11 ...	B×B
12 Q×P?	

Now White definitely loses. P×B is essential.

12 ...	Q—Kt4!
13 Q×R ch.	K—K2
14 Q×P	B×P ch.
15 K—R1	

Not 15. R×B, Q—B8 ch. 16. R—B1 Q—K6 ch. 17. K—R1, Kt—B7 ch. with a Philidor mate.

15 ...	R—KKt1
16 Q—R3	

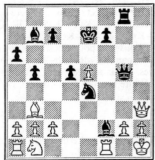

16 ...   P—Q5

This was Mardle's winning move; Rochlin preferred the less aesthetic 16... B—B1 17. P—Kt4 (if 17. Q—KB3 Kt—Kt6 ch. 18. P×Kt R—R1 ch. and mates) B×P; White resigns.

17 Kt—R3	Q×P ch.
18 Q×Q	Kt—Kt6 ch.
19 P×Kt	R—R1 mate.

8 WHITE: KARAKLAIC—BLACK: RELLSTAB

West Germany *v.* Yugoslavia, 1956

1 P—K4	P—K4
2 Kt—KB3	Kt—QB3
3 B—Kt5	P—QR3
4 B—R4	Kt—B3

The moves in the Moller Defence must be played in the exact order. If, for instance, 4... P—QKt4 5. B—Kt3 B—B4 6. Castles P—Q3 7. P—B3 B—K3? then 8. P—Q4 B×B 9. RP×B P×P 10. P×P B—Kt5 11. B—Kt5 Kt—B3 12. Q—B1 Q—Q2 13. P—K5 P×P 14. P×P Kt—K5 15. R—Q1 Q—K3 16. R×P! R×R 17. Q×Kt ch.! Q×Q 18. R—Q8 mate (won by *Soultanbéieff, Liège, 1923*). A finish on the lines of the famous Morphy opera box game.

5 Castles	P—QKt4
6 B—Kt3	B—B4
7 P—B3	

White could obtain the two bishops by 7. Kt×P Kt×Kt 8. P—Q4 B×P 9. Q×B, but after 9... Kt—B3 10. Q—B3, Castles; Black's superior development is adequate compensation.

7 ...	B—Kt3
8 P—Q4	P—Q3
9 P×P	P×P
10 Q×Q ch.	Kt×Q
11 Kt×P	B—Kt2

Black has to delay the recapture of the pawn, for if 11... Kt×P 12. B—Q5 B—Kt2 13. B×Kt B×B 14. R—K1, and the pin is fatal.

12 B—Kt5	Kt×P!

Black must still be careful, for if 12... B×P 13. R—K1 B×Kt 14. QR×B Castles 15. B×Kt P×B 16. Kt—Q7.

13 B×Kt	R×B
14 Kt×P	

If 14. B×P ch. K—K2, Black's attack on the KB file is more than enough for the pawn.

14 ...	R—KB1
15 Kt×R	K×Kt

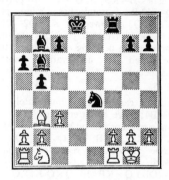

16 Kt—Q2

White must play very carefully, since the great activity of Black's pieces outweighs the material deficit. If 16. Kt—R3 B×P ch 17. K—R1 R—B3 18. P—R3 Kt—Kt6 ch. 19. K—R2 Kt×R ch. 20. R×Kt B—Kt6 ch. 21. K—Kt1 B—R7 ch.; it is Black who is the exchange up.

16 ...	Kt×KBP

Not 16... Kt×Kt 17. QR—Q1.

17 Kt—B3	Kt—R6 dis. ch.
18 K—R1	Kt—B7 ch.
19 K—Kt1	

Not 19. R×Kt B×R; when the black bishops dominate the ending.

19 ...	Kt—R6 dis. ch.

Black also has no choice, for White threatens 20. Kt—Q4.

20 K—R1	Kt—B7 ch.

Drawn by repetition of position. Even a short draw in which the queens come off early can be full of interesting points.

3. RUY LOPEZ

9 WHITE: SCHMID—BLACK: HERZOG
Dresden, 1943

1 P—K4	P—K4
2 Kt—KB3	Kt—QB3
3 B—Kt5	P—QR3
4 B—R4	Kt—B3
5 Q—K2	

This Wormald Attack is more flexible than the commoner Worrall line 5. Castles B—K2 6. Q—K2. In playing Q—K2 White usually has in mind a plan of P—Q3 followed by Kt—Q2—B1—Kt3, and in closed positions a tempo sacrificed in delaying castling can often be used in accelerating another manoeuvre.

| 5 ... | P—QKt4 |

Black can also play immediately 5... B—B4; since an attempt by White to win a pawn recoils on his own head after 6. B×Kt QP×B 7. Kt×P Q—Q5. A game, *Eriksen-Dreyer, Johannesburg, 1956*, went on 8. Kt—Q3 Castles 9. P—QB3 Q×KP 10. Q×Q Kt×Q 11. P—B3 R—Q1 12. K—K2 R×Kt 13. K×R Kt—B7 ch.; 14. K—B4 B—K3 ch. 15. K×B Kt×R 16. P—Q4 Kt—B7 17. P—Q5 B—B4 18. B—Kt5 Kt—Q6 ch. 19. K—Q4 P—R3 20. B—R4 P×P 21. K×P P—KKt4 22. B—Kt3 R—Q1 ch. 23. K—B4 B—K3 mate. An entertaining king hunt.

6 B—Kt3	B—B4
7 P—QR4	R—QKt1
8 P×P	P×P
9 Kt—B3	Castles
10 P—Q3	

10. Kt×KtP Kt×KP; is good for Black.

| 10 ... | P—Q3 |
| 11 B—Kt5 | |

A pin of a KKt is particularly effective if the opponent has castled and has his KB outside the pawn chain. But now Black should at least have played 11... B—K3; so as to answer 12. Kt—Q5, by 12... B×Kt.

| 11 ... | B—KKt5? |
| 12 Kt—Q5 | Kt—Q5 |

Follow my leader, in the Ruy Lopez as in the Four Knights' usually results in trouble. 12... B—K3 is still best.

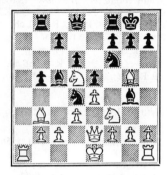

13 Kt×Kt!

An unusual variation on the Legal trap theme.

| 13 ... | B×Q |
| 14 B×Kt | P×B |

If 14... Q—Q2 15. Kt—B5, and the threatened 15. Kt(Q5)—K7 ch. K—R1 16. B×P mate, leaves Black with no time to save his bishop, so that White comes out with three pieces for the queen and a winning attack.

| 15 Kt—B6 | Resigns. |

After 15... Q—K1 16. Kt×P ch., White comes out a piece up. A remarkable little combination considering that the winner, the well-known German master, was only 15 at the time.

10 WHITE: TAL—BLACK: TESCHNER
Vienna, 1957

1 P—K4	P—K4
2 Kt—KB3	Kt—QB3
3 B—Kt5	P—QR3
4 B—R4	Kt—B3
5 Castles	P—Q3
6 P—B3	B—K2
7 P—Q4	P—QKt4

This and the following three moves constitute a risky pawn snatch, particularly when White is the world's greatest

8

attacking master. Correct is 7... B—Q2.

8 B—Kt3	B—Kt5
9 P—KR3	B×Kt
10 Q×B	P×P
11 Q—Kt3	P—Kt3

Only now does Black realize the extent of his difficulties. If 11... Castles 12. B—R6 Kt—K1 13. B—Q5 Q—Q2 14. R—Q1 K—R1 15. P×P! P×B 16. Q—QB3 with a tremendous advantage. However, a rather better defence is 11... Kt—KR4 12. Q—Kt4 P—Kt3 13. B—Q5 Kt—K4, although White in his turn could improve by 12. Q—Q3 P×P 13. Kt×P, with a persistent attack.

| 12 B—Q5 | Q—Q2 |

Also after 12... Kt×B 13. P×Kt Kt—K4 14. P×P Kt—B5 15. B—R6 Q—Q2 16. P—QR4, White has the initiative on both wings.

| 13 B—R6 | QR—Kt1 |

Now the king stays permanently in the centre, but if 13... Castles 14. P—QR4 P—Kt5 15. Q—Q3 with a strong attack, while if 13... P—Kt4, then not 14. B×P R—KKt1, with counterplay, but 14. P—KB4 R—KKt1 15. P×KtP Kt×B 16. P×Kt.

| 14 P—KB4 | Kt—Q1 |
| 15 Kt—Q2 | |

But not 15. P×P P—B3 16. B—Kt3 Kt×P.

15 ...	P—B3
16 B—Kt3	P×P
17 Q×BP	Q—R2 ch.
18 K—R1	Q—B4
19 Q—Q3	Kt—Q2

As so often in a position where a player has a permanent positional weakness in return for a pawn, Black must have recourse to unnatural contortions to stave off White's threats, in this case 20. B—Kt7 R—Kt1 21. B×Kt B×B 22. P—K5 P×P 23. Kt—K4 Q—K2 24. Kt—Q6 ch. K—B1 25. P×P, with a quick win.

| 20 P—K5 | P—Q4 |

If 20... P×P 21. P×P Kt×P 22. Q—K2, with a triple threat of 23. B—Kt7 23. Kt—K4, and 23. QR—K1.

| 21 P—B5 | P×P |

Or 21... Kt×P 22. Q—K2 P—B3 23. B—Kt7 R—Kt1 24. Kt—K4, winning at least the exchange.

| 22 Q×BP | Kt—B1 |

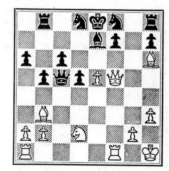

23 Kt—K4
Finally, opening all the centre lines.

23 ...	P×Kt
24 QR—B1	Q—Kt3
25 QR—Q1	

A pleasingly quiet finishing touch. If 25... Kt(B1)—K3 26. B×Kt P×B 27. Q—R5 ch, and mate next move.

| 25 ... | Resigns. |

11 White: Farré—Black: Pomar

Spain, 1958

1 P—K4	P—K4
2 Kt—KB3	Kt—QB3
3 B—Kt5	P—QR3
4 B—R4	Kt—B3
5 Castles	B—K2
6 B×Kt	KtP×B

For 6... QP×B, see the next game.

7 P—Q4

White continues on orthodox lines, instead of challenging Black to prove his compensation for the pawn after 7. Kt×P, and if 7... Kt×P 8. Q—Kt4.

7 ...	Castles
8 Kt—B3	P×P
9 Kt×P	P—B4
10 Kt—B5	P—Q3
11 Kt×B ch.	Q×Kt
12 B—Kt5	R—Kt1

If now 13. P—Kt3 Q—K4, Black has a promising initiative.

13 Kt—Q5	Q×P!
14 B×Kt	

Falling into a profound trap; better is 14. Kt×Kt ch. P×Kt 15. B×P B—Kt2 16. P—KB3 Q—Kt3 17. B—B3 P—KB3, with only a slight advantage for Black.

14 ...	B—Kt2
15 R—K1	Q×Kt
16 Q—Kt4	

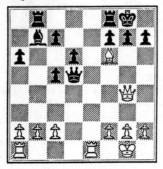

16 ...	Q×P ch.
17 Q×Q	B×Q
18 B—K7	

If 18. K×B, P×B, Black wins easily with two pawns up.

18 ...	KR—K1
19 K×B	P—KB3

This curious trapping of the bishop does not win it directly, but enables the black rook to have a good time gobbling on the queen's side.

20 R—K4	K—B2
21 QR—K1	R×P
22 P—QB4	R×P
23 P—R4	P—QR4
24 K—Kt3	R—Q7
25 P—B4	R—Q6 ch.
26 Resigns.	

For if 26. K—B2 R—Q5 and Black wins a fifth pawn, or if 26. K—Kt4 P—B4 ch. 27. K×P R—KKt6, and White is helpless against 28... P—Kt3 mate.

12 White: Madame Zvorykina
Black: Gladkov

White Russian Championship, 1958

1 P—K4	P—K4
2 Kt—KB3	Kt—QB3
3 B—Kt5	P—QR3
4 B—R4	Kt—B3
5 Castles	B—K2
6 B×Kt	QP×B
7 Q—K1	Kt—Q2
8 P—Q4	P×P
9 Kt×P	Castles
10 Kt—QB3	Kt—Kt3
11 B—K3	Kt—B5

This loses time. Preferable is either 11... P—QB4 or 11... Q—K1.

12 R—Q1	Q—K1

Not 12... Kt×B 13. Kt—K6 Q—K1 14. Kt×BP, winning the queen.

13 B—B1	P—QB4
14 KKt—K2	P—QKt4

Black's loss of time with his knight now makes it hard for him to prevent the creation of a king side pawn roller. If 14... P—B4 15. Kt—Q5 B—Q3 16. P—QKt3 Kt—K4 17. P—KB4, with great advantage to White.

15 Kt—Q5	B—Q1
16 Kt—Kt3	Kt—Kt3
17 Kt—K3	

Not only following the principle that the player of the greater command of space should avoid exchanges, but preparing for a full scale attack against the black king.

17 ...	B—B3
18 K—R1	P—Kt3
19 P—KB4	B—R5

Passive play is hopeless, so now and in the next two moves Black flails out wildly in a desperate effort to stem the attack.

| 20 P—B5 | B—Kt2 |
| 21 Kt—Kt4 | P—KR4 |

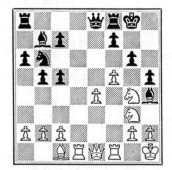

22 Kt×P!

Not just an exchanging combination, but a real queen sacrifice.

| 22 ... | B×Q |
| 23 Kt(R5)—B6 ch. | K—R1 |

If 23... K—Kt2, Peter Clarke in the *British Chess Magazine* has demonstrated a win by 24. B—R6 ch. K—R1 25. R—Q3 P×P 26. R×P, and now if 26... B×P 27. R—KR3 B×P ch. 28. K×B Q—B3 ch. 29. R(B5)—B3, or if 26... Q×P 27. Kt×Q B×Kt 28. R—KR3 B×R 29. B—Kt5 dis. ch. K—Kt2 (if 29... K—Kt1 30. B—B6) 30. B—B6 ch. K—Kt3 31. R—R6 mate.

| 24 R—Q3 | Q×P |
| 25 R—R3 ch. | Resigns. |

For Black is neatly mated after 25... B—R5 26. R×B ch. K—Kt2 27. R—R7.

13 WHITE: SCHMID—BLACK:
ENEVOLDSEN
Travemünde, 1951

1 P—K4	P—K4
2 Kt—KB3	Kt—QB3
3 B—Kt5	P—QR3
4 B—R4	P—Q3
5 P—B3	B—Q2
6 P—Q4	Kt—B3
7 QKt—Q2	B—K2

| 8 Castles | Castles |
| 9 R—K1 | P—QKt4 |

A common error; in almost all Ruy Lopez positions, Black should play P—QKt4 before White has a chance to retreat his bishop directly to QB2. Better here is the freeing manoeuvre 9... P×P 10. P×P Kt—QKt5.

| 10 B—B2 | B—Kt5 |

If now 10... P×P 11. Kt×P Kt×Kt 12. P×Kt, and White has an ideal Lopez set-up in which his KB can be opened against the black king by P—K5 at the right moment.

| 11 P—KR3 | B—R4 |

Another common, but fairly fundamental error. With the bishop driven into a restricted position on the king's side White can either gain tempi for a king's side-attack by Kt—B1—Kt3 or, as in the present case, exploit the white square weaknesses on the queen's wing. Better is 11... B×Kt.

| 12 P—Q5 | Kt—Kt1 |

12... Kt—R4 13. P—QKt4 Kt—Kt2 (if 13... Kt—B5 14. Kt×Kt P×Kt 15. Q—K2) 14. P—QR4 also gives White a strong initiative.

| 13 P—QR4 | QKt—Q2 |
| 14 Q—K2 | |

Beginning a fine manoeuvre to exploit Black's Achilles heel at QB3.

14 ...	R—Kt1
15 Kt—Kt3	Kt—B4
16 Kt—R5	Q—Q2
17 Kt—B6	R—R1

If 17... R—Kt3 18. P×P P×P 19. P—QKt4, followed by 20. B—K3.

18 P×P	P×P
19 R×R	R×R
20 Q×P	B—Kt3
21 B—Kt5	K—R1

Black overlooks the threat to his knight, but the alternative 21... Kt×QP 22. P×Kt KB×B 23. B×B RP×B 24. Kt×B also loses a piece.

3. RUY LOPEZ

| 22 B×Kt | B×B |
| 23 P—QKt4 | Resigns. |

For if 23... Kt—R3 24. R—R1 Q—B1 25. B—Q3.

14 WHITE: BISGUIER—BLACK: TORAN

Munich, 1958

1 P—K4	P—K4
2 Kt—KB3	Kt—QB3
3 B—Kt5	Kt—B3
4 Q—K2	

A harmless reply to the Berlin Defence. After the more aggressive 4. Castles, a game won by Varain in Leipzig in 1890 continued 4... Kt×P 5. P—Q4 Kt—Q3 6. Kt×P, Kt×B 7. R—K1, Kt—K2 (much better is 7... B—K2, when White has trouble in regaining the piece which he optimistically sacrificed on move 6 in place of the normal 6. B×Kt) 8. Q—R5 P—KKt3 9. Q—B3 Kt—Q3 10. Kt—B3 P—QB3 11. Kt—K4, Q—B2 12. Q×P ch.! K—Q1 (if 12... Kt×Q 13. Kt—B6 ch. K—Q1 14. Kt×Kt mate) 13. Kt—B6 (threatening 14. Q—K8 ch.!) Q—Kt3 14. B—B4 Kt(K2)—B4 15. Q—K8 ch.! K—B2 16. Kt—B7 B—Kt2 17. Kt×Kt R×Q 18. Kt—Kt5 db. ch. K—Q1 19. R×R mate. A quaint finish in view of White's previous attempts to get a smothered mate with the two knights.

4 ...	B—K2
5 P—B3	P—Q3
6 P—Q4	B—Q2

7 Castles	Castles
8 QKt—Q2	P×P
9 P×P	P—QR3
10 B×Kt	

Giving the two bishops in a position which is not completely closed hands the initiative to Black. If 10. B—R4 Kt×QP or if 10. B—Q3 Kt—QKt5 11. B—Kt1 B—Kt4 12. Kt—B4 P—Q4; but 10. B—B4 is better.

10 ...	B×B
11 P—Q5	B—Q2
12 P—QKt3	R—K1
13 Kt—Q4	

The natural 13. B—Kt2 fails against 13... Kt×QP 14. P×Kt B—KB3.

13 ...	P—B4
14 P×P e.p.	P×P
15 Q—B3	Kt—Kt5!

In return for this pawn sacrifice Black gets full command of the centre.

16 Kt×P	B×Kt
17 Q×Kt	B—B3
18 R—Kt1	P—Q4
19 P×P	Q×P
20 B—Kt2	P—KR4
21 Q—Kt3	B×B
22 R×B	R—K3

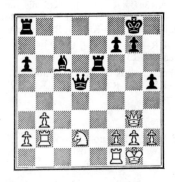

23 Kt—B3

White is curiously helpless against the attack. If 23. P—B3 Q—Q5 ch., or 23. Q—KB3 Q—Q5.

| 23 ... | R—Kt3 |
| 24 R—Q2 | Q—KB4 |

25 Kt—Q4	R×Q
26 Resigns.	

For if 26. Kt×Q R×P ch. 27. K—R1 R×BP dis. ch. After this game, Toran told his opponent that he was especially pleased to win since it was his birthday. "Ah!" replied Bisguier, sadly, "it's my birthday too!"

15 WHITE: MATANOVIC—BLACK: JANOSEVIC

Yugoslav Championship, 1953

1 P—K4	P—K4
2 Kt—KB3	Kt—QB3
3 B—Kt5	P—B4
4 Kt—B3	Kt—B3

The alternative 4... Kt—Q5 should lead to some advantage for White after 5. B—B4 P—Q3 6. Castles P—B3 7. R—K1, Kt×Kt ch. 8. Q×Kt.

5 P×P	B—B4

Kostic's continuation, which is more difficult to meet than 5... B—K2 or 5... P—K5.

6 Castles	Castles
7 R—K1	

This weakening of KB2 is the root cause of White's later troubles. The best plan is the quiet 7. P—Q3 P—Q3 8. Kt—K4 B—Kt3 9. Kt—Kt3 Kt—K2 10. Kt—R4, and Black has difficulty in regaining the pawn.

7 ...	P—Q3
8 Kt—QR4	

Eliminating one dangerous attacking piece, but at the cost of falling further behind in development. Better is 8. P—Q3.

8 ...	P—K5
9 Kt×B	QP×Kt
10 B×Kt	P×B
11 Kt—R4	P—Kt4!

Black vigorously opens all the lines for attack.

12 P×P e.p.	Kt—Kt5

13 P×P ch.	K—Kt2
14 P—KKt3	Q—Q5
15 Q—K2	R×P
16 Q×P	

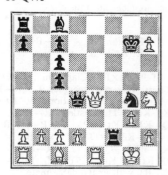

16 ...	R—B8 db. ch.
17 Resigns.	

If 17. K×R Q—B7 mate, or 17. K—Kt2 Q—B7 ch. 18. K—R3 Q×RP mate.

16 WHITE: ZAITSEV—BLACK: TIMCHENKO

Moscow, 1956

1 P—K4	P—K4
2 Kt—KB3	Kt—QB3
3 B—Kt5	Kt—Q5
4 B—B4	P—QKt4

Like all rarely employed gambits, this has the essential value of surprise. If Black is content with safe equality, he should rather play 4... Kt×Kt ch. 5. Q×Kt Q—B3.

5 B×P ch.	K×B
6 Kt×Kt	Q—R5

The point; after 6... P×Kt? 7. Q—R5 ch. K—K2 8. Q—K5 ch., followed by Q—Q5 ch., White wins the QR.

7 Q—B3 ch.	

White goes pawn hunting at the expense of development and conse-

13

quently loses the initiative. Much better is 7. Kt—K2, Q×KP 8. Castles, followed by 9. QKt—B3, when White has good prospects of utilizing his development advantage.

7 ...	Kt—B3
8 Kt×P	B—B4
9 Kt(Kt5)—B3	

If 9. Kt×BP, Clarke in the *British Chess Magazine* suggests 9... R—B1; when a likely continuation is 10. Kt×R K—Kt1 11. Castles Kt—Kt5 12. Q—KKt3 Kt×BP! 13. P—Q4 B×P 14. B—K3 Q×Q 15. P×Q B×B 16. Kt—B3 B—QR3 17. KR—K1 B—B4 18. Kt—B7 Kt—Kt5 dis. ch. 19. K—R1 R—B3, with unavoidable mate.

9 ...	R—B1
10 P—Q3	K—Kt1
11 Q—Kt3	Q—R4
12 Castles	Kt—Kt5
13 Kt—Q1	

Trying to keep his pawn formation intact, White allows a decisive combination. After 13. B—K3 Kt×B 14. P×Kt R×R ch. 15. K×R R—Kt1 16. P—Kt3 R—Kt3 17. Kt—Q2 R—KKt3 18. Q—R3 Q×Q 19. P×Q B×P 20. Kt—B3 P—Q3 21. K—K2 B—QB4; White has no adequate defence against the threats of R—Kt7 ch. and B×P.

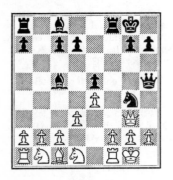

| 13 ... | Kt×BP |
| 14 B—K3 | |

If 14. Kt×Kt B×Kt ch. 15. R×B Q—Q8 ch., followed by mate.

| 14 ... | Kt—R6 ch. |
| 15 P×Kt | |

Or if 15. Q×Kt R×R ch. 16. K×R Q×Kt ch. 17. K—B2 P—Q4.

15 ...	R×R ch.
16 K×R	Q×Kt ch.
17 K—Kt2	B×B
18 Q×B	P—Q3
19 Q—Q2	B×P ch.!

Finally driving the king into the wide open spaces, for if 20. K—B2 R—B1 ch. 21. K—K3 Q—B6 mate.

20 K×B	Q—B6 ch.
21 K—R4	P—KR3
22 Resigns.	

22... P—Kt4 ch. will win the queen and the king shortly afterwards.

17 WHITE: SCHMID—BLACK: WELZ
Radebeul, 1945

1 P—K4	P—K4
2 Kt—KB3	Kt—QB3
3 B—Kt5	P—Q3
4 P—Q4	P×P
5 Kt×P	Kt—K2

A very passive defence. The interest of the game lies in the elegant way in which White cuts it to ribbons.

| 6 Castles | B—Q2 |
| 7 Kt—QB3 | Kt—K4 |

At least he should get rid of a couple of minor pieces by 7... Kt×Kt.

8 P—B4	B×B
9 Kt(Q4)×B	Kt(K4)—B3
10 Kt—Q5	Kt×Kt
11 P×Kt	Kt—K2
12 P—B5	P—QR3
13 Kt—B3	Q—Q2
14 Q—Q4!	

Many players know the art of reaching a good middle game position after the opponent has mishandled the opening. Many of them, however, gradually lose their initiative in a situation such as this without quite knowing why. The instinctive reaction is to defend the attacked pawn by 14. Q—Q3, or 14. Q—B3, but this would tie down the queen to defence and allow Black to consolidate gradually. After the actual move, however, Black's king cannot escape from the centre by 14... Castles, because of 15. Q—R7, so that he must accept the pawn sacrifice and expose his king to the blizzard.

14 ...	Kt×BP
15 Q—B2	P—KKt3
16 B—Kt5	

But not 16. P—KKt4 Kt—R3 17. Q—B6 Q×P ch. 18. K—R1 Kt—B4 19. Q×R Kt—Kt6 ch.! 20. P×Kt Q—R6 ch. and draws.

| 16 ... | B—Kt2 |

Now if 16... B—K2 17. B×B K×B 18. P—KKt4.

17 QR—K1 ch.

17 ...   K—B1

If 17... B—K4, White has a sparkling finish by 18. R×B ch. P×R 19. Kt—K4 K—B1 20. Q—B5 ch. Kt—Q3 21. B—R6 ch. K—K2 22. Kt—B6 Q—B1 23. Q—B3 P—QKt4 24. Q×KP ch. K—Q1 25. B—Kt5, and Black is helpless.

18 Kt—K4!	B—Q5
19 Q×B!	Kt×Q
20 Kt—B6	Resigns.

He loses the queen or is mated by 21. B—R6.

4. FOUR KNIGHTS' GAME

18 WHITE: POSCH—BLACK: DORRER
Vienna, 1957 (?)

1 P—K4	P—K4
2 Kt—KB3	Kt—QB3
3 Kt—B3	Kt—B3
4 B—Kt5	Kt—Q5
5 Kt×Kt	

5. Kt×P has often been tried and found wanting.

5 ...	P×Kt
6 P—K5	P×Kt
7 P×Kt	

The game has now become a four-knight-less game. If now 7... Q×P

8. QP×P leads to a very drawish position. But Black sees a pawn and grabs it—to pay a terrible penalty.

7 ...	P×P ch.?
8 B×P	Q×P
9 Castles	B—K2
10 B—B3	

The Australian master, Purdy, has introduced a method of counting tempi that is not in the "books": since the ultimate aim of the development is to bring the rooks into action, he compares the relative number of moves each side requires to connect the rooks. Here White needs one (with his queen); Black on the face of it three (with K, QP and

4. FOUR KNIGHTS' GAME

QB), but actually more because his KB is an object of attack as soon as he prepares for castling. Thus White has an overwhelming lead in exchange for his pawn.

| 10 ... | Q—Kt4 |
| 11 R—K1! | |

He can already give up a piece for if 11... Q×B 12. Q—Kt4, and now (a) 12... P—Q4 13. Q×P R—B1 14. R×B ch. K×R 15. B—B6 ch. K—K1 16. R—K1 ch. B—K3 17. R×B ch. P×R 18. Q—K7 mate; or (b) 12... R—KKt1 13. R×B ch. K×R 14. R—K1 ch. K—Q3 15. B—K5 ch. K—B3 16. P—QB4 and the king will be chased to death. As he plays, Black succeeds in castling, but that is about all he succeeds in.

11 ...	Castles
12 R—K5	Q—B3
13 B—Q3	

This position is the outcome of Black's misguided pawn snatch. White threatens 14. R—KR5, and there is no defence (13... P—KKt3 14. R—R5 Q—K3 15. R×P K×R 16. Q—R5 ch. and mate on R8).

13 ...	P—KR3
14 Q—Kt4	Q—R5
15 Q×P ch.	K×Q
16 R—Kt5 mate.	

5. PETROFF'S DEFENCE

19 White: Sanguinetti—Black: Puiggros

Mar del Plata, 1957

| 1 P—K4 | P—K4 |
| 2 Kt—KB3 | Kt—KB3 |

Beloved of Marshall, the Petroff is today almost out of business—perhaps because simple development will usually give White a small positional advantage —something that is true of neither the Ruy Lopez nor the Two Knights' Defence. It is only against attempts to "refute" the Petroff move out of hand that Black can hit back with a variety of attacking manoeuvres as often shown by Marshall.

3 Kt×P	P—Q3
4 Kt—KB3	Kt×P
5 P—Q4	P—Q4
6 B—Q3	B—Q3

| 7 Castles | Castles |
| 8 P—B4 | P—QB3 |

8... B—KKt5 (Marshall) leads to interesting play, but is not quite sufficient. The accepted continuation is 8... B—K3; but after 9. Q—K2 Kt—KB3 10. P—B5 B—K2 11. P—QKt4 White certainly has the pull. The text is too passive, hampering Black in the development of his queen side.

| 9 Q—B2 | B—KKt5 |

Played with a view to 10. B×Kt P×B 11. Q×P B×Kt 12. Q×B Q—R5 —regaining the pawn and easing his development problems. But White counters with a fine combination.

10 Kt—K5!	B×Kt
11 P×B	B—B4
12 P—B3!	Q—Kt3 ch
13 P—B5!	

16

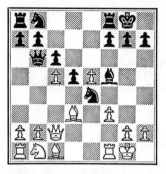

If 13. K—R1 Kt—B7 ch. The sacrifice in the text is decisive.

13 ...	Kt×P
14 B×B	Kt—Kt6 ch.
15 R—B2	Kt×R
16 B×P ch.	K—R1
17 Q—KB5	

Leaving Black defenceless against the threat, Q—R5.

17 ...	R—K1
18 Q—R5	R×P
19 B—B5 ch.	K—Kt1
20 Q—R7 ch.	K—B1
21 Q—R8 ch.	Resigns.

For if 21... K—K2 22. B—Kt5 ch. P—B3 23. Q×P ch., etc.—if 22... K—Q3 23. Q—B8 ch. K—B2 24. B—Q8 mate.

20 White: Keres—Black: Alexander
Hastings, 1954/55

1 P—K4	P—K4
2 Kt—KB3	Kt—KB3
3 Kt×P	P—Q3
4 Kt—KB3	Kt×P
5 P—Q4	P—Q4
6 B—Q3	B—K2

With this move, instead of 6... B—Q3 Black virtually allows the opponent the fine outpost, K5, for his knight, for White will always be able to work out of the pin that follows.

| 7 Castles | Kt—QB3 |

| 8 R—K1 | B—KKt5 |
| 9 P—B3 | Kt—B3 |

If 9... P—B4 10. Q—Kt3 with the threat of 11. Kt—K5, and if then 10... B×Kt 11. P×B, Black loses either the BP or the QP, while he has not sufficient force at his command to exploit the weakened white pawns.

| 10 B—KKt5 | Q—Q2 |

Alexander dislikes positions in which he has slightly the worse game without counterplay and therefore discards 10..., Castles in favour of Castles (Q).

11 QKt—Q2	Castles (Q)
12 Q—R4	P—KR3
13 B—R4	P—KKt4
14 B—Kt3	B×Kt
15 Kt×B	P—Kt5

Hoping to force the knight away before Kt—K5 becomes a threat—but it is a threat already! However, after 15... Kt—K5 16. B×Kt P×B 17. R×P P—Kt5 18. Kt—K5 Kt×Kt 19. P×Kt! White retains his plus pawn.

16 Kt—K5!

An elegant way of deciding the game. Also possible, as Golombek points out, was 16. B—Kt5 P×Kt 17. B×Kt Q×B (P×B? 18. Q×RP) 18. R×B Q×Q 19. R×P ch. K—Kt1 20. R—B4 ch., with a sound plus pawn.

| 16 ... | Kt×Kt |
| 17 B—B5! | |

The surprising point of his previous move.

17 ...	Q×B
18 R×Kt	Q—Q6

If 18... Q—Kt3 19. R×B R—Q2 20. R×R (but not 20. Q×P? R×R 21. Q—R8 ch. K—Q2 22. Q×R R—K1) Kt×R 21. R—K1! P—R3 22. P—QB4! wins. Even clearer is 18... Q—Q2 19.

Q×P Q—Q3 20. QR—K1 B—B1 21. R—B5! Q—B3 22. B—R4 B—Kt2 23. R—K7, etc.

19 R×B	R—Q2
20 R—K3	Q—R3
21 Q×Q	P×Q
22 B—K5	Resigns.

6. EVANS GAMBIT

21 WHITE: CIOCALTEA—BLACK: BRZOZKA

Polanica, 1958

1 P—K4	P—K4
2 Kt—KB3	Kt—QB3
3 B—B4	B—B4
4 P—QKt4	B×P
5 P—B3	B—R4
6 P—Q4	

White has an equally good alternative in 6. Castles. A game won by Tchigorin at odds of queen's knight continued 6... P—Q3? (better is 6... Kt—B3 7. P—Q4 Castles) 7. P—Q4 B×P 8. Q—Kt3! B×R 9. B×P ch. K—K2 10. B—Kt5 ch. Kt—B3 11. R×B Kt×QP 12. Kt×Kt P×Kt 13. R—K1 Q—B1 14. P—K5 Q×B 15. P×Kt db. ch. K—B1 16. R—K7 Resigns; for if 16... Q×Q 17. P×P ch. K—Kt1 18. P×Q P—KR4 19. B—B6 R—R3 20. R—K8 ch. and wins. A droll finish.

6 ...	Q—B3

Black could carry out the plan in the present game and save a vital tempo by avoiding the need for P—KR3 by moving 6... Q—K2 7. Castles B—Kt3 8. Kt×P Kt×Kt 9. P×Kt Q×P 10. Q—Kt3 Q—QR4 11. B—R3 Kt—K2 12. P—K5 Kt—B3 13. Kt—Q2 Kt×P 14. KR—K1 P—Q3, when Black held on to his extra material and eventually won (*Barden-Gereben, Hastings, 1958/59*).

The alternative idea is 6... P—Q3 7. Q—Kt3 Q—Q2 8. P×P, but a

number of Russian games have demonstrated that this is favourable to White, which explains why there has been a semi-revival of the Evans in the last few years.

7 Castles	P—KR3

If he continues naturally with 7... KKt—K2, White continues as in a famous game between Tchigorin and Steinitz by 8. P—Q5 Kt—Q1 9. Q—R4 B—Kt3 10. B—KKt5 Q—Q3 11. Kt—R3, with a big advantage.

8 P×P	Kt×P
9 Kt×Kt	Q×Kt
10 Q—Kt3	Q—R4

If 10... Q—B3 11. P—K5 Q×P 12. B×P ch., and the black king is a sitting duck in the centre.

11 P—K5	Kt—K2
12 B—R3	Kt—B3
13 Kt—Q2	B—Kt3

If 13... Kt×P 14. KR—K1 P—Q3, White utilizes his extra tempo over the Barden-Gereben game by 15. Q—Kt5 ch.

14 QR—K1	Kt—R4
15 Q—R4	K—Q1

Confession of failure, but if 15... Kt×B, White breaks through by 16. P—K6 P×P 17. R×P ch. K—B2 18. R—K7 ch., followed by 19. Q×Kt.

16 B—Q3	R—K1
17 Kt—B3	R—K3

If 17... Kt—B3 18. Q—KB4, still leaves Black entangled.

18 P—R4

White has designs on the queen (19. P—Kt4) as well as on the king.

18 ...	P—B3
19 P×P	P×P
20 R×R	P×R

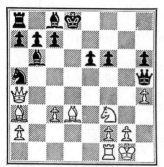

21 B—Kt6

Suddenly Black is left without resource, for if 21... Q×B 22. R—Q1 ch., and mate in three.

21 ...	B—Q2
22 R—Q1	Resigns.

Either the king or the queen goes.

22 WHITE: CLEMENZ—BLACK: EISENSCHMIDT

Dorpat, 1862

1 P—K4	P—K4
2 Kt—KB3	Kt—QB3
3 B—B4	B—B4
4 P—QKt4	B×P
5 P—B3	B—B4

An inferior line which enables White to get a quick advantage in the centre.

6 P—Q4	P×P
7 P×P	B—Kt3
8 Castles	P—Q3
9 Kt—B3	B—Q2

It is said that Morphy once attended a spiritualist seance and asked the medium what was Black's best move in this position; for the only time in the evening the spirit and the medium were completely tongue-tied. The answer, at any rate, is certainly not the move which Black plays here. 9... B—Kt5 10. B—QKt5 K—B1 has been suggested as equalizing, but it remains to be tested.

10 P—K5	P×P
11 R—K1	KKt—K2
12 Kt—KKt5	B—K3

Black is already in great trouble, for if 12... Castles 13. Q—R5 wins quickly.

13 B×B	P×B
14 Kt×KP	Q—Q3
15 Kt×KtP ch.	K—B1
16 Q—Kt4	B×P

If 16... Q—Kt3 17. Kt—K6 ch. K—Kt1, White's best would be to swap queens and win the ending after 18. Q×Q ch. P×Q 19. P×P Kt—Q5 20. Kt×Kt B×Kt 21. B—Q2—although, considering the climate of chess thought in 1862, he would probably have continued to play for the attack and lost.

17 Kt(B3)—K4	Q—Kt5
18 Kt—K6 ch.	K—K1

If 18... K—B2 19. Kt(K4)—Kt5 ch. K—K1 20. Kt×P ch. K—Q1 21. Kt(Kt5)—K6 ch. K—B1 22. B—R3! Q×B 23. Kt—QKt5 Q—R4 24. Kt—B4 dis. ch. K—Kt1 25. Kt—Q7 ch. K—B1 26. Kt—Kt6 db. ch., with a typical Philidor mate after 26... K—Kt1 27. Q—B8 ch. R×Q 28. Kt—Q7 mate.

19 Kt—B6 ch.	K—B2
20 Kt—Kt5 ch.	K—B1

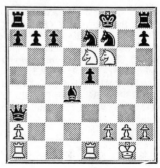

6. EVANS GAMBIT

If 20... K×Kt 21. Q—K6 ch. followed by Q—B7 ch. and Kt—K6 dis. ch. If 20... K—Kt2 21. Kt—R5 ch. K—B1 22. B—R3 Q×B 23. Q—K6.

21 B—R3!	Q×B
22 Q—K6	Kt—Q1
23 Q—B7 ch.	Kt×Q
24 Kt—K6 mate.	

The final position certainly deserves a diagram.

7. SCOTCH GAME AND SCOTCH GAMBIT

23 WHITE: PENROSE—BLACK: BLAU

Hastings, 1957/8

1 P—K4	P—K4
2 Kt—KB3	Kt—QB3
3 P—Q4	P×P
4 P—B3	

The gambit is also playable with 4. B—QB4. A game, *Martin-Pompei, Rapperswil, 1955*, continued 4... B—B4 5. Castles P—Q3 6. P—B3 P×P 7. Kt×P B—K3 8. Kt—Q5 Q—Q2 9. P—QR3 Kt—K4 10. Kt×Kt P×Kt 11. Q—Kt3 P—QB3 12. R—Q1! B—Q5 (not 12... P×Kt 13. B—QKt5, but 12... Q—B1 is better) 13. B—K3 Castles 14. QR—B1, K—Kt1 15. R×B! P×R (the main alternative is 15... P×Kt 16. P×P P×R 17. B—B4 ch. K—R1 18. P×B P×P 19. B×P, followed by 20. R—B7); 16. B—B4 ch. K—B1 17. Q—R4, B×Kt 18. P×B Q—Kt5 19. P—KKt3 Kt—K2 20. P×P Kt×P 21. B—QR6 Resigns.

4 ...	Kt—B3

Black's soundest procedure is to accept the pawn by 4... P×P 5. Kt×P B—Kt5 6. B—QB4 Kt—B3 7. Castles B×Kt 8. P×B P—Q3; and now neither 9. B—R3 B—Kt5 (*Penrose-Smyslov, Münich, 1958*), nor 9. P—K5, Kt×P 10. Kt×Kt P×Kt 11. Q—Kt3 Q—K2 12. B—R3 P—B4 13. Q—Kt5 ch. Kt—Q2 give White enough for his sacrifice.

5 P—K5	Kt—KKt5?

5... Kt—K5 6. Q—K2 puts Black in some difficulty, but the decentralizing text-move is still worse.

6 P×P	P—Q4
7 B—QKt5	

White could, of course, drive back the knight and wreck Black's pawns by 7. P—KR3 Kt—R3 8. B×Kt, but reasons that this can wait since the knight is misplaced in any case.

7 ...	B—Q2
8 Kt—B3	Kt—K2
9 Castles	P—QB3

Exchanges in this position don't relieve Black's game, for if 9... B×B 10. Kt×B Kt—Kt3 11. Kt—Kt5 Kt—R3 12. P—K6 is deadly.

10 B—Q3	Q—B1

Black can no longer play natural moves. If 10... Kt—Kt3 11. Kt—KKt5 (threatening P—K6) Kt—R3 12. P—B4, and the pawn roller is overwhelming.

11 R—K1	B—K3
12 Kt—KKt5	P—KKt3
13 Kt×B	Q×Kt
14 B—KKt5	P—KR4
15 Q—Kt3	Q—Q2
16 R—K2	B—Kt2
17 Q—R3	

Black's king is now permanently confined to the centre, and the opening of the king's file is looming up. If 17... Q—K3 18. Kt—R4 P—Kt3 19. Kt×P. Black's next move is intended as a preparation for ... Q—K3, but White strikes first.

17 ...	P—Kt3
18 P—K6	P×P

19 Kt×P!

The knight cannot be accepted in any of the four ways, for if 19... KP×Kt 20. R×Kt ch., or if 19... Kt×Kt 20. B×P ch., or 19... BP×Kt 20. B—Kt5, or finally 19... Q×Kt 20. Q×Kt mate.

19 ...   Kt—B4
20 B×Kt   Resigns.

For if 20... P×B 21. R×P ch. Q×R 22. Kt—B7 ch.

24 WHITE: LEPICHIN—BLACK: TARASOV

Novosibirsk, 1958

1 P—K4	P—K4
2 Kt—KB3	Kt—QB3
3 P—Q4	P×P
4 Kt×P	B—B4

This gives more winning chances to Black than the alternative 4... Kt—B3.

5 B—K3	Q—B3
6 P—QB3	KKt—K2
7 Kt—B2	

This is rather passive. White's best way of maintaining equality (he cannot well hope for more in this opening) is 7. B—QB4.

| 7 ... | P—Q3 |
| 8 B×B | |

Not good, since Black's increased hold on the centre and possession of the open Q file outweighs the doubled pawns. 8. Kt—Q2 B—K3 9. B—K2

B×B 10. Kt×B Castles KR 11. Castles P—Q4, still keeps the game about level.

8 ...	P×B
9 Kt—K3	Castles
10 Kt—Q2	B—K3
11 B—K2	QR—Q1
12 Castles	Q—R3
13 B—B4	

This and the following exchange allow Black's rooks to invade the king's side. Although White's position is passive, there is only one open file and there is no reason for him to lose if he chooses a plan which leads to simplifying exchanges of the rooks. A sound idea is 13. P—KB4 R—Q2 (if 13... P—B4, then not 14. P—K5 because of 14... Kt×P; but 14. P×P Kt×P 15. Kt×Kt R×Kt 16. B—Kt4); 14. Q—B2 KR—Q1 15. QR—Q1, followed by P—KKt3 and Kt—Kt3.

13 ...	Kt—K4
14 B×B	P×B
15 Q—B2	R—B5
16 P—KR3	R—R5
17 Kt(K3)—B4	Kt(K2)—Kt3
18 QR—Q1	R—Q6
19 Kt×Kt	R(Q6)×RP

This is a refinement of White's torture, for Black could also win by the simple 19... Kt×Kt, e.g. 20. Kt—Kt3 R(Q6)×RP 21. P×R Q—Kt4 ch. 22. K—R2 Kt—B5 ch.; or 20. P—KB4, R(R5)×RP 21. P×R (if 21. P—KKt R—R8 ch. 22. K—B2 Q—K6 mate)

R—Kt6 ch. 22. K—B2 Q×P ch. 23.
K—K1 R—K6 mate.

| 20 P×R | R×RP |
| 21 P—B3 | |

Otherwise 21... R—R8 ch. and 22...
Q—R6 mate.

| 21 ... | R—R8 ch. |

| 22 K—B2 | R—R7 ch. |
| 23 K—Kt1 | |

White here lost in a graceful way by exceeding the time limit with 17 moves still to make, but he could have equally well have resigned since 23... Q—R6 wins immediately (24. R—B2 R—R8 mate; or 24. Kt(Q2)—B4 R×Q).

8. DANISH GAMBIT

25 WHITE: WYSOWSKI—BLACK: ROZMAN

By Correspondence, 1951

1 P—K4	P—K4
2 P—Q4	P×P
3 P—QB3	P×P
4 B—QB4	P×P
5 B×P	P—Q3

There is an entirely erroneous impression about that the double pawn sacrifice in the Danish Gambit can be refuted out of hand by Schlechter's 5... P—Q4 6. B×QP Kt—KB3 7. B×P ch. K×B 8. Q×Q B—Kt5 ch. 9. Q—Q2 B×Q ch. 10. Kt×B P—B4; but if White does not now lose time by P—B4 and concentrates on his lead in piece development (11. KKt—B3!) it is very doubtful who has the better ending.

6 Q—Kt3	Q—K2
7 Kt—QB3	P—QB3
8 Castles	B—K3
9 B×B	P×B
10 Kt—B3	Kt—QR3
11 B—R3!	

One glance at the position shows that White has a tremendous lead in development which ought to tell as soon as the game opens up. In the face of the two threats 12. B×P and 12. P—K5, how is Black to prevent this? If 11... Castles 12. P—K5 Q—KB2 (if 12... Kt—B4 13. B×Kt P×B 14. R×R ch. K×R 15. Kt—K4 poses much the same problems as the game); 13. P×P plants a nasty

thorn in Black's side:—the pawn cannot be removed by 13... Q—B5 ch. 14. K—B2 B×P, because of 15. Q×KP ch. K—B2 16. R—Q4.

| 11 ... | Kt—B4 |

Meeting both threats, but allowing the fatal opening of the game.

| 12 B×Kt | P×B |

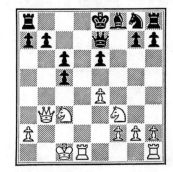

13 Kt—QKt5!

Clever and decisive in view of the threat 14. Kt—Q6 ch. If 13... Q—KB2 14. Kt—Kt5! Q—B5 ch. 15. K—Kt1 Q×Kt 16. Q×P ch., any 17. Kt—B7 mate. Black's trouble is that neither here nor later can he afford to give the queen for rook and minor piece, because his backward development would cost him further material.

13 ...	R—Q1
14 R×R ch.	K×R
15 Kt—Q6!	P—QKt3

8. DANISH GAMBIT

(...15 Q×Kt 16. R—Q1)

16 Kt—K5!	K—B2
17 Kt(6)—B7	Kt—R3
18 Q—R4	Kt×Kt

The double threat of Q×BP ch. and Q×RP ch. can no longer be met.

19 Q×RP ch.	K—B1
20 Q—R8 ch.	K—B2
21 Q×P ch.	K—Kt1
22 Kt—Q7 ch.	Resigns.

A game of which any grandmaster could be proud.

9. KING'S GAMBIT

26 WHITE: STOLTZ—BLACK: SÄMISCH

Swinemünde, 1932

1 P—K4	P—K4
2 P—KB4	P×P
3 Kt—KB3	P—KKt4
4 P—KR4	P—Kt5
5 Kt—K5	Kt—KB3
6 P—Q4	

This move in the Kieseritzky Gambit is originally a recommendation by Rubinstein. It complements the idea of 4. P—KR4: to break up the black pawn position on the K-side rather than play for the imaginary weakness of KB7 (by either 4. B—B4 or now 6. B—B4), which can always be stopped by Black's P—Q4. The basic idea of the King's Gambit is the opening of the KB file, and to this end the black pawn on KB4 must be removed—either this is right or the King's Gambit is wrong. Which of the two alternatives is the correct one, is still doubtful.

6 ,...	P—Q3
7 Kt—Q3	Kt×P
8 B×P	Q—K2
9 Q—K2	B—Kt2
10 P—B3	P—KR4?

Black is trying to safeguard his extra pawn, completely unaware of the fact that the opponent, a pawn down and with no advantage in development, will actually invite an exchange of queens. The reason for this seeming anomaly is that, after P—KR4, the black pawn position is irremediably weakened. Much better was rapid development by

10... B—B4 in preparation for queen side castling. It is not clear whether in that case White has sufficient compensation for his pawn.

11 Kt—Q2!	Kt×Kt
12 K×Kt	Q×Q ch.
13 B×Q	B—B4

13... Castles would be answered with 14. B—K3 B—B4 15. Kt—B4 B—Kt3 16. Kt—Q5 as indicated by König, whose excellent appreciation of this game in *Chess from Morphy to Botvinnik* we follow throughout.

| 14 KR—KB1 | Kt—Q2 |

Becker discusses the alternative 14... Kt—B3 15. B—Kt5 B—Kt3 16. Kt—B4 Castles 17. B—Q3 B×B 18. Kt×B P—B3 19. B—K3 K—B2 20. Kt—B4 R—R1 21. Kt—Q5 QR—QB1 22. B—Kt5, regaining his pawn with a strong attack.

| 15 Kt—Kt4 | Kt—B3 |
| 16 B—Kt5 ch. | B—Q2 |

Or 16... P—B3 17. Kt×P P×Kt 18. B×P ch. K—K2 19. B×R R×B 20. B—Kt5 B—K3 21. R—B2 followed by 22. QR—KB1.

| 17 QR—K1 ch. | K—Q1 |

If 17... K—B1 18. B×B Kt×B 19. Kt—Q5 R—Q1 (the BP cannot be protected: 19... R—B1 20. Kt×P R×Kt 21. B×P ch.) 20. Kt×P Kt—B3 21. B—Kt5 and wins.

| 18 B—Kt5 | B×B |

23

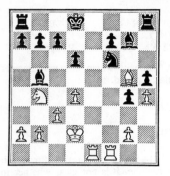

19 R × Kt!   Resigns.

The finish could be 19... B×R 20. B×B ch. K—Q2 21. R—K7 ch. K—Q1 22. R×KBP ch. K—K1 23. R—K7 ch. K—B1 24. Kt—Q5! and the triple threat of B×R, Kt×P and Kt—B4 is unanswerable. This game is one of the greatest *strategic* miniatures of all time.

27 WHITE: HORSEMAN—BLACK: HORNE

Hastings, 1955/56

1 P—K4	P—K4
2 P—KB4	P×P
3 Kt—KB3	P—KKt4
4 P—KR4	P—Kt5
5 Kt—Kt5	P—KR3
6 Kt×P	K×Kt
7 Kt—B3?!	

With this move Horseman introduces an innovation in the old Allgaier Gambit. The usual continuations are 7. P—Q4 or 7. B—B4 ch. By being able to capture on Q5 with a knight White creates interesting new attacking possibilities, which the opponent could have avoided by answering 7... Kt—KB3! 8. P—Q4 P—Q4 9. B×P B—Kt5 leading back to known positions.

7 . . .	P—Q4
8 Kt×P	B—K2
9 B—B4	B×P ch.
10 K—B1	P—Kt4

Black intends to play K—Kt2 without having to worry about P—QKt3 and

B—Kt2 ch. and thus drives the bishop to Kt3, though in doing so he seriously weakens his QR1—Q4 diagonal. 10... B—K3 (with the threat of P—B3) looks superior to us.

11 B—Kt3	K—Kt2
12 P—Q3	B—Kt4
13 B×P	Kt—KB3

Black is in difficulties. If 13... B×B 14. Kt×B Kt—KB3 15. P—K5 with the threat of 16. P—K6. If in this line 14.... Q—B3 15. P—Kt3 followed by 16. K—Kt2 and an attack along the KB file very much as in the game.

14 B×B

Heading for an "irresistible" attack along the KB file, White disdains the complexities of 14. B×P Kt×Kt 15. B×Q Kt—K6 ch. In view of the possibility indicated at Black's 18th move, however, one may well ask whether this line would not have been preferable.

14 . . .	P×B
15 R×R	Q×R!

If 15... K×R 16. Q—Q2 Kt×Kt 17. B×Kt Q—B3 ch. 18. K—K2! P—B3 (if Kt—B3 19. B×Kt Q×B 20. R—R1 ch. and 21. Q×P ch., etc.) 19. R—KB1 Q—Kt2 20. R—B7.

16 K—Kt1!   Kt×Kt

16... P—Kt6? would be useless: 17. Q—B3! Kt×Kt 18. B×Kt and if now 18... Q—R7 ch. 19. K—B1 Q—R8 ch. 20. K—K2 Q×R 21. Q—B7 ch. K—R3 22. Q—B6 ch. K—R2 23. B—B7 forces mate.

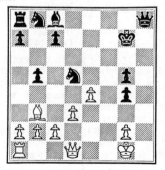

17 B×Kt	P—B3
18 Q—Q2	Q—R3?

Only this loses. In the heat of battle few players would consider letting the KtP go with check, yet 18... P×B would have set White a very difficult and perhaps insoluble problem. If then 19. Q×P ch. K—B2 20. R—B1 ch. K—K1 21. R—B6? B—Q2! (so as to provide a retreat on Q1 for the king in case of 22. Q—K5 ch.), the white attack fizzles out. Best would be 21. P×P Q—Q5 ch. 22. K—R2 P—Kt6 ch.! 23. Q×P (if 23. K×P Q—Kt5 ch.) Q—R1 ch. 24. K—Kt1 Q—Q5 ch. 25. R—B2—but the outcome would be doubtful.

19 R—KB1!

Now this is decisive, for if 19... P×B 20. Q—B3 ch. K—R2 21. R—B7 ch. K—Kt1 22. R—B6 Q—Kt2 23. Q×B ch., etc.

19 . . .	Kt—Q2
20 R—B7 ch	K—Kt3
21 Q—B2!	P×B
22 Q—B5 ch.	K—R4
23 R—R7	Resigns.

28 WHITE: PODGORNY—BLACK: STULIK

Czechoslovakia, 1956

1 P—K4	P—K4
2 P—KB4	P×P
3 Kt—KB3	B—K2
4 B—B4	Kt—KB3
5 Kt—B3	Kt×P
6 Kt—K5	

A suggestion of Levenfish's against the modern Cunningham Defence. However, after 6... Kt—Kt4! (Diemer), it is likely to disappear quickly from tournament practice. Other replies are far more dangerous, as this and the following game demonstrate.

6 . . .	Kt—Q3
7 B—Kt3	B—R5 ch.
8 P—Kt3	P×P
9 Castles	P×P ch.
10 K—R1	B—B3?

The decisive mistake. Brinckmann recommends 10... Castles 11. Q—R5 P—QKt3! (with the threat of 12... Q—K2, since Kt—Q5 can be countered by B—Kt2) 12. Kt×BP Kt×Kt 13. R×Kt R×R 14. B×R ch. K—R1 15. B—Kt6 B—Kt2 ch. 16. K×P P—KR3 17. P—Q4 B—Kt4 18. B×B Q×B 19. Q×Q P×Q 20. R—K1 Kt—B3—and it is very doubtful whether White has any advantage.

11 P—Q4	P—QKt3
12 Q—R5	B—Kt2 ch.
13 K×P	P—Kt3

Since this meets with a brilliant refutation, 13... Castles has been suggested as a better defence. However, after 14. Kt—Kt4, B×P 15. B—Kt5 Black is lost: 15... Q—B1 16. QR—Q1! P—Kt3 17. Kt—B6 ch.! B×Kt 18. B×B Kt—K1 (if 18... P×Q? 19. R—Kt1 ch.) 19. B—Q4 P—Q4 (preparing to capture the queen because the black queen can now interpose on Kt5, and also stopping the sacrifice on B2) 20. Q—K5 P—KB3 21. B×P ch. K—R1 22. Q—K7. Or 15...Q—K1 16.QR—K1 Kt—K5 17. R×P! R×R (if 17... B—K4 ch. 18. B—B4! wins a piece) 18. Kt×Kt and it is not apparent how Black can defend himself against the numerous threats.

14 Q—R6	B—Kt2

So as to punish 15. Q×B with Q—R5 ch. But:

15 Kt×BP!

25

15 ...	B×Q
16 Kt×Kt ch	P×Kt

If 16... K—K2 17. B×B K×Kt (or
17... P×Kt 18. QR—K1 ch. and mate
next move) 18. B—B4 ch. K—B3 19.
B—Q5 mate.

17 B—B7 ch	K—K2
18 B×B	Q—Kt1

White threatened both QR—K1 ch.
with mate next move, and B—Kt5 ch.
winning the queen and remaining a piece
up. There are four moves to cope with
both threats, but all are insufficient:

(a) 18... Q—B2 19. B—Kt5 ch. K—B1
20. B—Q5 ch. K—Kt2 21. R—B7 ch.
K—Kt1 22. B—R6! with mate on B8.

(b) 18... Q—QB1 19. B—Kt5 ch.
K—B1 20. B—Q5 ch. K—Kt2 21.
B—B6 ch. K—R3 22. K—Kt3!
P—KKt4 23. B—B7 Q—B3 24. P—Q5!
and the eventual mate on White's KR1
is unavoidable.

(c) 18... P—Q4! 19. B—Kt5 ch.
K—Q3 20. B×Q R×B 21. Kt—Kt 5
ch. K—B3 22. P—R4 B—R3 (if 22...
P—QR3 23. R—B6 ch. P—Q3 24.
B—K8 ch. R×B 25. R×P mate) 23.
R—B6 ch. P—Q3 24. Kt—B3 Kt—Q2
25. B×P ch. K—B2 26. R—B7 and
Black cannot break the bind of the white
pieces. This is the least spectacular and
most beautiful variation. The text reply
offers no chance at all.

19 B×Q	Resigns.

For if 19... R×B 20. B—Kt5 ch.
followed by QR—K1 ch. A return to the
Romantic era.

29 WHITE: SCHUSTER—BLACK: KARL

Heilbronn, 1957

1 P—K4	P—K4
2 P—KB4	P×P
3 Kt—KB3	B—K2
4 B—B4	Kt—KB3
5 Kt—B3	Kt×P
6 Kt—K5	P—Q4

7 B×P	Kt×Kt
8 B×P ch.	K—B1
9 KtP×Kt	B—Q3

This wins a piece and it does not seem
as though White gets anything for it.
However, he gives two pieces and gets a
great deal!

10 Castles!	B×Kt

He wants his pound of flesh. But the
alternative, 10... Q—K2 11. P—Q4
B×Kt 12. B×P! B—B3 13. B—QKt3
also leaves Black awkwardly placed
(13... B—K3 14. R—K1!).

11 B—R3 ch.!	K×B

Now he is committed, for if 11...
B—Q3 12. R×P and the bishop cannot
be taken because of 12... B×B 13.
B—Kt3 ch. K—K2 14. Q—K2 ch., etc.

12 Q—R5 ch.

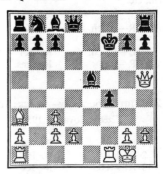

12 ..	K—B3

A hard decision. Jl12... P—Kt3 13.
Q×B R—K1 14. Q×KBP ch. K—Kt1
15. Q—B7 ch. K—R1 16. B—Kt2!
Kt—B3 17. P—B4 ch. Kt—Q5 18.
QR—K1 R×R 19. R×R B—B4 20.
R—K8 ch.! followed by mate. If 12...
K—Kt1 13. Q×B Kt—B3 14. Q—K4!
P—KR3 15. R×P B—Q2 16. QR—
KB1 Q—K1 17. R—B8 ch. Q×R 18.
B×Q, and if 18... R×B 19. Q—Q5 ch.
However, 12... K—K3 promises rescue,
for it is doubtful whether the white
attack after 13. QR—K1 Q—B3 14.
P—Q4 Kt—B3 is sufficient.

9. KING'S GAMBIT

13 QR—K1	B—B4

13... Kt—B3 is not good enough:
14. R×B Kt×R 15. R×P ch., K—K3
16. Q—B5 ch., etc.

14 R×B!

Again—but with an even finer point.

14 ...	K×R
15 Q—B7!	Q×P

The only move since White threatened both P—Q4 ch. and R—K1 ch. (followed by P—Q3).

16 B—B1	Q×B

17 R×Q	Kt—B3
18 R—K1 ch.	B—K5
19 Q×KtP ch.	K—Q4
20 Q—B7 ch.	K—B4

(or 20... K—K4 21. Q—R5 ch.)

21 R×B	QR—QB1
22 Q—B4 ch.	K—Kt3
23 Q—Kt3 ch.	K—R3
24 R—R4 ch.	Resigns.

If 24... Kt—R4 25. Q—B4 ch.
P—Kt4 26. Q—B6 mate; or 25...
K—Kt3 26. R—Kt4 mate.

10. FALKBEER COUNTER GAMBIT

30 WHITE: MARSHALL—BLACK:
VON SOLDATENKOV
New York, 1926 (?)

1 P—K4	P—K4
2 P—KB4	P—Q4
3 P×QP	P—K5
4 P—Q3	Kt—KB3
5 P×P	Kt×KP
6 Q—K2	Q×P
7 Kt—Q2	P—KB4
8 P—KKt4?	

Charousek's system against the Falkbeer, as played, *inter alia*, in the famous encounter Charousek-Pillsbury, Nuremberg, 1896. Later it was Pillsbury himself who found the knock-out 8...
Kt—B3! Today we know that 8.
P—KKt3! is the correct move.

8 ...	Kt—B3!
9 P—B3	

If 9. P×P B×P (9... Kt—Q5 10.
Q×Kt ch., etc., only leads to an ending in which Black has to struggle with R+P against two minor pieces) 10. B—Kt2
Castles! 11. Kt×Kt Kt—Q5! and wins; or if 11. B×Kt B×B 12. Kt×B (12.
Q×Kt Q×Q 13. Kt×Q R—K1 with a clear end game advantage) B—Kt5 ch.
13. P—B3 KR—K1 and wins.

9 ...	B—K2
10 B—Kt2	B—R5 ch.

11 K—B1	Castles
12 P×P	Kt×Kt ch.
13 B×Kt	Q×BP
14 B—K4?	

White has concluded the opening with an exposed king, an inferior development and weakened pawns, and still thinks he can make attacking moves.
14. Kt—B3! was imperative.

14 ...	Q—B3
15 Kt—B3	B—R6 ch.
16 K—Kt1	

From now on Black makes brilliant use of the imprisonment of the white king.

16 ...	QR—K1
17 Q—Q3	R—Q1

18 B×P ch.

27

10. FALKBEER COUNTER GAMBIT

Mainly to gain square Kt6 for the queen. The alternative 18. Q—B2 would be answered with 18... Kt—K4! and now (a) 19. P×Kt Q—QKt3 ch. 20. Kt—Q4 B—B7 mate; (b) 19. Kt×Kt Q—Kt4 ch.! 20. P×Q B—B7 mate; (c) 19. Q—Kt3 ch. K—R1 20. P×Kt R×B with an early mate.

18 . . .	K—R1
19 Q—Kt6	R×B!
20 Kt×R	Kt—Q5!
21 Q—R5	Q—Kt4 ch.!

Resigns.

If 21. Q×Q Kt—K7 mate; if 21... P×Q B—B7 mate. The brilliant finish is worthy of the winner's opponent.

11. VIENNA GAMBIT

31 WHITE: MILNER-BARRY—BLACK: HANNINEN

Moscow, 1956

1 P—K4	P—K4
2 Kt—QB3	Kt—KB3
3 P—B4	P—Q4
4 P×KP	Kt×P
5 P—Q3	

This interesting move, instead of the more usual 5. Kt—B3, allows two wild variations, starting with 5... Q—R5 ch. and 5... B—QKt5 respectively. A game, *Honfi-Kluger, Budapest, 1958*, went: 5... B—QKt5 6. P×Kt Q—R5 ch. 7. K—K2 P×P 8. Q—Q4? (P—KKt3!) B—Kt5 ch. 9. Kt—B3 P×Kt ch. 10. K—K3 Kt—B3 11. B—Kt5 P×P 12. R—KKt1 B—QR4 13. B×Kt ch. P×B 14. Q—K4 B—Kt3 ch. 15. K—Q3 Castles ch.! Resigns. In the present game Black chooses the quiet positional main line which, however, is not without danger.

5 . . .	Kt×Kt
6 P×Kt	P—Q5
7 Kt—B3	P—QB4
8 B—K2	B—K2
9 Castles	Castles
10 Q—K1	P—B3
11 Q—Kt3	

Also strong is 11. P×P B×P 12. Q—Kt3 P×P 13. B—Kt5 Kt—QB3 14. B×B Q×B 15. Kt—Kt5 B—B4 16. B—B3, as in a game *Horseman-Barden. Oxford, 1952*.

| 11 . . . | BP×P |

But this is too obliging. The following assault had to be nipped in the bud by 11... K—R1!

| 12 B—R6 | B—B3 |
| 13 Kt×KP! | B×Kt? |

Apparently under the delusion that he was going to win a piece; otherwise Black should at least have completed his development by 13... Kt—B3!

| 14 Q×B | R—B3 |

Now he finds that the white bishop is taboo: if 14... P×B 15. R×R ch. Q×R 16. R—KB1 Q—Q1 17. B—B3 followed by B—Q5 ch. would finish quickly. Meanwhile, however, Black's position is in shreds.

| 15 B×P! | R—K3 |

If 15... K×B 16. Q—Kt5 ch. K—B2 17. B—R5 ch.

16 Q—R5!	Q—K2
17 B—R6	Kt—Q2
18 B—Kt4	R—K4

28

11. VIENNA GAMBIT

19 Q—R3
After this Black has no reasonable move left. The immediate threat is 20. B—B4.

19 ...	Kt—Kt3
20 R—B8 ch.	Q × R
21 B × Q	K × B
22 Q × P	Resigns.

12. PHILIDOR'S DEFENCE

32 White: E. Z. Adams—Black: Torre

New Orleans, 1920

1 P—K4	P—K4
2 Kt—KB3	P—Q3
3 P—Q4	P × P

This "surrender of the centre" is rarely played. Either 3... Kt—KB3 or 3... Kt—Q2 are the usual moves here.

4 Q × P	Kt—QB3
5 B—QKt5	B—Q2
6 B × Kt	B × B
7 Kt—B3	Kt—B3
8 Castles	B—K2
9 Kt—Q5	B × Kt

After this move Black will have slight difficulties because of the pressure exerted by the QP. Much simpler was 9... Castles, for if then, as has been suggested, 10. Kt × B ch. Q × Kt 11. B—K5, the simple 11... Q × P 12. B × Kt P × B 13. Q × BP Q—Kt3 would give Black the slightly superior game.

10 P × B	Castles
11 B—Kt5	P—B3
12 P—B4	P × P
13 P × P	P—QR4?

This move allows White to double his rooks on the K-file—a factor which decides the game. Either the "loophole move" 13... P—KR3, or the immediate 13... R—K1 was superior.

14 KR—K1	R—K1
15 R—K2	QR—B1
16 QR—K1	

Threatening 17. B × Kt P × B 18. Q—Kt4 ch. K—B1 (if K—R1 19. R × B R × R 20. R × R Q × R 21. Q × R ch); 19. Kt—R4 and the attack against KKt7 (via KB5) is unanswerable.

Black's reply seems to meet the danger.

16 ...	Q—Q2
17 B × Kt!	

Most surprising. Doesn't the man see that the bishop can recapture now?

17 ...   B × B

This position looks perfectly harmless for Black. It seems that White's preponderance on the K-file will be broken by exchanges, and the remaining endgame is clearly in Black's favour: White's QP is weak and Black's bishop superior to the knight. However, the middle game is not over yet.

18 Q—KKt4!

With this move starts the most famous queen sacrifice combination in the literature of chess. Everything that follows is based on White's threat to the rook on K8.

18 ...	Q—Kt4
19 Q—QB4!	

This time the queen is offered to two different pieces, neither of which can capture.

19 ...   Q—Q2

29

20 Q—B7!	Q—Kt4
21 P—QR4!	

The decisive finesse, which finally forces the black queen from the protection of the rook.

21 ...	Q×RP
22 R—K4	Q—Kt4
23 Q×KtP!	Resigns.

Black's queen can no longer defend the rook.

33 White: Heidenfeld—Black: Wolpert

Johannesburg, 1955

1 P—K4	P—K4
2 Kt—KB3	P—Q3
3 P—Q4	Kt—KB3
4 Kt—B3	QKt—Q2
5 B—QB4	B—K2
6 B×P ch.?	

In this form the sacrifice is insufficient; White should first close the square K5 to a black piece, as in *Pachman-Guimard, Göteborg, 1955*, which continued: 6. P×P P×P 7. B×P ch. K×B 8. Kt—Kt5 ch. K—Kt1 9. Kt—K6 Q—K1 10. Kt×BP Q—Kt3 11. Kt×R Q×P 12. R—B1 Kt—B4 13. Q—K2 B—R6 14. B—K3 Q×R ch. 15. Q×Q B×Q 16. K×B with an insignificant white advantage.

6 ...	K×B
7 Kt—Kt5 ch.	K—Kt1
8 Kt—K6	Q—K1
9 Kt×BP	Q—Kt3
10 Kt×R?	

After this capture the game is lost by force, though the demonstration requires ingenious and precise play. An interesting idea is to be satisfied with the two pawns and general dislocation of the black game, and play 10. Castles R—Kt1 11. Q—Q3 P—KR3 12. P—B4 (*Brinckmann-Romih, Hamburg, 1930*).

11 ...	Q×P
11 R—B1	P×P
12 Q×P	

Keres gives 12. Q—K2 P×Kt 13. Q—B4 ch. P—Q4 14. Q×B ch. K—B2, which is also in Black's favour.

12 ...	Kt—K4
13 P—B4	

This is the move White had relied on; now Black can answer neither 13... Kt—B6 ch. 14. R×Kt Q×R 15. Q—B4 ch., nor 13... B—R6 14. Q—B2 Q×R ch., etc., as in the Pachman-Guimard game.

13 ...	Kt(B3)—Kt5!

Indirectly protecting the other knight through the threat of B—R5 ch.

14 Q—Q5 ch.

The only defence, forcing back the attacked knight, because after 14... K—B1? it would be taken with check. Thus the white queen is able to protect KB1.

14 ...	Kt—B2
15 Q—B4	B—R5 ch.
16 K—Q1	B—K3!

The third offer of a piece; if now 17. Q—Kt5? B—Q2! and White will not even be able to keep the bishop out by a direct attack (see move 19).

17 Q—K2	Kt—B7 ch.
18 R×Kt	

Even worse is 18. K—Q2 B—Kt5 19. R×Kt B×R 20. Q—Kt5, and now simply 20... P—KKt3, retaining his deadly discovered check.

18 ...	B×R
19 P—B5	Q—Kt8 ch.
20 K—Q2	Kt—K4!

The fourth piece offer rounds off the game harmoniously. White's best chance now was to accept the dare and hope for 21. P×B B—K6 ch.? 22. Q×B Kt—B5 ch. 23. K—Q3 Kt×Q 24. B×Kt Q×R 25. Kt—B7—when Black, though having the colossal material superiority of queen and rook for three minor pieces and a strong passed pawn, will find it difficult to stop the pawn without losing a whole rook. But Black has better:

12. PHILIDOR'S DEFENCE

21. P×B B—K8 ch.! 22. Q×B Kt—B6 ch. 23. K—K2 Kt×Q 24. B—K3 Q×P ch.! 25. K×Kt Q—R8 ch. 26. K—K2 Q×R 27. Kt—Q5 P—KR4! and the KRP is quickly decisive.

(*See diagram.*)

21 Kt—Q1?

Providing against B—K6 ch., but not against the alternative threat.

21 ...	B—K8 ch.
22 Q×B	Q—Q5 ch.
23 K—K2	B—B5 mate.

---

13. FRENCH DEFENCE

34 WHITE: ROSSETTO—BLACK: STAHLBERG

Vina del Mar, 1947

1 P—K4	P—K3
2 P—Q4	P—Q4
3 Kt—QB3	Kt—KB3
4 B—Kt5	B—K2
5 P—K5	KKt—Q2
6 P—KR4	P—QB4

Today regarded as the best method of meeting the Alekhine-Chatard Attack. For acceptance of the pawn see Keres-Wade.

7 Kt—Kt5

General preference is for 7. B×B, when Black has the choice between the solid 7... K×B and the chancey 7... Q×B 8. Kt—Kt5 Castles 9. Kt—B7, a sacrifice condemned by theory but usually successful in practice.

7 ...   P—B3

Keres suggests, as a promising alternative, 7... Kt—QB3 8. Kt—Q6 ch. K—B1 9. Q—R5 P—KKt3 10. Q—R6 ch. (10. Q—B3? Kt(Q2)×KP!) K—Kt1 11. B×B Q×B 12. P—KB4 Kt×QP 13. B—Q3 "with some attack for the pawn sacrificed". The text leads to a lovely scramble.

8 B—Q3   P—QR3!

Consistently maintaining the attack on the white centre, 8... P×B? 9. Q—R5 ch. K—B1 10. P×KtP would give White a tremendous attack. If then 10... B×P 11. Kt—Q6.

9 Q—R5 ch.   K—B1
10 R—R3

10. Kt—KR3 is too slow, as was shown in *Ragosin-Yanofsky, Saltjöbaden, 1948*; 10... P×QP 11. Kt—B4 Kt×P 12. QKt×P Q—Kt3 13. Castles (Q) Q×Kt! 14. B—Kt5 Q×R ch. 15. K×Q P×KB, and White has given up too much material.

10 ...   P×Kt
11 B—R6!   Q—R4 ch.!

Black, a piece up and with the white centre on the point of disintegration, naturally plays for a win. A draw could be had by 11... P×B 12. Q×P ch. K—B2, as given by Keres. If 12... K—K1, on the other hand, John Rather in *Chess Review*, suggests the interesting winning attempt 13. B—Kt6 ch. P×B 14. Q×P ch. K—B1 15. R—Kt3. If then 15... Kt—Kt3 16. Q—Kt7 ch. K—K1 17. Q×R ch. K—Q2 18. Q×Q ch. B×Q and though Black will have three minor pieces for a rook, the white KRP threatens to march through.

31

13. FRENCH DEFENCE

12 B—Q2

Now that the queen has vacated the square Q1 for the king, the perpetual check is no longer on, and White has to recall the bishop. Has he overreached himself?

12 ...   Q—B2
13 R—Kt3   P×QP

Threatening the exchange of queens by Q×P ch. Where is White's attack?

14 Kt—B3   Kt×P

There is nothing better against the threats of B—R6, R×P and Q—Kt4, but the text looks good enough:

15 R×P!

And suddenly it seems that Black is lost, for if now 15... Kt×Kt ch. so as to answer 16. P×Kt? with Q—K4 ch., White sidesteps by 16. K—Q1! And if 15... K×R 16. B—R6 ch. K—Kt1 17. Q—K8 ch. and mate next move.

15 ...   P—R3!

An equally ingenious defence. If now 16. B×RP? R×B 17. Q×R B—Kt5 ch. and wins.

16 B—R7!
The final surprise.

16 ...   K×R
17 Q×P ch.   K—B2
18 Q—R5 ch.

and draws by perpetual check. This is one of the finest games ever played, though far too many, who want to see blood for their money, will refer to it as "only a draw".

35 WHITE: KERES—BLACK: WADE

Anglo-Soviet Match, 1954

1 P—K4   P—K3
2 P—Q4   P—Q4
3 Kt—QB3   Kt—KB3
4 B—Kt5   B—K2
5 P—K5   KKt—Q2
6 P—KR4   B×B
7 P×B   Q×P

The acceptance of the pawn is regarded as "unplayable" by the books—but no determined attempt has yet been made to play it as it should be played. Fahrni, against Alekhine (Mannheim, 1914), and Spielmann, against Bogolyubov (Stockholm, 1919), both made the mistake of keeping their king in the centre, an error Wade repeats in aggravated form. With such a preponderance of force facing him on the king side, Black must do his utmost to effect Castles (Q).

8 Kt—R3   Q—K2
9 Kt—B4   P—QR3
10 Q—Kt4   K—B1?

Completely at variance with the spirit of the opening. Correct, as H. Müller has pointed out, is 10... P—KKt3 11. Castles, Kt—Kt3! (protecting both Q4 and QB1 and thus stopping an eventual Kt×QP) 12. B—Q3 QKt—Q2 13. R—R6 Kt—B1 14. QR—R1 B—Q2 followed by Castles (Q), with a somewhat cramped but perfectly tenable game.

11 Q—B3!

Threatening 12. Kt—Kt6 ch. and much stronger than the previously played 11. Castles P—QB4 12. Q—Kt3 to which Wade intended replying 12... P×P 13. Kt(3)×P Q—B4.

11 ...   K—Kt1
12 B—Q3   P—QB4?

Either 12... P—R3 or Kt—B1 had to be played to stop the following sacrifice. Of course, White would then have had the time to support his centre by Kt(3)—K2 and P—QB3 and continue his king side attack at leisure.

13 B×P ch.	R×B
14 R×R	K×R
15 Castles	P—B4?

Unaware of the danger. No better would have been 15... Q—Kt4 16. R—R1 ch. K—Kt1 17. R—R5. Wade gives 15... K—Kt1 as the best defence, with the possible sequel 16. R—R1 Kt—B1 17. Q—R3 P—B4 18. Q—R8 ch. K—B2 19. Q—R5 ch. K—Kt1 20. P—KKt4! (threatening to advance further) P×P 21. R—R4, followed by Q—R8 ch. and R×P, and the White attack wins through.

| 16 R—R1 ch. | K—Kt1 |
| 17 R—R8 ch.! | Resigns. |

If 17... K×R 18. Kt—Kt6 ch.; if 17... K—B2 18. Q—R5 ch. and mate next move.

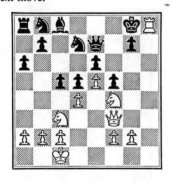

36 White: Giusti—Black: Cipriani

Correspondence, 1954/55

1 P—K4	P—K3
2 P—Q4	P—Q4
3 Kt—QB3	B—Kt5
4 P—K5	P—QB4
5 B—Q2	Kt—K2
6 Kt—Kt5	B×B ch.
7 Q×B	Castles
8 P—QB3	QKt—B3
9 Kt—Q6	Q—Kt3
10 Kt—B3	B—Q2
11 B—Q3	Kt—B1

This sequence of moves has often been seen in the Winawer variation characterized by 3... B—Kt5. Of the present position, Schwarz (*Die Französische Verteidigung*) says that Black has an "absolutely equal game", and Keres, in his famous work, commits the same error!

12. B×P ch!

In view of the above quotations, it is obvious that this is not "just another sacrifice on KR7".

| 12 ... | K×B |

If 12... K—R1 13. Q—Kt5 leaves Black no hope.

| 13 Kt—Kt5 ch. | K—Kt3 |

If 13... K—Kt1 14. Q—Q3 P—B4 15. Q—R3 R—K1 16. Kt×R B×Kt 17. Q—R7 ch. K—B1 18. Q—R8 ch. K—K2 19. Q×P ch. K—Q1 20. Kt×P mate. If, in this line, immediately 14... R—K1 15. Q—R7 ch. K—B1 16. Q—R8 ch. K—K2 17. Q×P Kt×Kt 18. Q—B6 ch. K—B1 19. P×Kt— threatening mate on R8 and B7.

| 14 Q—Q3 ch! | K×Kt |

White here announced mate in six moves, but Black's alternatives are no better :

14... P—B4 15. Q—R3 and now (*a*) 15... Kt×KP 16. Q—R7 ch. K×Kt 17. P—B4 ch. K×P 18. Q—R4 ch. Kt—Kt5 19. R—B1 ch. K—K6 20. Q—Kt3 mate; or (*b*) 15... K×Kt 16. P—B4 ch. K—Kt3 17. P—KKt4 P×P 18. Q×P ch. K—R2 19. R—KKt1 and mate cannot be averted; or (c) 15... Kt×Kt 16. Q—R7 ch. K×Kt 17. P—B4 ch. K×P 18. Q—R4 ch. K—K6 19. Q—Kt3 ch. K—K5 20. Q—B3 mate.

15 P—B4 ch.   Resigns.

For he is mated by 15... K—R3 16. Q—R3 ch. K—Kt3 17. P—KKt4 R—R1 18. Q×R Kt×KP 19. Q—R5 ch. K—B3 20. Q—Kt5 mate.

37 White: Oxford University— Black: Canisius College

By Correspondence, 1958

1	P—K4	P—K3
2	P—Q4	P—Q4
3	Kt—QB3	B—Kt5
4	P—K5	P—QB4
5	P—QR3	B—R4
6	P—QKt4	P×KtP
7	Kt—Kt5	P×P ch.?

Botvinnik used to continue with 7... B—B2, but the whole system is suspect. The text, allowing the white QB a fine diagonal, makes matters much worse.

8 P—B3   P—QKt3?

Hard to understand. Merely in order to develop his bishop to QR3, Black buries his other bishop alive. In effect, he will conduct the rest of the game without both his bishops.

9	Q—B3	P—B4
10	B×P	K—Q2
11	K—Q1	

Forestalling, in case of B—Q3, the reply P—QR3 followed by check on QB6.

11	...	B—R3
12	B—Q3	Kt—R3
13	Kt—K2	Q—Kt1

In order to deny the white knight the square KB4, Black wants to play P—KKt4. This he could not have done earlier because of Q—R5, which can now be answered by Q—Kt3. Therefore:

14 P—R4!   Kt—B3

15	Kt—B4	P—Kt3
16	R—K1	

Threatening 17. Kt×QP followed by P—K6 ch. and Q×P

16	...	Kt—K2
17	B—Q6	Kt—Kt5
18	R—K2	

Threatening 19. Kt—B7 which, if played immediately, could be answered with 19... B×B, forcing White to remove his KKt from the scene of action.

18 ...   P—Kt4

Played with desperate ingenuity. Black intends to open the KR file and plant a knight on KR7 in order to dislodge the white queen from her commanding post. But the relief comes too late.

19	P×P	P—R3
20	Kt×KP!	

The invasion begins: if now 20... K×Kt 21. B×P ch. Kt×B 22. Kt—B7 ch., regaining both pieces; if 20... Q×Kt 21. Kt—B7 Q—Kt3 (if 21... B×B 22. Q×B! but not 22. Kt×Q? B×R ch. 23. Q×B K×Kt) 22. B×B P×P 23. R×B P×R 24. Kt×P and wins in short order.

20	...	Kt—R7
21	Kt—B5 ch.!	K—B3

Acceptance would have led to the following exquisite finish: 21... P×Kt 22. P—K6 ch. K—B3 23. R×B! Kt×Q 24. R×B ch. K—Kt2 25. R—Kt2! K×R (if 25... P—B5 to stop the threat-

ened mate by Kt×P 26. Kt—B7 ch.
K—B1 27. Kt×R wins) 26. Kt—B7 ch.
K—R4 27. R—Kt5 ch. K—R5 28.
B—B2 ch. K—R6 29. B×P ch. K—R7
30. R—R5 ch. K—Kt7 31. Kt—Kt5
Kt—B3 32. B—R3 ch. K—R8 33.
R—R4 followed by 34. B—B1 mate.

22	R×B	Kt×Q

If 22... P×R 23. B×P! Kt×Q 24.
B—Q7 ch. K—Kt3 25. B—B7 mate.

23	R×B	Kt—B1
24	R—Kt2	Resigns.

White threatens 25. Kt×P ch, followed
by either B—Kt5 mate or R×P mate
according to Black's reply. The only
defence 24... Kt×B merely delays the
inevitable for a few moves after 25.
Kt×P ch. K—B2 (still quicker would be
25.... R×Kt 26. R(2)×P ch. K—B2
27. P×Kt ch. K—B1 28. R×R and
mate next move) 26. R(2)×P.

38 WHITE: SCHMEIL—BLACK: MERTINS

Berlin, 1957

1	P—K4	P—K3
2	P—Q4	P—Q4
3	Kt—QB3	B—Kt5
4	Kt—K2	P×P
5	P—QR3	B—K2

A safer line than the exchange followed by P—KB4, with which Nimzovitch
once lost a miniature to Alekhine (*200
Miniature Games of Chess*, p. 160).

6	Kt×P	Kt—KB3
7	KKt—B3	Kt—B3
8	B—K3	Kt×Kt
9	Kt×Kt	P—B4
10	Kt—B3	B—B3
11	B—QKt5	Castles
12	B×Kt	P×B

White aims at reaching an ending of
good knight *v.* bad bishop. In that case,
however, he should have refrained from
castling (Q), after which Tarrasch's
dictum that the Gods have placed the

middle-game before the endgame, gains
additional point.

13 P—B4

Trying to stop P—K4, but the cure is
worse than the disease. 13. Castles was
indicated.

13 ...	B—R3!
14 Q—Q2	R—Kt1
15 Castles?	

Instead of carefully making up for
past sins (15. Kt—R4—B5, chasing the
black bishop off the dominant diagonal),
White castles into it! Punishment is
swift and terrible.

15 ...	Q—Q3
16 Kt—R4	

Black threatened 16... R×P! 17.
K×R R—Kt1 ch., etc. This the text
move is designed to meet, threatening
in its turn to cut off the black queen by
17. Kt—B5. However, 16. Q—B2, preparing to "uncastle" in case of need, was
necessary.

16 ...	R×P!

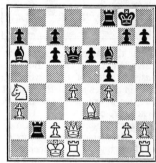

17 Kt×R	Q×RP
18 P—B3	R—Kt1
19 Q—QB2	R—Kt6!
20 B—Q2	

Immediate disaster could only be
averted by 20. Q×R, Q×Q 21. B—Q2,
but the position would have remained
hopeless.

20 ...	B—Q6!
21 Q×R	Q—R8 mate.

13. FRENCH DEFENCE

39 WHITE: BARENDREGT—BLACK:
VAN OOSTERWIJK BRUIN

Dutch Championship Elimination,
1951

1 P—K4	P—K3
2 P—Q4	P—Q4
3 Kt—QB3	B—Kt5
4 B—Q2	P×P
5 Q—Kt4	Q×P
6 Castles	Kt—KB3
7 Q×KtP	R—Kt1
8 Q—R6	B—B1
9 Q—R4	R—Kt5
10 Q—R3	Q×P
11 B—K2!	

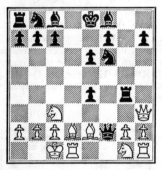

So far the game is identical with the
decisive game in the Boleslavsky-
Bronstein match of 1950, which made
Bronstein challenger for the world title.
Black, two pawns up, threatens to force
the exchange of queens by 11... R—R5
—a threat Boleslavsky tried to meet by
11. Kt—Kt5, which lost in short order.
Barendregt finds a very ingenious way
of coping with Black's simplification
desire.

11 ...   R—Kt3?

Obviously, if 11... R×P 12. R—B1!
And if 11... R—R5 as per plan, White
would win the exchange by 12. Q×R!
Q×Q 13. P—KKt3. Whether, however,
he then would have an advantage after
the further moves 13... Q—R3! 14.
B×Q B×B ch. 15. K—Kt1 B—Q2 is
doubtful: Black has two pawns for the

exchange, and it would not be easy for
White to get at the exposed KP. After
the timid text Black is murdered.

12 P—KKt4

Threatening 13. B—K3 Q×B 14.
Q×Q B—R3 15. Q×B, R×Q 16.
P—Kt5. The businesslike way in which
both sides "invest" their queens throughout the game is an unusual feature.

12 ...	B—B4
13 P—Kt5	KKt—Q2
14 Kt×P	Q—B4
15 B—Q3!	

Now White actually seeks the exchange of queens.

15 ...	Q×Q
16 Kt×Q	B—Q5
17 Kt—B4	

The four minor pieces completely
dominate Black's game; so White is no
longer interested in "winning" the
exchange for two pawns, which he could
have done by 17. Kt—B6 ch.

17 ...	R—Kt1
18 Kt—R5	K—K2
19 Kt(4)—B6	Kt×Kt
20 P×Kt ch.	K—K1

If 20... B×P 21. B—Kt4 ch.

21 B—KR6	B—Q2
22 B—K4	Resigns.

40 WHITE: KUNIN—BLACK: OCHSENGOIT
Moscow, 1958

1 P—K4	P—K3
2 P—Q4	P—Q4
3 Kt—QB3	B—Kt5
4 B—Q2	P×P
5 Q—Kt4	Q×P
6 Castles	P—KB4
7 B—Kt5	

Not a very strong line for White; with
the simple 7... P×Q! 8. R×Q B—K2
9. Kt×P Kt—KB3 Black gets a comfortable game with a pawn up.

7 ...	Q—K4
8 R—Q8 ch.	K—B2

36

9 Kt—B3!

Threatens 10. Kt × Q mate. In the face of such brutality Black should have energetically headed for the draw, which was to be had by 9... P × Kt 10. Q × B P—B4 (or 10... Q—K8 ch. 11. R—Q1 Q × P 12. P × P Kt—QB3, and the Black position, though a little open, can probably be held) 11. Q—KR4 Kt—QB3 12. B—KB4 Q—B3 13. B—KKt5 Q—Kt3 14. Q—Kt3! Kt × R 15. Q—B7 ch. and draws by perpetual check. Black cannot escape by delaying Kt × R and playing 14... Q—R4, because White wins after 15. P × P! Kt × R 16. Q—B7 ch., K—Kt3 17. R—Kt1.

9 ...   Q—R4?
10 B—Kt5!

Re-establishing the mating threat on K5 and adding another one: 11. B—K8 ch. K—B1 12. B—Kt6 mate. If now 10... Kt—KB3 11. Q—R5 ch.! P—Kt3 (of course not 11... Kt × Q? 12. Kt—K5 mate). 12. Kt—K5 ch. K—K2 13. R × R P × Q 14. R—K8 ch. K—Q3 15. Kt—B4 ch. K—B4 16. B—K3 mate. Best is 10... P—KKt3 11. Kt—K5 ch. K—Kt2 12. Q—R4. Now White threatens both 13. Kt—B4 and 13. R × B and none of the possible replies seem to be sufficient:

(*a*) 12... Kt—QB3 13. R × Kt ch. K × R 14. Kt—B4 winning the queen;

(*b*) 12... B × Kt 13. B—R6 ch.! Kt × B 14. Q—K7 ch. Kt—B2 15.

Q × Kt ch. K—R3 16. R × R and Black will soon be mated.

(*c*) 12...P—KR3 13. B—B6 ch.! Kt × B 14. R × R K × R 15. Q × Kt ch. and mate in two.

(*d*) 12... P—B3! 13. R × B P × B 14. R × Kt ch. K × R 15. B—Q8! B × Kt (otherwise 16. Q—B6 is decisive) 16. B × Q B × Kt 17. Q—K7 wins. We have been following throughout the excellent notes by G. Fridstein in *Schachmaty*.

10 ...   Kt—QB3?

This does not meet the threat at all.

11 Kt—K5 ch.!   Resigns.

The white queen has been *en prise* for five moves—it could be taken the first time, but not thereafter.

41 WHITE: FICHTL—BLACK: WINIWARTER

Salzbrunn, 1957

1 P—K4	P—K3
2 P—Q4	P—Q4
3 Kt—QB3	B—Kt5
4 P—QR3	B × Kt ch.
5 P × B	P × P
6 Q—Kt4	Kt—KB3
7 Q × KtP	R—Kt1
8 Q—R6	P—B4
9 Kt—K2	R—Kt3
10 Q—K3	Kt—B3
11 P × P	

So far identical with the 7th match game, Smyslov-Botvinnik, 1954. Botvinnik now simplified with 11... Kt—KKt5? 12. Q × P Q—Q8 ch. 13. K × Q Kt × P ch. 14. K—K1 Kt × Q; but after 15. Kt—B4, R—KKt1 16. B—Q3 had the inferior game. In the present game Black employs an improvement first suggested by van Scheltinga.

11 ...   P—K4!

A multi-purpose move. It gives the QB an outlet, the QKt (in certain variations) a hold on Q5 and stops Kt—KB4, so that Botvinnik's combination becomes possible.

13. FRENCH DEFENCE

12 Kt—Kt3	B—Kt5

Since the queen would now be protected on K4, 12... Kt—Kt5 is no longer playable.

13 B—Kt2?

Black threatened R—Q8 mate as well as Kt—Q4, the latter possibility rendering B—K2 ineffective. However, 13. B—Q2 was preferable to the text, which buries the bishop for the rest of the game.

13 ...	Q—R4
14 Kt×P	

This leaves the white pieces in a fatal bind. But even after 14. B—B4! Castles 15. Castles (not 15. B×P because of 15... Kt—Q5) P—R4! Black seems to retain the better chances.

14 ...	Kt×Kt
15 Q×Kt	Kt—Q5!

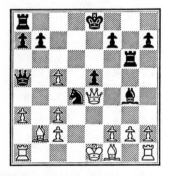

16 B—Q3

Black threatened 16... B—B4, followed by Kt×P ch.

16 ...	Castles
17 Q—K3	

If 17. Castles B—B6 wins, but 17. K—B1 had to be considered. This would have protected the KtP, unpinned the BP, and got the king out of the K-file. However, after 17... P—B4 18. Q—K1 Kt—B6! 19. P×Kt B—R6 ch. 20. K—K2 P—K5 21. P×P P×P 22. B×P Q—Kt4 ch. the black attack wins through.

17 ...	P—K5!

Pawns are there to be sacrificed.

18 B×P	P—B4!
19 B×KtP ch.	K×B
20 Q—K7 ch.	K—B1
21 Castles	B—B6
Resigns.	

An elegant win which, at the time, was of great theoretical importance.

---

42 WHITE: BONSDORFF—BLACK: LIIPOLA

Helsinki, 1957

1 P—K4	P—K3
2 P—Q4	P—Q4
3 Kt—QB3	B—Kt5
4 Q—Kt4	

A rarely-played continuation, which acquired ephemeral notoriety when Alekhine overran Euwe with it in one of their games for the world championship.

4 ...	Kt—KB3
5 Q×P	R—Kt1
6 Q—R6	Kt×P

Avoiding the complicated lines beginning with 6... R—Kt3 or 6... P—B4, by allowing the exchange of queens.

7 Q×P	R—Kt3
8 Q—R8 ch.	K—Q2
9 Q×Q ch.	K×Q
10 B—Q2	Kt×B
11 K×Kt	

While White is a pawn up, Black has considerable positional compensation in the two bishops, which would become very powerful if Black can force P—K4. Quite correctly Black therefore tries to remove the white QP, but then goes in for an altogether uncalled-for simplification, which nullifies his positional trumps.

11 ...	P—QB4
12 P—QR3	P×P? (B—R4!)
13 P×B	P×Kt ch.
14 P×P	Kt—B3
15 Kt—B3	P—K4?

38

13. FRENCH DEFENCE

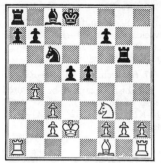

Allowing an amusing finish. After 15... P—B3 White's task would not have been easy.

16 P—Kt5	P—K5
17 P×Kt	P×Kt
18 P×P	P×P
19 P×R(Q)	P×R(Q)
20 Q×B ch.!	K×Q
21 B—R3 ch.	Resigns.

43 White: Janosevic—Black: Ugrinovic

Belgrade, 1958

1 P—K4	P—K3
2 P—Q4	P—Q4
3 Kt—Q2	Kt—QB3

First played by Tarrasch, White's move is designed to avoid the 3...B—Kt5 variation. Black's reply, variously called the Guimard or Groningen variation, aims at an early P—K4 instead of the usual P—QB4.

4 KKt—B3	Kt—B3
5 P—K5	Kt—Q2
6 Kt—Kt3	P—B3
7 B—QKt5	

This "half-pin" of the two black knights maintains control of the black central squares. After, e.g., 7. P×P Q×P 8. B—KKt5 Q—B2 9. B—R4 P—K4! Black would have freed his game completely.

7 ...	P×P
8 B×Kt	

Whether this move is really superior to Pachman's 8. P×P, which in practice has always led to some advantage for White, is very doubtful.

8 ...	P×B
9 P×P	B—K2

Against 9... P—B4! White planned 10. B—Kt5 B—K2 11. Kt—R5 Kt—Kt1 12. P—KR4, but after 12... P—KR3 he would certainly have no advantage.

10 Kt—R5	B—Kt5 ch.

A completely wrong idea, which robs the black king side of its best protector. Even now 10... Kt—Kt1! was playable.

11 P—B3	B×Kt
12 B—Kt5	Kt—B3
13 P×Kt	P×P

14 Kt—K5!

This is probably what Black overlooked. If now 14... P×B 15. Q—R5 ch. mates or wins the queen; if 14... Castles 15. B—R6 P×Kt 16. Q—Kt4 ch. K—B2 17. Q—Kt7 ch. K—K1 18. Q×R ch. and wins.

14 ...	B—Kt2
15 Q—R5 ch.	K—K2
16 Q—B7 ch.	K—Q3
17 B×P	Resigns.

There is no hope in 17... Q—K1 18. B×R Q×B 19. P—KB4.

44 White: Perfors—Black: van Seters

Wageningen, 1955

1 P—K4	P—K3
2 P—Q4	P—Q4
3 Kt—Q2	Kt—KB3

4 P—K5	KKt—Q2
5 B—Q3	P—QB4
6 P—QB3	Kt—QB3
7 Kt—K2	Q—Kt3
8 Kt—B3	P×P
9 P×P	P—B3

This line, which owes a great deal to the researches of the German master, Lothar Schmid, is one of those most frequently seen nowadays, especially in recent Russian tournaments. This is no doubt due to the fact that it always leads to very sharp, double-edged positions, with the "book" assessment see-sawing all the time between advantage for White and advantage for Black.

10 P×P	Kt×BP
11 Castles	B—Q3
12 Kt—B4	

Consistently attacking the weak square K6. A frequent alternative is 12. Kt—B3 Castles 13. B—KKt5; while the Argentinian grandmaster, Pilnik, pleads for 12. B—Q2 followed by B—B3, safeguarding the key square Q4.

12 ...	Castles
13 R—K1	B—Q2

A pawn sacrifice introduced by Lothar Schmid, the correctness of which has remained in the balance to this day.

14 Kt×KP	KR—K1
15 B—B5	P—KR3?

Designed to stop B—Kt5, this move allows a decisive sacrifice. Correct is 15... B—Kt5! 16. B—Q2 B×B 17. Q×B Kt—K5!, as played in a game Arulide-Tal.

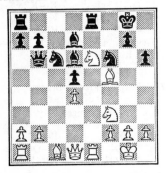

16 Kt×P!	K×Kt

16... R×R ch. facilitates White's task by clearing the Q1—Kt4 diagonal (17. Kt×R K×Kt 18. B×B Kt×B 19. Q—Kt4 ch.).

17 B×P ch.!	K—R1

The bishop cannot be captured because of 18. Q—Q2 ch. K—Kt2 19. Q—Kt5 ch. K—B2 20. Q—Kt6 ch., etc.

18 B×B	Kt×B
19 R×R ch.	R×R
20 Kt—Kt5!	

Clearing the queen's diagonal and threatening 21. Kt—B7 ch. followed by Kt×B.

20 ...	R—K2
21 Q—R5	Q×KtP
22 Kt—B7 ch.	Resigns.

for if 22... R×Kt 23. B—B1 ch. R—R2 24. Q—K8 ch. and Black loses his queen.

45 WHITE: RABAR—BLACK: MATULOVIC

Sombor, 1957

1 P—K4	P—K3
2 P—Q4	P—Q4
3 Kt—Q2	P—QB4

Generally regarded as the safest line against the Tarrasch variation, yet not often seen these days because it "promises Black no more than a draw". As will be seen, rules have exceptions.

4 P×QP	KP×P
5 B—Kt5 ch.	B—Q2
6 Q—K2 ch.	B—K2
7 P×P	Kt—KB3
8 Kt—Kt3	

Beginning a long series of moves designed to hold the extra pawn—an impossible task. In pursuing this will-o'-the-wisp White gets fatally behind in development.

8 ...	Castles
9 B—K3	R—K1
10 Castles	P—QR3
11 B×B	QKt×B
12 Q—B3	

Still with the same idea. On the developing 12. Kt—B3 Black could have recaptured the pawn.

12 ...	P—QR4
13 P—QR4?	Q—B2
14 KKt—K2	

Now the pawn can no longer be defended, but meanwhile White has contracted many weaknesses.

14 ...   B×P

It is important to retain both knights, because the black attack will be carried on the white squares (K5, QKt6, QB7).

| 15 Kt×B | Kt×Kt |
| 16 Kt—B3 | QR—B1 |

Threatening 17... Kt×P. If now 17. Kt×P Kt—Kt6 ch. 18. K—Kt1 Q×P ch. 19. K—R2 Kt×Kt 20. Q×Kt R—B5! If 17. R—Q2 Kt(3)—K5 18. Kt×Kt (or 18. Kt×P Q—B3) Kt—Kt6 ch., winning the exchange after 19... P×Kt. If 17. B×Kt, Q×B 18. R—Q2 P—Q5 or if 18. Q—B5 R—K5! Best was 17. Q—K2, so as to protect QB2 and threaten 18. Q—Kt5.

17 Q—B4?

Understandable, but fatal.

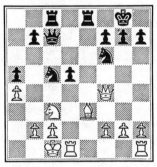

17 ...	Q×Q
18 B×Q	P—Q5!
19 Kt—Kt5	

Not 19. R×P Kt—K3! and the white rook has no square from which to protect the bishop.

| 19 ... | P—Q6! |
| 20 Kt—B3 | |

Back to plug the QB-file, for 20. P—B3 would have been answered with R—K7. But Black keeps hammering at the weakness QB7.

| 20 ... | Kt—Q4! |
| 21 B—Q2 | |

Leading to an amusing finish, but after, e.g. 21. B—Kt3 Kt×Kt, followed by P×P would leave White with a hopeless ending.

21 ...   Kt—Kt5!
      Resigns.

The threat of 22... P×P, followed by Kt—Kt6 mate can be parried only by 22. P×P, but then Kt×P ch., with Kt×BP next, costs White too much material.

46 WHITE: FOULDS—BLACK: LANG

New Zealand, 1956

1 P—K4	P—K3
2 P—Q4	P—Q4
3 P—K5	P—QB4
4 P—QB3	Kt—QB3
5 Kt—B3	Q—Kt3
6 B—Q3	

6. P—QR3 or 6. B—K2 are more usual, but White aims at a sacrificial variation ascribed to Milner-Barry, which had quite a vogue in New Zealand.

6 ...	P×P
7 P×P	B—Q2
8 Castles	Kt×QP
9 Kt×Kt	Q×Kt
10 Kt—B3	

This double pawn sacrifice is the idea. It is undoubtedly incorrect, but the refutation is far from easy. How dangerous this clearance of the centre can become was also shown in a game, *Herter-Nievergelt, Stuttgart, 1957*, which had gone 4. Kt—KB3 Kt—QB3 5. B—Q3 KKt—K2 6. Castles B—Q2 7. P—B3 P×P 8. P×P Q—Kt3 9. Kt—B3! Kt×QP 10. Kt×Kt Q×Kt,

and now continued 11. Kt—Kt5 Q×KP
12. R—K1 Q—Kt1 13. Q—B3! Kt—Kt3
14. B×Kt RP×B 15. B—B4 Q—Q1
16. Kt—B7 ch. K—K2 17. Kt×P ch.
K—K1 18. Kt—B7 ch. K—K2 19.
Q—R3 ch. K—B3 20. Q—B3 ch.
Resigns.

10 ...	Q×KP
11 R—K1	Q—Q3
12 Kt—Kt5	B×Kt
13 B×B ch.	K—Q1
14 B—K3	Kt—K2

With the intention of challenging the
white bishop by Kt—B4—the logical
plan.

15 R—QB1	Kt—B4
16 B—B5	Q—B5?

Undoing the good work of the previous moves. White has brought so much
force to bear on the centre pawns that
he now threatens to break the barrier by
a sacrifice. Black therefore should have
reduced the opponent's attacking power
by 16... Q×B! 17. R×Q B×R—with
R+Kt+2P's for the queen, and a
beautiful square (Q3) for the knight,
from which it protects the two weak
squares in Black's camp QKt2 and KB2.
Black would have had winning chances.

17 P—KKt3	Q—Kt4

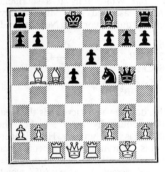

18 Q×P ch.!	P×Q
19 B—Kt6 ch.!	P×B
20 R—K8 mate.	

A most surprising finish, which illus-

trates the power of the cleared centre
files.

47 White: Diemer—Black: Illig
By Correspondence, 1954

1 P—Q4	P—K3
2 P—K4	P—Q4
3 B—K3	P×P
4 P—KB3!	

The so-called Alapin Gambit, re-
juvenated and improved by Diemer.
Originally it was no gambit at all:
Alapin used to continue with Kt—Q2,
P—QB3, Q—B2, P—KKt3, B—Kt2,
etc., recovering the pawn, and played
P—KB3 only after Black had committed
himself to P—KB4. This is a very slow
and cumbersome way of treating the
French; but as a proper gambit the line
has considerable merit. The present
game is typical of White's attacking
chances.

4 ...	P×P
5 Kt×P	Kt—KB3
6 B—Q3	QKt—Q2
7 Castles	P—B4
8 P—B3	B—K2
9 Kt—K5	P×P

With the idea of isolating the QP and
then conducting the defence from the
protected square Q4. This, however,
proves too slow for the tempo of the
white attack.

10 P×P	Castles
11 Kt—QB3	Kt—Kt3
12 R—B3	Kt(Kt3)—Q4
13 R—R3	P—KKt3

If 13... Kt×B 14. B×P ch. K—R1
(not 14... Kt×B 15. Q—R5) 15. Q—Q3
Kt(K6)—Q4 16. R—KB1 with the
double threat of 17. Kt×Kt P×Kt 18.
B—B5 ch. K—Kt1 19. B×B R×B
20. R×Kt, and 17. B—Kt6 ch. K—Kt1
18. B×P ch. R×B 19. Kt—Kt6! R—B1
20. R—R8 ch. K—B2 21. Kt—K5 ch.
K—K1 22. Q—Kt6 mate.

14 B—KR6	R—K1
15 Q—Q2	P—QR3

13. FRENCH DEFENCE

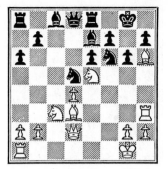

The immediate 15... Kt—QKt5 would allow 16. B—QKt5 B—Q2 16. Kt×B Kt×Kt 17. Kt—K4 (threatening 18. B×Kt Q×B 19. Q×Kt! B×Q 20. Kt—B6 ch.) Kt—Q4 21. B—Kt7 B—B1 22. B×B K×B 23. B×Kt! Q×B 24. Q—R6 ch. K—K2 25. Q—Kt5 ch. K—B1 26. R×P. But now the white QR enters the fray and the black game collapses.

| 16 R—KB1 | Kt—QKt5 |
| 17 B×KtP! | |

With the subtle point not of smashing the king's position, but guarding against Q×P ch., and thus preparing the final combination.

| 17 ... | BP×B |
| 18 B—Kt7! | Kt—B3 |

If 18... K×B 19. Q—R6 ch. K—Kt1 20. R×Kt! followed by mate.

| 19 Kt×Kt | P×Kt |
| 20 Q—R6 | Kt—R4 |

Or 20... Q×P ch. 21. K—R1 Q—K4 22. B×Kt B×B 23. Kt—K4; if 21... Q—QB5 22. R×Kt! etc.

| 21 R×Kt | Resigns. |

If 21... P×R 22. B—K5 B—B1 23. R×B ch. R×R 24. Q—Kt7 mate; or 22... B—B3 23. B×B Q—Q2 24. Q—Kt5 ch., and mate next move.

14. SICILIAN DEFENCE

48 WHITE: FARRÉ—BLACK: GUDMUNDSSON

Munich, 1958

1 P—K4	P—QB4
2 Kt—KB3	P—Q3
3 P—Q4	P×P
4 Kt×P	Kt—KB3
5 Kt—QB3	P—KKt3
6 B—K3	B—Kt2
7 P—B3	Kt—B3
8 Q—Q2	P—QR3

In positions where the players castle on opposite sides the loss of a move in attack is often well nigh fatal. However, this variation in any case has always tended to favour White in practical play. Here are three other examples which show the same pattern of a white attack arriving well before Black has been able to react incisively on the opposite wing.

White: *Rubenchik*—Black: *Kanayan*. *White Russia, 1957.* 8... Castles 9. B—QB4 Kt—QR4? (better 9... Kt×Kt 10. B×Kt B—K3) 10. B—Kt3 B—Q2 11. B—R6 R—B1 12. P—KR4 Kt—B5 13. B×Kt R×B 14. B×B K×B 15. P—R5! P—K4 16. KKt—K2 Kt×RP 17. P—KKt4 Kt—B3 18. Q—R6 ch. K—Kt1 19. P—Kt5 Kt—R4 20. R×Kt! P×R 21. Kt—Q5 P—B4 22. P—Kt6 P×P 23. Q×P ch. K—R1 24. Castles. Resigns.

White: *Joppen*—Black: *Schneider*. *West Germany, 1958.* 8... Castles 9. Castles P—QR3 (the same mistake as in the Farré-Gudmundsson game) 10. P—KKt4 Kt—K4 11. B—R6 P—QKt4 12. P—KR4 R—K1 13. B×B K×B 14. P—R5 Kt—Kt1 15. P—Kt5 P×P 16.

R×P Kt—Kt3 17. Q—R2 Kt—B1 18. B—Q3 Q—Kt3 19. Kt—B5 ch. B×Kt 20. P×B Q—K6 ch. 21. K—Kt1 P—Kt5 22. R—Kt1! P×Kt 23. P—B6 ch. P×P 24. P×P ch. Resigns. If 24... K×P 25. Q×P ch., followed by R—B5 mate.

White: *Rhodin*—Black: *Siegel. Landau, 1958.* 8... Castles 9. Castles B—K3 10. Kt×B P×Kt 11. B—KR6 R—B1? (much better is 11... P—K4) 12. B—QB4 Q—Q2 13. B—Kt3 Kt—QR4 14. B×B Kt×B ch. 15. RP×Kt K×B 16. P—K5 Kt—K1 17. P—R4 R—KB4 18. P—KKt4 R×KP (in a previous game, *Rhodin-Behrenbruch, Hamburg, 1957,* Black also lost quickly after 18... R×BP 19. P—R5 P—KKt4 20. Q×P ch. K—R1 21. KR—B1 Resigns. The present move was meant as an "improvement") 19. Q—Q4 (threatening both 20. Q×R ch. and 20. P—B4) Kt—B3 20. P—Kt5 Kt—Q4 21. P—B4 Kt×P 22. Q×R ch. Resigns.

9 Castles	B—Q2
10 P—KKt4	R—QB1
11 B—K2	Castles
12 P—KR4	Kt×Kt

This manoeuvre does not fit in well with Black's 8th and 10th moves. Better is either 12... Kt—K4, or 12... Kt—QR4.

13 B×Kt	Q—R4
14 K—Kt1	P—K4
15 B—K3	B—K3
16 P—R3	KR—Q1
17 B—KKt5	R—Q2
18 P—R5	R(Q2)—B2
19 P—R6	R×Kt

Superficially it seems that Black's counter attack is gaining strength; but White has calculated further. If 19... B—R1 20. B×Kt B×B 21. Kt—Q5 wins a piece.

20 P×B	R(B1)—B3
21 B×Kt	R—Kt3

Black's attack now looks very dangerous because of the threat of 22... R×P ch. 23. K×R Q×P ch. and mates.

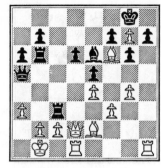

22 B—QKt5!   R×B

There is nothing better. If 22... P×B or Q×B 23. Q×R.

23 Q×P

Protecting QR3 and threatening 24. Q—B8 mate.

23 ...   R—B1
24 Q—B8 ch.!

Very pretty and the only way to win. If 24. R×P? R×P ch.! 25. K×R Q—B6 ch. and it is Black who wins.

24 ...   R×Q
25 P×R(Q) ch.   Resigns.

After 25... K×Q 26. R×P, there is nothing to be done.

49 WHITE: GALULA—BLACK: LEONE

Paris, 1955

1 P—K4	P—QB4
2 Kt—KB3	P—Q3
3 P—Q4	P×P
4 Kt×P	Kt—KB3
5 Kt—QB3	Kt—B3
6 B—K2	P—KKt3
7 B—K3	B—Kt2
8 Castles	Castles
9 Q—Q2	P—QR3

Inferior is 9... Kt—KKt5 10. B×Kt B×B 11. P—B4 B—Q2 12. QR—Q1 R—B1 13. P—B5! Kt—K4 14. R—R6 Kt—B5 15. Q—B1 Kt×P 16. B×B Kt×R 17. Q—R6 Kt×Kt (*Unzicker-Giustolisi, Lugano, 1959*) 18. P×

BP×P 19. R×R ch. Q×R 20. B×Q
R×B 21. Q—K3, with an easy win.

10 P—B4	B—Q2
11 B—B3	R—B1
12 QR—Q1	Kt—QR4?

Any mishandling of his queen's side
counterplay by Black in the Sicilian
usually enables White to come with a
rush on the other wing. Here a much
better line is 12... B—Kt5.

13 Q—B2

Now White makes a mistake. Simply
13. P—QKt3 Kt—Kt5 14. B×Kt B×B
15. R—B1, followed by 16. Kt—Q5,
gives him an excellent position.

13 ...   Kt—B5

Black is still windmill tilting; much
better is 12... Kt—Kt5, which really
does force the exchange of one of White's
bishops.

14 B—B1	Q—Kt3
15 P—QKt3	Kt—QR4
16 B—Kt2	Kt—Kt5

The right move at the wrong moment.
He could still obtain a reasonable game
by 16... P—K4 17. P×P P×P 18.
Kt(Q4)—K2 Q×Q ch. 19. R×Q
KR—K1.

17 B×Kt	B×B
18 Kt—Q5	

Once White has established a knight
on this square in the Sicilian, he has a
clear advantage.

18 ...   Q—Q1

19 Q—R4!	B×R
20 Kt×P ch.	K—R1

21 P—B5   P—KKt4

Seemingly refuting the combination,
for if 22. Q×P P—B3. In any case, he
has no defence to the threatened P—B6,
e.g., 21... P—B3 22. Kt×P ch. K—Kt1
23. Kt—K6 Q—K1 24. Kt(Kt6)×R
B×Kt 25. Q×P, or if 21... B×Kt ch.
22. B×B ch. P—B3 23. Q×BP ch.
R×Q 24. B×R mate.

22 P—B6

The pattern of a mate worked by a
pawn or piece on the long black
diagonal supported by a knight or rook
is quite common in the Sicilian. If now
22... P×Q 23. P×B ch. K×P 24.
Kt(Q4)—B5 mate.

22 ...	Q×Kt
23 P×B ch.	K—Kt1
24 Kt—B5	Resigns.

50 White: Moran—Black: Franco
Gijon, 1955

1 P—K4	P—QB4
2 Kt—KB3	Kt—QB3
3 P—Q4	P×P
4 Kt×P	Kt—B3
5 Kt—QB3	P—Q3
6 B—KKt5	P—K3
7 Q—Q2	B—K2
8 Castles	Castles
9 P—B4	P—K4

9... P—KR3 10. B—R4 P—K4 11.
Kt—B5 makes little difference to White's
advantage. A game, *Kondratjev-Rovner,
Leningrad, 1956,* continued 11... B×Kt
12. P×B P×P 13. K—Kt1 Kt—K4 14.
B—K2 R—B1 15. KR—B1 P—B6?
(better is the immediate 15... Kt—B5
16. B×Kt R×B 17. R×P R×R 18.
Q×R Kt—R4 19. Q—B3 B×B 20.
Q×Kt B—B3 21. Kt—Q5, although
White is still clearly on top) 16. P×P
Kt—B5 17. Q—Q4 Q—B2 18. R—Kt1
Kt—K4 19. P—B4 Kt(K4)—Q2 20.
B—QKt5 K—R2 21. KB×Kt Q×B
22. Kt—Q5 R—KKt1 23. B×Kt P×B
24. Q×P! Resigns. If 24... R×R 25.
R×R B—B1 26. Q—Q4, followed by

Kt—B6 ch., and otherwise Black loses at least a piece.

10 Kt—B3

This move has been discontinued among masters, since 10. Kt—B5, on the lines of the game in the previous note, gives White a more enduring advantage.

10 . . .	B—Kt5
11 P—KR3	B × Kt
12 P × B	Kt—Q5
13 P × P	P × P
14 P—B4	

If 14. R—Kt1 Kt × KBP 15. Q—B2 Q—Kt3 16. B—K3 Kt—Q5 17. R × Kt P × R 18. B × P, with a winning attack, as in a well known game between Korchnoi and Geller; but a better line for Black is 14... R—B1 15. B—K2 R × Kt 16. B × Kt B × B 17. P × R B—K2; and it is Black's attack which is conclusive.

14 . . .	Q—R4?

Now White wins practically by force. Black's only adequate defence is 14... Kt—K3, e.g., 15. P × P Kt × B 16. Q × Kt Kt × P.

15 P × P	Kt—B6

Not 15... Q × KP 16. B—KB4, winning a piece.

16 P × Kt	Kt × Q

Another line which also results in a queen sacrifice is 16... B × P 17. B × B Kt × Q 18. R—Kt1 P—KKt3 19. R × Kt, with three pieces for the queen and good attacking chances.

17 P × B	Kt × B?

Black could put up a tougher fight by 17... Kt—Kt6 ch. 18. K—Kt1! KR—K1 19. Kt—Q5 Kt—B4 20. P—QKt4, Q—R6 21. P × Kt Q × BP 22. B—K3, when White should win since Black must soon sacrifice the exchange for the passed pawn.

18 P × R(Q) ch.	K × Q

18... R × Q; also loses after 19. B—B4 Kt—Kt6 20. KR—Kt1! Kt × P 21.

Kt × Kt Q—KB4 22. B—R6! Q × Kt 23. B × P R—B1 24. B—K5 dis. ch. K—B1 25. B—Q6 ch. K—K1 26. QR—K1 R × P ch. 27. K—Q1.

19 B—B4	Kt—Kt6

A last hope to save the knight, for if 20. B × Kt Q—Kt4 ch.

20 KR—Kt1	Kt × P

If 20... Kt—R4 21. R—Kt5.

| 21 Kt × Kt | Q × P |
| 22 B—Q6 ch. | K—Kt1 |

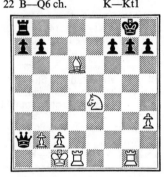

23 R × P ch.!

The final stroke of an energetic attack; if 23... K × R 24. R—Kt1 ch. K—R3 (24... K—R1 25. B—K5 ch.) 25. B—B4 ch. K—R4 26. R—Kt5 ch. K—R5 27. R—Kt4 ch. K × P 28. Kt—B2 mate.

23 . . .	K—R1
24 R—Kt8 ch.!	Resigns.

For if 24... R × R 25. B—K5 ch. P—B3 26. B × P ch. R—Kt2 27. R—Q8 ch. Q—Kt1 28. R × Q ch. K × R 29. B × R, and White emerges from the slaughter house a piece up.

51 WHITE: STERNER—BLACK: BOLESLAVSKY
Russia v. Sweden, 1954

1 P—K4	P—QB4
2 Kt—KB3	Kt—QB3
3 P—Q4	P × P
4 Kt × P	Kt—B3
5 Kt—QB3	P—Q3

6 B—K2	P—K4

Boleslavsky's own variation and one with which he has gained many fine victories in master play. Black's backward QP is hard to attack and he constantly threatens to play ... P—Q4. Furthermore, Black often obtains attacking chances on the queen's side by advancing his QRP.

7 Kt—Kt3

Probably weaker than either 7. Kt—B3, after which the positional threat of B—KKt5, B×Kt, and Kt—Q5 makes Black lose an important tempo by 7... P—KR3, or than 7. Kt×Kt P×Kt 8. Castles B—K2 9. K—R1, followed by 10. P—B4, when White has good chances of attack on the king's wing.

7 ...	B—K2
8 Castles	

A game, *Kalkstein-Gligoric, Montevideo, 1953*, illustrates how quickly White can come to grief if Black is permitted to play ... P—Q4 without hindrance. 8. B—K3 Castles 9. Q—Q2 P—QR4 10. P—QR4 Kt—QKt5 11. R—Q1 B—K3 12. Castles P—Q4 13. P×P KKt×P 14. Kt×Kt B×Kt 15. P—QB4 B—QB3 15. Q×Q B×Q, 16. B—B5 R—K1 17. R—R1 Kt—B7 18. R—R2 P—QKt3 19. B—Q6 R—K3 20. R—Q1 Kt—Q5 21. Kt×Kt P×Kt 22. Resigns. One of the bishops is lost.

8 ...	Castles
9 B—K3	B—K3
10 P—B4	

Obvious, but antipositional. Stronger is 10. B—B3, in order to consolidate his hold on Q5.

10 ...	P—QR4

Beginning the queen's side counterattack. If White replies 11. P—QR4, the following trap has occurred more than once in master play: 11... Kt—QKt5 12. Q—Q2 P×P 13. B×P Kt×BP 14. Q×Kt Q—Kt3 ch., winning a pawn.

11 P×P

More obvious is 11. P—B5, but then Black can systematically prepare ...

P—Q4, e.g., 11... B—Q2 12. P—QR4 Kt—QKt5 13. B—B3 B—B3, followed by ... Q—Q2 and ... QR—Q1.

11 ...	P×P
12 Q×Q	KR×Q

By exchanging queens, White exemplifies the type of error often made by players with a conservative style when they meet opponents with a first class reputation. White expects that the exchange of queens will make it easier for him to draw, but he does not realize the extent to which Black can exploit his lead in development.

13 KR—Q1

More active is Kt—B5, but White is still thinking in terms of a quick draw.

13 ...	Kt—QKt5
14 R×R ch.	B×R
15 B—Q3	

White is in a dilemma: if he holds his QBP by 15. R—QB1, then 15... P—QKt3, with the strong threat of 16... P—R5 (16. P—QR4 Kt×BP).

15 ...	P—R5

The advance of this pawn to the sixth rank is a frequent motif in the Boleslavsky variation.

16 Kt—Q2	P—R6
17 P—QKt3	

17 ...	Kt—Kt5
18 B—B5	Kt×B
19 P×Kt	R—B1
20 B—Kt4	B—Kt3 ch.
21 K—B1	

Or 21. K—R1 Kt—B7 ch. 22.
K—Kt1, Kt×QP dis. ch.

21 ...	Kt—K6 ch.
22 K—K2	Kt—B7
23 Resigns.	

52 WHITE: SÖDERBORG—BLACK:
OLAFSSON

Reykjavik, 1957

1 P—K4	P—QB4
2 Kt—KB3	Kt—QB3
3 P—Q4	P×P
4 Kt×P	Kt—B3
5 Kt—QB3	P—Q3
6 B—KKt5	P—K3
7 Q—Q2	B—K2
8 Castles	Castles
9 P—B4	P—Q4

One of the strengths of the Richter Attack is that neither this move nor the other attempt to counter-attack in the centre by 9... P—K4 are quite satisfactory.

10 P—K5	Kt—Q2
11 B×B	Q×B
12 P—KKt4	Kt—Kt3
13 P—Kt5	B—Q2?

The problem of what style to adopt when meeting a clearly stronger opponent is one which White here solves in cavalier and remarkably successful fashion. Yet the border line between a storming success and a quick loss is a narrow one. Black could and should have played here 13... P—B3 14. KtP×P P×P 15. R—Kt1 ch. K—R1 16. P×P Q×P, and White has difficulty in holding his weak KBP. Now, however, White's attack rolls along on oiled wheels.

14 R—Kt1	QR—B1
15 R—Kt3	Kt—R4
16 Q—B2	P—Kt3
17 R—R3	K—Kt2
18 R(Q1)—Q3	R—KR1
19 R—R6	Kt(R4)—B5
20 R(Q3)—R3	R(QB1)—KKt1

An unsuccessful attempt to make a get-away with the king. He must have overlooked White's reply, for a better defence is 20... Q—B1 21. Q—R4 Q—Kt1, when although Black's position is completely immobile White has no clear way of making his attack decisive.

21 R×RP ch.	R×R
22 R×R ch.	K—B1

For if 22... K×R 23. Q—R4 ch., and mate next move.

23 P—QR3

Preventing any counter-attack by 23... Q—Kt5.

23 ...	B—K1
24 Q—R4	Q—B4
25 Kt×P ch.	

The last trump. If 25... P×Kt 26. Q—R6 ch., and mate next move.

25 ...   Resigns.

53 WHITE: SHERBAKOV—BLACK:
TAIMANOV

Russian Championship Semi-Finals, 1954

1 P—K4	P—QB4
2 Kt—KB3	Kt—QB3
3 P—Q4	P×P
4 Kt×P	Kt—B3
5 Kt—QB3	P—Q3
6 B—KKt5	P—K3
7 Q—Q3	

An idea of Keres in place of the usual

7. Q—Q2. In some variations the white queen helps in a king's side-attack at KR3 or KKt3.

> **7 ...**   **P—QR3**

Not essential; Black can obtain enough counterplay in the centre by 7... B—K2 8. R—Q1 Castles 9. B—K2 P—Q4 10. P×P Kt—QKt5 11. Q—Kt3 QKt×QP.

8 Castles?

This, however, is wrong, since it sets up a potential family fork of the white queen and rooks at KB2. The best play for both sides is 8. R—Q1 B—Q2 9. B—K2 B—K2 10. Castles KR Kt×Kt 11. Q×Kt B—B3 12. K—R1 Q—R4 with about equal chances.

8 ...	B—Q2
9 P—B4	P—R3
10 B—R4	P—KKt4!
11 P×P	Kt—KKt5
12 Q—Kt3	

A lesser evil is 12. K—Kt1 P×P 13. B—Kt3 Kt(Kt5)—K4, although then Black has full command of an important central square at K4.

12 ...	P×P
13 Kt—B3?	

The final error, but if 13. Q×Kt R×B 14. Q—Kt3 Kt×Kt 15. R×Kt B—B3, when Black has the two bishops and a persistent initiative.

13 ...	P×B
14 Q×Kt	

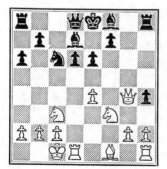

14 ...	P—K4

So concluding a typical history of an over-ambitious queen. If 15. Q—Kt5 B—R3

15 Resigns.

---

54 WHITE: GELLER—BLACK: VATNIKOV

Kiev, 1950

1 P—K4	P—QB4
2 Kt—KB3	Kt—QB3
3 P—Q4	P×P
4 Kt×P	Kt—B3
5 Kt—QB3	P—Q3
6 B—QB4	P—K3
7 Castles	B—K2
8 B—K3	Castles
9 B—Kt3	Kt—QR4
10 P—B4	P—QKt3

Whether this is playable or very bad is still the subject of dispute among analysts. A game, *Padevsky-Botvinnik, Moscow, 1956*, went on 11. Q—B3 B—Kt2 12. P—Kt4 R—B1 13. P—Kt5 R×Kt! and Black has the initiative.

11 P—K5	Kt—K1
12 P—B5	QP×P?

Very much better is 12... P×BP 13. P—K6 Kt—B2 14. P×P ch. K—R1 15. Kt×P Kt×B 16. RP×Kt R×P 17. Kt×B R×R ch. 18. Q×R Q×Kt 19. B—Kt5 Q—K1 20. Q—QB4 Q—Q2 21. Q—K4 P—Q4 22. Q—B3 (*Balanel-Botez, Rumania, 1956*) Kt—K3! with equal chances.

13 P×P	P—B3?

This loses very quickly, but if 13... Kt×B 14. Kt—B6 Q—Q3 15. Q×Q B×Q 16. RP×Kt B×P 17. Kt×RP B—QB4 18. B×B P×B 19. Kt—B6 R×R 20. R×R P—B3 21. Kt—K4, and White wins a pawn with a decisive advantage in the ending.

14 Kt—B5	Kt×B

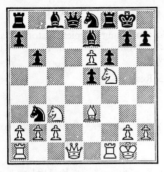

15 Kt—Q5!   **Kt—Q5**

If 15... K—R1 16. Kt(B5)×B Kt×R 17. Q—R5. If 15... Kt×R 16. QKt×B ch., winning the queen.

16 Kt(Q5)×B ch.   **K—R1**
17 Kt—Kt6 ch.   **Resigns.**

A game with the element of force characteristic of Geller on top of his form.

55 WHITE: PEREZ—BLACK: TORAN

Gijon, 1956

1 P—K4	P—QB4
2 Kt—KB3	Kt—QB3
3 P—Q4	P×P
4 Kt×P	Kt—B3
5 Kt—QB3	P—Q3
6 P—B4	P—K3
7 B—K3	B—K2
8 B—K2	Castles
9 Castles	P—Q4

The counter-attack in the centre at this point is insufficient, since Black has not enough space to withstand White's pressure on the king's side. Correct is 9... P—QR3, followed by 10... Q—B2, transposing into the Scheveningen variation.

10 P—K5   **Kt—Q2**

If 10... Kt—K5 11. QKt×Kt, P×Kt 12. Kt×Kt P×Kt 13. Q×Q R×Q 14. KR—Q1, with the better ending for White because of the isolated black pawns.

11 K—R1   **Kt—Kt3**
12 B—Q3   **Kt—Kt5**

Black underestimates the sacrifice, since the stock criterion for a successful bishop offer on KR7 is the presence of a knight on the king's side to support the attack; and this is not available here. In compensation, however, White's rook comes into the attack very quickly and Black's minor pieces are far removed from the defence of his king. Black is in difficulties in any case, since if 12... P—B4 13. P×P e.p. B×P 14. Q—R5 P—Kt3 15. B×P.

13 B×P ch.   **K×B**
14 Q—R5 ch.   **K—Kt1**
15 R—B3   **P—B4**
16 R—R3   **Q—K1**

Black has no satisfactory defence. If 16... B—B4 17. Q—R7 ch. K—B2 18. Kt×BP, P×Kt 19. B×B Kt—B3 20. R—Kt3 and wins, while if 16... B—Q2 17. Q—R7 ch. K—B2 18. R—R6. White now threatens 19. Q—Kt6 ch. K—Kt1 20. R—R7 R—B2 21. Q—R5, and if Black replies (a) 18... R—R1 19. Q—Kt6 ch. K—Kt1 20. Kt×KP; (b) 18... Q—K1 19. R—Kt6 R—KKt1 20. P—Kt4; (c) 18... R—KKt1 19. P—Kt4.

17 Q—R7 ch.   **K—B2**
18 P—Kt4!

Opening lines is what counts in such an attack. If 18... P×P 19. R—KKt1.

18 ...   **B—Q2**
19 Kt×BP!

Very precise; the immediate 19. P×P would be inferior owing to 19... R—R1.

19 ...   **P×Kt**
20 P×P   **R—KKt1**

20... R—R1 fails against 21. P—K6 ch. B×P 22. Q—Kt6 ch. K—Kt1 23. Q×B ch. Q—B2 24. R×R ch.

21 B—Q4

The culmination of the attack;

14. SICILIAN DEFENCE

although Black is two pieces up he cannot save himself.

21 ...   B—QB3

Darga in the *Deutsche Schachzeitung* shows that Black can't save himself by either 21... Kt—B3 22. P—K6 ch. B×P 23. P×B ch. K×P 24. R—K1 ch. K—Q2 25. Q—B5 ch. K—Q1 26. B×Kt ch. P×B 27. Q×P ch. K—B2 28. Kt—Kt5 ch. K—Kt1 29. R×B, and wins or by 21... K—B1. Against this last move White has the quiet and beautiful reply 22. R—KKt1 with the following possibilities: (*a*) 22... B×P 23. Q×B ch. Q—B2 24. Q—Kt4 P—Kt3 25. P—K6 Q—B4 26. Q×Q ch. P×Q 27. R×R ch. K×R 28. R—R8 mate ; (*b*) 22... Q—B2 23. P—K6 B×P 24. P×B Q×KP 25. P—B5 Q—B2 26. R(R3)—Kt3 B—B3 27. B—B5 ch. B—K2 28. P—B6 Q×P 29. B×B ch. K×B 30. R×P ch.

22 P—K6 ch.   K—B1
23 R—Kt3

But not 23. R—KKt1 B—B3 24. B×B P—Q5 dis. ch.

23 ...   B—KKt4

Now if 23... B—B3; simply 24. B×B wins.

24 R×B   Resigns.

For if 24... Q—K2 25. B×P ch. R×B 26. Q—R8 ch.

---

56 White: Hearst—Black: Franklin
Marshall Chess Club *v.* National Chess Centre, Correspondence, 1955

1 P—K4	P—QB4
2 Kt—KB3	P—Q3
3 P—Q4	P×P
4 Kt×P	Kt—KB3
5 Kt—QB3	P—QR3
6 P—B4	

6. B—K2 is usually considered the most solid method of meeting the Najdorf variation, but in a game, *Lepikhin-Alekseev, White Russia, 1955,* it formed the basis for an early violent attack after 6... P—K4 7. Kt—Kt3 B—K2 8. B—K3 QKt—Q2 9. P—Kt4 P—R3 10. P—KR4 P—QKt4 11. P—QR4 P—Kt5 (much better is 11... P×P 12. R×P Kt—Kt3 13. R—R1 B—Kt2) 12. Kt—Q5 Kt×Kt 13. Q×Kt R—QKt1 14. B—QB4 Castles 15. P—Kt5 P×P 16. P×P Kt—Kt3 17. B×Kt Q×B 18. P—Kt6 B—K3 19. Q×B! Resigns. If 19... P×Q 20. B×P ch. R—B2 21. B×R ch. K—B1 22. R—R8 mate, while if 19... Q×P ch. White is a whole piece up.

6 ...	Q—B2
7 B—Q3	P—KKt3
8 Castles	B—Kt2
9 Kt—B3	Kt—B3
10 K—R1	Castles
11 Q—K1	B—K3

Strategically good (Black wants K4 for his knight) but tactically wrong. Sounder is 11... P—QKt4 and ... B—Kt2 so as to prepare for an eventual ... P—Q4.

12 P—B5	B—Q2
13 Q—R4	Kt—K4

A better chance is 13... KR—Q1; and if 14. P—KKt4 P—Q4.

14 Kt×Kt	P×Kt
15 P—KKt4	B—B3
16 P—Kt5	Kt—Q2
17 P—B6	P×P
18 P×P	B—R1

The boxing in of a Dragon bishop almost always means disaster; from now

51

on Black is effectively a piece down.

19 R—B3	P—QKt4

Admitting that he is devoid of a constructive plan. If 19... KR—Q1 20. R—R3 B×P 21. Q×P ch. K—B1 22. Kt—Q5 B×Kt 23. P×B, with an overwhelming attack.

20 B—Kt5	KR—Q1
21 R—R3	Kt—B1
22 R—KB1	R—Q3
23 Kt—Q5	B×Kt
24 P×B	Q—Q1

The only move which would have met White's double threat of 25. B—R6 and 25. B×KKtP is 24... P—KR4; but then comes 25. Q—Kt3 and if 25... Kt—R2 26. R×P P×R 27. B—R6 dis. ch., or if 25... Q—Q1 26. R×P P×R 27. B—R6 dis. ch. Kt—Kt3 28. B×Kt B×P 29. B—Q3 dis. ch. K—R1 30. Q—B3, winning because of the threats of Q—B5 and Q×P.

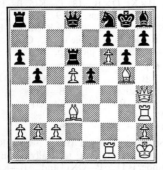

25 B×KKtP!	Resigns.

If 25... RP×B 26. Q×B mate, or if 25... BP×B 26. P—B7 ch. K—Kt2 27. Q—R6 mate, or if 25... Kt×B 26. Q×P ch. K—B1 27. Q×B ch. Kt×Q 28. R×Kt mate. A very neat finish.

57 WHITE: BOEY—BLACK: O'KELLY
Belgian Championship, 1957

1 P—K4	P—QB4
2 Kt—KB3	P—Q3
3 P—Q4	P×P
4 Kt×P	Kt—KB3
5 Kt—QB3	P—QR3
6 B—KKt5	P—K3
7 P—B4	Q—Kt3
8 Q—Q2	Q×P
9 R—QKt1	Q—R6
10 P—K5	P×P
11 P×P	KKt—Q2
12 Kt—K4	

One of the most discussed variations in the whole of current master practice. The main alternatives are for Black 7... P—KR3 before capturing the QKtP, and for White 12. B—QB4 or 12. B—K2 and, earlier, 8. Kt—Kt3. It seems likely that in every case Black has sufficient counterchances so long as he can remember the analysis.

12 ...	P—R3
13 B—R4	Q×P
14 R—Kt3	Kt—QB3

This has now been abandoned in favour of a still more Wild West line, 14... Q—R8 ch. 15. K—B2 Q—R5 16. B—QKt5 P×B 17. Kt×KtP B—B4 ch. 18. Kt×B Q×B ch. 19. P—Kt3 Q—Q1 20. Q—Q6 Kt×P 21. Kt—B7 ch. Q×Kt 22. Q×Q QKt—R3 23. Q—Kt6 Kt×R; and Black's three pieces outweigh the queen (*Korchnoi-Tolush, Riga, 1958*).

15 Kt×Kt	P×Kt
16 Kt—Q6 ch.?	

Darga later pointed out the much stronger line 16. Q—B3 Q—R5 17. B—QB4 Kt×P 18. Castles Kt×B 19. Kt—B6 ch., with a tremendous attack.

16 ...	B×Kt
17 P×B	

White overlooked that the natural 17. Q×B is met by 17... Q—R4 ch., followed by ... Q×KP ch. or ... Q—B4 ch., forcing the exchange of queens.

17 ...	P—QR4!

It is extraordinary that this pawn can win the game off its own bat—but it does.

14. SICILIAN DEFENCE

18	B—K2	P—R5
19	R—QB3	Q—R8 ch.
20	B—Q1	P—R6
21	Castles	P—R7
22	Q—K3	

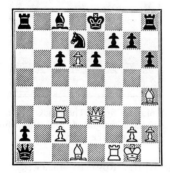

22 ...	Castles!

Avoiding the last trap 22... Q—Kt7
23. Q×P ch. P×Q 24. B—R5 ch.
P—Kt3 25. B×P mate.

23 Resigns.

58 WHITE: KERES—BLACK: SAJTAR
Amsterdam, 1954

1	P—K4	P—QB4
2	Kt—KB3	P—Q3
3	P—Q4	P×P
4	Kt×P	Kt—KB3
5	Kt—QB3	P—QR3
6	B—Kt5	QKt—Q2
7	B—QB4	P—K3

The correct reply here is 7... P—KKt3
but not 7... Q—B2 8. B—Kt3 P—Kt4;
when a game, *Goldin-Ambarian, Armen-
ian Championship, 1955*, went on 9.
Castles B—Kt2 10. R—K1 Kt—Kt3
11. B×Kt KP×B 12. P—QR4 P—Kt5
13. P—R5 P×Kt 14. P×Kt Q—B4
15. B—R4 ch. K—Q1 16. Q—Kt4
Q—B1 17. Q—R5 P—Kt3 18. Q—Q5!
B×Q 19. P×B, Resigns, for if 19...
B—K2 20. Kt—B6 ch., K—K1 21.
R×B ch. K—B1 22. P—Kt7.

8 Castles	Q—B2

Black obviously has no idea of the
storm which is about to break over his
king. 8... B—K2 would be met by a
similar combination, so that Black's
only reasonable defence is 8... Kt—Kt3.
Even this move would represent a
positional success for White, since the
knight blocks the advance of Black's
QKtP.

9 B×KP

The sacrifice of a minor piece on K6
is almost a commonplace in the Najdorf
variation in 1959—but in 1954 it was a
sensational brilliancy.

9 ...	P×B
10 Kt×P	Q—B5
11 Kt—Q5	K—B2

11... Kt×Kt 12. P×Kt leaves the
black king terribly exposed in the centre,
while if 11... Kt×P, then 12. P—QKt3
Q—B3 13. Kt(K6)—B7 ch. K—B2
14. Q—R5 ch. P—Kt3 15. Q—B3 ch.
Kt(K5)—B3 16. B×Kt Kt×B 17.
Q×Kt ch. K—Kt1 18. QR—K1 B—Q2
19. R—K7 and wins.

12 B×Kt	K×Kt

A considerably stronger defence here
is 12... Kt×B! and if 13. Kt—Kt6
Q×Kt 14. Kt×R B—K2 and, despite
his slight material disadvantage, Black
has plenty of fight left as his pieces are
at last co-ordinated.

13 B—B3	Kt—B3
14 B×Kt	P×B
15 Kt—Kt6	Q—B3
16 Kt×R	B—K2
17 P—QR4	P—Kt3
18 Q—Q5 ch.	K—Q2

Black is hoping to trap the knight. If
18... Q×Q 19. Kt—B7 ch. followed by
Kt×Q, and White's knight dominates
the centre.

19 R—R3	B—Q1

It seems that Black is home and dry,
for he threatens 20... Q×Q and 21...
B—Kt2, but...

14. SICILIAN DEFENCE

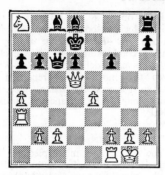

20 Kt×P ch.!   Resigns.

A delightful finish. If 20... B×Kt
21. Q—B7 ch. K—Q1   22. Q×P ch.
K—Q2 23. Q—Kt7 ch. K—Q1 24.
Q×R ch. or 20... Q×Kt 21. Q—B5 ch.
K—B2 22. R—B3 ch.

59 WHITE: KLUGER—BLACK: NAGY

Budapest, 1942

1 P—K4	P—QB4
2 Kt—KB3	Kt—QB3
3 P—Q4	P×P
4 Kt×P	Kt—B3
5 Kt—QB3	P—Q3
6 B—KKt5	P—QR3

An inferior defence, which White
could answer by the immediate 7. B×Kt.
However, he is well justified in delaying
this, since Black immediately commits
another indiscretion.

7 Q—Q2	Kt—Q2
8 B—K2	P—KKt3
9 Kt—Q5	P—B3

Black gives in without a fight, justifi-
ably so in view of the variation 9...
P—R3 (if 9... B—Kt2 10. Kt×Kt
P×Kt 11. B×KP) 10. B—R4 P—KKt4
11. Kt—K6!

10 Kt—K6

Ring around the roses.

10 ...	Q—R4
11 Kt(Q5)—B7 ch.	K—B2
12 Kt—Q8 ch.	K—Kt2
13 Kt—K8 ch.	Resigns.

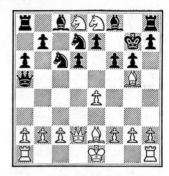

A piquant finish. The Black king and
queen have emigrated, and the white
knights occupy their thrones.

60 WHITE: ROSSETTO—BLACK: BEHRENSEN

Mar del Plata, 1958

1 P—K4	P—QB4
2 Kt—KB3	P—Q3
3 P—Q4	P×P
4 Kt×P	Kt—KB3
5 Kt—QB3	P—QR3
6 B—QB4	

Although this is played less often than
the various other alternatives against the
Najdorf variation, it is probably just as
good.

6 ...	P—K3
7 P—QR3	

An idea of Bronstein's, to preserve the
bishop from exchange.

7 ...	Q—B2
8 B—R2	Kt—B3
9 Castles	B—K2
10 K—R1	B—Q2
11 P—B4	Castles KR
12 P—B5	Kt×Kt
13 Q×Kt	Kt—K1?

It is remarkable how this single weak
move allows White to obtain a winning
attack. Correct is either 13... Kt—Kt5
or 13... Q—B4.

14 P×P	P×P
15 R×R ch.	B×R
16 B—Kt5	Q—R4

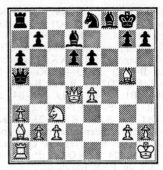

17 Kt—Q5!

A most economic move, since it not only brings a fresh piece into the attack but shuts out the black queen from the king's side. If 17... P×Kt 18. B×P ch. K—R1 19. R—KB1 Kt—B3 (if 19... Kt—B2 20. B—R6, followed by 21. R×B ch) 20. P—QKt4 Q×RP 21. R×Kt! and wins.

17 ...	R—Kt1
18 R—KB1	P—R3
19 Q—B2	P×B
20 Q×B ch.	K—R2
21 Kt—K7	Resigns.

61 WHITE: JEZEK—BLACK: BOLESLAVSKY

Vienna, 1957

1 P—K4	P—QB4
2 Kt—KB3	Kt—QB3
3 P—Q4	P×P
4 Kt×P	Kt—B3
5 Kt—QB3	P—Q3
6 B—QB4	P—K3
7 Castles	B—K2
8 B—Kt3	Castles
9 K—R1	

A more dangerous line for Black is the immediate 9. P—B4, after which a game, *Wade-Boxall, Bognor, 1953,* continued 9... P—QR3? (better 9... Kt—QR4) 10. P—B5 Kt×Kt 11. Q×Kt Q—B2 12. K—R1 B—Q2 13. B—Kt5 QR—Q1 14. QR—Q1 P—Kt4 15. R—Q3 Q—B4 16. P×P Q×B 17. P×B R×P 18. R—Kt3 Q—R5 19. Kt—Q5 K—R1

20. R—R3 Q—Kt4 21. Kt—B4 Q—K4 22. B×P! Resigns.

9 ...	Kt×Kt
10 Q×Kt	P—QKt3

This now saves a tempo as against the manoeuvre ... P—QR3 and ... P—QKt4.

11 B—Kt5

This move is out of harmony with White's normal plan in this variation, which consists of advancing P—B4—B5, forcing Black to play ... P—K4, and only then carrying out the manoeuvre B—KKt5×Kt so as to occupy Q5 with a minor piece. K—R1 has no place in this scheme, so that Black is presented with an extra tempo for defence.

11 ...	B—Kt2
12 P—B4	R—B1
13 P—B5	R—B4!

The point of Black's defence, which prevents White from capturing at K6, and enables Black on the next move to block the KB file and open the long diagonal for his QB.

14 B—KR4

The attempt to continue the attack by 14. P—Kt4 would give Black a winning advantage after 14... Kt×KP 15. Kt×Kt B×B 16. K—Kt1 R—K4.

14 ...	P×P
15 P×P	

If 15. R×P Kt×P, wins a pawn.

15 ...	Q—B1
16 QR—K1	

This permits a series of neat combinations which decide the game quickly. 16. Q—KB4 is necessary, but after 16... Q—B3 17. R—B2 B—B1 White is still in great difficulties.

16 ...	R×P
17 R×R	Q×R
18 B—B4	

If 18. R×B Q—B8 ch. 19. Q—Kt1 B×P mate.

18 ...	B—Q1
19 B—Q3	Q—Q2
20 R—KB1	Q—R6
21 R—KKt1	

If 21. R—B2 Kt—Kt5, or if 21. Q—B2 B×P ch., wins another pawn.

21 ...   Kt—Kt5

22 B—Kt3   B—KB3
23 Kt—K4

If 23. Q—QB4, Black has a pretty mate by 23... Q×RP ch. 24. B×Q Kt—B7. But if 23. Q—KB4 B—K4 24. B—K4 Q—R4 25. Q—B3 B×QB 26. Q×B Q×P ch. 27. Q×Q Kt—B7 mate.

23 ...   B×Kt
24 B×B   Q×B
25 Resigns.

Black wins a piece.

A game with the power typical of Boleslavsky at his best.

62 WHITE: JUNGE—BLACK: SAHLMANN

Hamburg, 1944

1 P—K4   P—QB4
2 Kt—KB3   P—K3
3 P—Q4   P×P
4 Kt×P   Kt—KB3
5 Kt—QB3   P—Q3
6 B—K2   P—QR3

A game, *Olafsson-Gudmundsson, Reykjavik, 1953*, illustrates a typical pawn storm by White if Black plays without aggression in the Scheveningen: 6... Kt—B3 7. B—K3 B—K2 8. Castles Castles 9. P—B4 Q—B2 10. P—KKt4 P—QR3? (correct is 10...

Kt×Kt and 11... P—K4) 11. P—Kt5 Kt—K1 12. P—B5 Q—Q1 13. P—KR4 Kt×Kt 14. Q×Kt P—K4? (giving White complete control of Q5 and of the white diagonal QR2—KKt8; correct is 14... B—Q2) 15. Q—Q2 Kt—B2 16. B—Kt6 Q—Q2 17. R—B2 B—Q1 18. QR—KB1 P—B3   19. B—B4 ch. K—R1 20. P—Kt6 P—R3 21. B—B7 Q—B3 22. B×Kt B×B 23. R—Kt2 P—Q4 (the counter-attack comes a good dozen moves too late) 24. Q×P ch.! Resigns. If 24... P×Q 25. P—Kt7 ch. K—R2 26. P×R(Kt) ch.

7 Castles   Q—B2
8 P—B4   P—QKt4

Premature, and the cause of Black's later troubles. Right is 8... Kt—B3.

9 B—B3   B—Kt2
10 P—K5   P×P
11 P×P   Kt(B3)—Q2
12 B×B   Q×B
13 Q—R5   P—Kt3

Black is obliged to weaken his king's position for if 13... Kt—B4 14. P—QKt4 followed by 15. Kt×KP, while if 13... Kt—Kt3   14. Kt×KP P—Kt3   15. Q—R3 P×Kt 16. Q×P ch. B—K2 17. B—Kt5 Kt—B3 18. Q—B7 ch. K—Q1 19. QR—Q1 ch., with a decisive attack.

14 Q—R4   B—Kt2
15 Kt—K4!   B×P
16 Kt—KB3   Q—Kt3 ch.
17 K—R1   B—Kt2

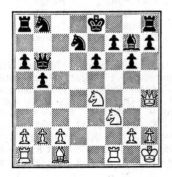

56

18 B—K3!

A pretty stroke, which brings the last White minor piece into play with gain of time, for if 18... Q×B 19. Kt—Q6 ch. K—B1 20. Q—Q8 mate.

18 ...	Q—B2
19 Kt(B3)—Kt5	P—KR4
20 R×P	Q—K4
21 B—B4	Q×Kt

Despair, but if 21... Q×P 22. Kt—Q6 ch. K—Q1 23. Kt×P mate.

22 Kt×Q	K×R
23 Kt—Kt5 ch.	Resigns.

This was the last game played by the young German master, who was killed in action in the very last days of the war. The clock times for the game make interesting reading. White took sixteen minutes, Black an hour and twenty-eight minutes, which indicates that Junge, had he lived, might have had a speed of calculation equal to Tal's at the present day.

63 WHITE: KLOVAN—BLACK: PUKUDRUVA

Latvian Championship, 1955

1 P—K4	P—QB4
2 Kt—KB3	P—Q3
3 P—Q4	P×P
4 Kt×P	Kt—KB3
5 Kt—QB3	P—QR3
6 P—KKt3	Q—B2

More accurate than the immediate 6... P—QKt4, when a game, *Dubinin-Suetin, Moscow, 1953*, continued 7. B—Kt2 B—Kt2 8. Castles P—K3 9. Q—K2 QKt—Q2 10. R—Q1 Q—B2 11. P—QR4 P—Kt5 12. Kt—Q5! P×Kt 13. P×P dis. ch. K—Q1 14. Kt—B6 ch. K—B1 15. B—Kt5 B×Kt 16. P×B Kt—K4 17. B×Kt P×B 18. P—KB4 Kt×P 19. Q—B4 K—Kt2 20. P—B3 P—Kt6 21. P—R5 R—B1 22. Q×KtP ch. K—R2 23. R—R4 Kt—Q1

24. R—B4! Resigns (24... Q×R 25. Q—Kt6 mate).

7 B—Kt2	P—K3
8 Castles	B—K2
9 B—K3	Castles
10 Q—K2	B—Q2
11 QR—Q1	Kt—B3
12 Kt—Kt3	P—QKt4
13 P—QR3	QR—Kt1
14 P—B4	KR—Q1

One reason why the Sicilian is favoured by many masters both for White and Black is that the timing of White's normal king's side-attack and Black's natural counterplay on the queen's side and in the centre needs to be done very precisely. Black's mistake in the present game is that he is simultaneously trying to make progress in the centre and on the queen's side, and as a result both loses time and weakens his king's position. Better is 14... P—Kt5 15. P×P Kt×KtP followed by B—B3 and Q—Kt2 when the attack on the king's pawn restricts White's activities.

15 P—Kt4	P—Kt5
16 P×P	Kt×QKtP
17 P—Kt5	Kt—K1
18 P—B5	

White's attack is now very strong; Black cannot avoid the opening of the KB file, and if 18... Kt—QB3 19. P×P P×P 20. Q×P, his hold on K4 is insufficient compensation for the pawn minus.

18 ...	Kt×P

Positionally outplayed, Black goes in for the traditional remedy of a tactical mêlée.

19 Q×Kt	B—R5
20 P×P	B×Kt

If 20... P×P, White wins immediately by 21. Q—B2 B×Kt 22. Q—B7 ch. K—R1 23. Q—B8 ch., followed by mate.

21 P×P ch.	B×P

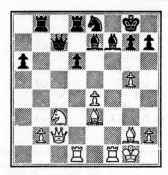

22 R×B!

An attack on KB7 is a rare bird in the Sicilian, where king's side-attacks are usually directed against KKt7 or KR7.

| 22 ... | K×R |
| 23 R—B1 ch. | K—Kt1 |

Overlooking White's drastic reply, but as Clarke shows in the *British Chess Magazine*, Black is lost in any case. If 23... K—K3 24. B—R3 ch. or 23... K—Kt3 24. P—K5 dis. ch., in both cases with a quick mate, while if 23... Kt—B3 24. P×Kt B×P 25. P—K5 P×P 26. R×B ch.! finally if 23... B—B3 24. P×B P×P 25. P—K5 QP×P 26. Q×P ch. Kt—Kt2 27. B—Q5 ch.

| 24 Kt—Q5! | Q—Kt2 |

If 24... Q×Q 25. Kt×B ch. K—R1 26. R—B8 mate.

| 25 Q—B2 | Resigns. |

The threatened mate costs Black a piece.

64 WHITE: OLAFSSON—BLACK: PILNIK
Reykjavik, 1957

1 P—K4	P—QB4
2 Kt—KB3	P—K3
3 P—Q4	P×P
4 Kt×P	P—QR3
B—K2	Kt—KB3

6 Kt—QB3	Q—B2
7 Castles	B—Kt5
8 Q—Q3	

Another idea is to sacrifice a pawn for the attack by 8. B—B3 B×Kt 9. P×B Q×P 10. R—Kt1 Q—B2 11. B—R3 Kt—B3 12. R—K1 Kt—K4 13. R—Kt3.

| 8 ... | Kt—B3 |
| 9 Kt×Kt | QP×Kt? |

A surprising error of judgment for a great master. Correct is ... KtP×Kt, followed by an early ... P—Q4 with a counter-attack in the centre.

10 P—B4	Castles
11 P—K5	R—Q1
12 Q—R3	B×Kt

White has already a promising position on the king's side, but this move helps him considerably. As Black will soon have to play ... P—KKt3 in any case, it is essential to retain the KB to help in the defence via KB1 and KKt2.

13 P×B	Kt—Q2
14 B—K3	P—QB4
15 R—B3	Kt—B1
16 B—Q3	P—QKt3
17 Q—R5	B—Kt2
18 R—R3	

Finally White succeeds in forcing Black to create a weakness in the pawn front defending his king, and this is the beginning of the end.

| 18 ... | P—Kt3 |
| 19 Q—R6 | Q—B3 |

Missing the last defensive chance, which was to drive the white KB off its good diagonal by 19... P—B5 20. B—KB1 R—Q2. If then 21. B—B2 QR—Q1, and White cannot play for an immediate mating attack because of 22. B—R4 Q—B4 ch. 23. K—R1 R—Q8 24. B—B6 B×P ch. 25. K×B R(Q1)—Q7 ch. and wins.

| 20 R—Kt3 | R—Q2 |

Now if 20... P—B5 21. P—B5 threatening P—B6 and mate.

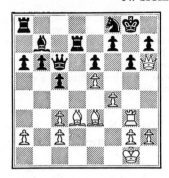

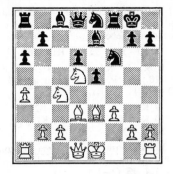

21 P—B5!	P×P
22 B—KKt5	Kt—K3

If 22... P—B3 23. B—B4 ch.

23 B—B6	P—KB5
24 Q×RP ch.	Resigns.

If 24... K×Q 25. R—R3 ch. K—Kt1 26. R—R8 mate.

65 WHITE: O'KELLY—BLACK: AHLBACH

Correspondence, 1938

1 P—K4	P—QB4
2 Kt—KB3	P—Q3
3 P—Q4	P×P
4 Kt×P	Kt—KB3
5 P—KB3	P—K4
6 Kt—Kt5	P—QR3
7 Kt(Kt5)—B3	QKt—Q2?

Very passive; correct is 7... B—K2; and if 8. B—Kt5 Kt×P!

8 P—QR4	B—K2
9 Kt—R3	Castles
10 Kt—B4	Kt—K1

Black seems determined to go into a huddle with himself: 10... Kt—B4; still gives some fighting chances, although after 11. P—R5, followed by Kt—Kt6, White has a permanent stranglehold on the queen's wing.

11 Kt—Q5	P—B4
12 P×P	R×P
13 B—Q3	R—B1
14 B—K3	Kt(Q2)—B3

15 B—QKt6	Q—Q2
16 B—KB5!	Resigns.

White has not moved any of his major pieces!

66 WHITE: CANAL—BLACK: SCAFARELLI

San Benedetto del Tronto, 1957

1 P—K4	P—QB4
2 P—QB3	Kt—KB3
3 P—K5	Kt—Q4
4 Kt—KB3	

The 2. P—QB3 system is a favourite one for masters giving simultaneous exhibitions, since it heaves an unimaginative player right out of the books. For instance, a game won by Horowitz (*White, Chicago, 1958*) continued 4. P—Q4 P×P 5. P×P P—Q3 6. Kt—B3 Kt—QB3 7. P×P Q×P 8. Kt—B3 B—B4 (better 8... P—K3) 9. B—QB4 Kt—Kt3 10. B—Kt3 P—K3 11. Castles Q—Q1 12. P—Q5 P×P 13. Kt×P Kt×Kt 14. B×Kt Q—Kt3 15. R—K1 ch. B—K2 16. B×P ch.! K×B 17. Q—Q5 ch. K—Kt3 18. R—K6 ch. B×R 19. Q×B ch. B—B3 20. Kt—R4 ch. K—R4 21. Q—K2 ch. Resigns; for if 21... K×Kt 22. P—Kt3 ch. K—R6 23. Q—K6 mate.

4 ...	P—Q3
5 P—Q4	BP×P
6 KP×P	Q×P
7 Kt×P	P—QR3

White threatened 8. Kt—Kt5, followed by 9. Q×Kt, but 7... P—K3 is a steadier defence.

8 Kt—R3   Kt—QB3

If 8... P—K4 9. Kt(Q4)—Kt5 P×Kt 10. Kt×P, wins a pawn after 10... Q—Q1 11 Q×Kt.

9 Kt—B4   Q—B2
10 Kt×Kt   P×Kt
11 Q—Q4   B—Kt2

Black's position is now very uncomfortable, for if 11... P—B3 12. B—Q3 P—K4 13. Q—R4.

12 B—K2   P—QB4
13 Q—R4   P—K3
14 B—B3   B—K2
15 Q—Kt3!

White's superior pawn structure and better placed minor pieces are shown to their full advantage in the ending.

15 ...   Q×Q
16 RP×Q   P—QR4
17 B—B4   Castles KR
18 B—Q6   B×B
19 Kt×B   B—R3
20 Castles

Now White wins a pawn; in trying to save it Black runs into still worse trouble.

20 ...   KR—Q1
21 B×Kt   P×B
22 R×QP   B—B5
23 Kt×B!   Resigns.

After 23... R×R   24. Kt—Kt6 R(Q4)—Q1 25. Kt×R R×Kt 26.

R—Q1, followed by R—Q5 or R—Q7, the ending is simple technique. This game shows that the 2. P—QB3 system, which has been worked out by Canal and Heidenfeld, deserves more attention than has been hitherto paid it by masters.

67 WHITE: HAAG—BLACK: KORANYI

Budapest, 1953

1 P—K4   P—QB4
2 Kt—KB3   Kt—QB3
3 B—Kt5   P—KKt3

An equally playable alternative is 3... P—Q3. A game, *Roiter-Boleslavsky, Kiev, 1958*, continued 4. Castles P—QR3 5. B×Kt ch. P×B 6. P—Q4 P×P 7. Q×P P—K4 8. Q—Q3 B—K2 9. R—Q1 Q—B2 10. Kt—R3 P—KB4 11. P×P Kt—B3 12. Kt—KKt5 Castles 13. Q—R3 P—Q4 14. P—QKt3 P—KR3 15. Kt—B3 Kt—K5 16. P—KKt4 B—B4 17. R—B1 Q—R2 18. Q—Kt2 B×P! 19. P—Kt4 (if 19. P×B R×P 20. B—Kt2 QR—KB1 21. Kt—K1 R×P and wins) B×P ch. 20. K—R1 (if 20. R×B B×P!) B—R2 21. P—B4 B—Q5 22. Kt×B Q×Kt 23. B—Kt2 Kt—B7 ch. 24. K—Kt1 Q×B 25. Resigns.

4 Castles   B—Kt2
5 R—K1   Q—Kt3

This early excursion, though theoretically playable, almost always gives Black practical troubles. Preferable is 5... P—Q3, followed by... B—Q2.

6 Kt—R3   P—Q3
7 P—R3   B—Q2
8 P—B3   Kt—B3

Not 8... P—K4 9. Kt—B4 Q—B2 10. Kt—K3, when White either secures Q5 for his knight or, after 10... Kt—B3, gets in P—Q4 just the same.

9 P—Q4   P×P
10 P×P   P—Q4
11 P×P   KKt×P
12 Q—Kt3   B—K3

Not 12... Kt—B2? 13. Kt—B4, while other knight moves are answered by 13. P—Q5.

13 R×B

Leading to very interesting complications; but a sounder way of holding White's advantage is 13. Kt—Kt5, Kt—B2 14. Kt×B.

13 ...	P×R
14 Kt—Kt5	K—Q2
15 Kt—B4	Q—B2

Wisely declining the QP for after 15... Q×P White wins by 16. B—K3 Q—B3 17. Kt—K4 Q—B4 18. Kt—B5 ch. K—B2 19. B×Kt.

16 Kt×KP!	K×Kt
17 Kt—K3	QR—Q1
18 B—B4	Q—R4
19 B—Q2!	Q×B
20 B×Kt ch.	K—B3
21 Kt—Kt4 ch.	K—Kt4

But not 21... K—B4 22. Q—B3 ch. Q—B5 23. B—K4 ch. K—Kt4 24. P—R4 ch., winning the queen.

22 P—R4 ch.!

An ingenious way of keeping the attack alive, for if now 22... K×Kt? 23. Q—B3 ch. K×P 24. Q—Kt3 ch. K—R4 25. B—B3 ch. K—R3 26. Q—R4 mate, while if 22... K×P? 23. Q—Kt3 ch. K—R4 24. B—B3 and wins.

22 ...   K—R4!

23 Q—KB3

Now, however, if 23. B—B3? K×P! and Black wins.

23 ...   Kt×P!

The razor-edge manoeuvring of both sides finally ends in a forced draw by perpetual check (24. Kt—B6 db. ch. K—R3 25. Kt—Kt4 ch.). The alternative 24. Kt—K5 dis. ch.? would be an hallucination after 24... Kt×Q ch. 25. B×Kt ch. K×P (25... K—R3? 26. Kt—B7 mate) 26. P—Kt3 ch. K—Kt4 (but not 26... K—R6? when 27. B—Kt4 is mate). A most entertaining game in which both sides show great imagination.

68 WHITE: FICHTL—BLACK: GEREBEN
Warsaw, 1956

1 P—K4	P—QB4
2 Kt—KB3	Kt—QB3
3 P—Q4	P×P
4 Kt×P	P—KKt3
5 B—K3	B—Kt2
6 Kt—QB3	

Declining the challenge, but according to the latest theory 6. P—QB4 allows Black enough counterplay after 6... Kt—B3 7. Kt—QB3 Kt—KKt5 8. Q×Kt Kt×Kt 9. Q—Q1 P—K4.

6 ...	Kt—B3
7 Kt×Kt	KtP×Kt
8 P—K5	Kt—Kt1
9 P—B4	

More promising is 9. B—Q4 Kt—R3 10. P—K6 B×B 11. Q×B Castles 12. P×QP Q×P 13. Q×Q B×Q 14. Castles, with winning prospects for White owing to the queen's side-pawn majority.

9 ...	Kt—R3
10 Q—B3	Castles
11 B—B4?	

Overlooking Black's deep pawn offer which follows, 11. B—K2, followed by Castles KR, gives about equal chances.

11 ...	P—Q4!
12 P×P e.p.	P×P!
13 Q×P	

With the king in the centre, White's game is very difficult; but 13. P—KR3 is a better defensive chance.

13 ...	B—Q2

14 Q—B3

Not 14. Q×P Kt—B4, winning material.

14 ...   R—B1
15 B—Q3   B—Kt5
16 Q—Q5

If 16. Q—B2 R×Kt, wins a piece, while if 16. Q—Kt3 B—B3 17. P—KR4 R—K1, and White's king cannot survive for long in the centre.

16 ...   R—K1
17 K—Q2

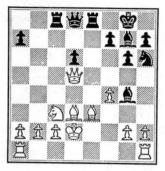

17 ...   R×B!
18 K×R   Q—Kt3 ch.
19 K—Q2   Q×P!

More precise than 19... Q—B7 ch. 20. K—B1 Q×KBP ch. 21. K—Kt1 B×Kt 22. P×B R—Kt1 ch. 23. B—Kt5 P—QR3 24. P—QR4.

20 Kt—K4   Q—Kt5 ch.
21 P—B3

Or 21. K—K3 B—Q5 ch. 22. Q×B Kt—B4 ch., and it's all over.

21 ...   B×P ch.
22 Kt×B   Q×Kt ch.
23 K—K3   Kt—B4 ch.
24 K—B2   Q—Kt7 ch.
25 Resigns.

69 WHITE: THAL—BLACK: GRANITZKY
East German Championship, 1958

1 P—K4   P—QB4
2 Kt—KB3   Kt—QB3

The Wing Gambit is a rare bird these days, but if Black does underestimate the attack it gives opportunities for beautiful combinations. A game, *Tartakower-Andor, Paris, 1952*, went on 2... P—Q3 3. P—QKt4 P—QKt3? 4. P×P QP×P 5. B—B4 Kt—QB3 6. Castles P—K3 7. B—Kt2 Kt—B3 8. P—Q4 Kt×KP 9. B—Kt5 B—Q2 10. P—Q5 Kt—R4 11. B×B ch. Q×B 12. P×P P×P 13. Q—K2 Kt—KB3 14. R—Q1 Q—B3 (if 14... B—Q3 15. B—K5 Kt—Q4 16. P—B4 B×B 17. Kt×B Kt—B5 18. Q—B3) 15. Kt—K5 Q—R5 16. Kt—QB3 Q—QKt5 17. B—R3! Q×B (White would win by an even more spectacular king hunt after 17... Q×Kt 18. Q—Kt5 ch. K—K2 19. R—Q7 ch. Kt×R 20. Q×Kt ch. K—B3 21. Kt—Kt4 ch. K—Kt4 22. B—B1 Kt—R5 23. P—Kt3 ch. K—R6 24. Q×KP Q—B5 25. P—KB3! Q—Q5 ch. 26. Kt—B2 mate) 18. Q—Kt5 ch. K—K2 19. R—Q7 ch. Kt×R 20. Q×Kt ch. K—B3 21. Q—B7 ch. K×Kt 22. R—K1 ch. K—Q5 23. Q—B3! Q×Kt 24. Q—K4 mate. A piquant finish.

3 P—QKt4   P×P
4 P—Q4   P—Q4

Opening of the position almost always favours a gambit player. Safer is 4... P—K3; for if 5. P—Q5 Q—B3.

5 P×P   Q×P
6 P—B4   Q—QR4?

Here 6... P×P e.p. is essential.

7 P—Q5   P—Kt6 dis. ch.

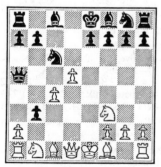

8 B—Q2!

14. SICILIAN DEFENCE

The young East German player Thal has based his style on his more famous Russian namesake Tal, and this extraordinary sacrifice is very reminiscent of the way in which Tal sacrifices pieces with gay abandon.

8	...	P—Kt7
9	B×Q	P×R(Q)
10	P×Kt	P—QKt3
11	B—B3	Q×P
12	B—K2	

With nearly all his pieces in play and Black's king's side completely undeveloped, White has more than enough compensation for his exchange sacrifice.

12	...	Kt—B3
13	Castles	P—K3
14	Q—Q3	B—K2
15	Kt—Kt5	P—QR4?

15... P—KR3 puts up a much better resistance, for if 16. B×Kt B×B 17. Kt×BP? K×Kt 18. B—R5 ch. K—K2 19. R—Q1 B—K4 20. P—B4! Q—R4! and Black should survive the attack.

16 Kt—Q2

From now on Black can only make defensive moves; here, for instance, White threatens 17. R—R1.

16	...	Q—R6
17	Kt(Kt5)—K4	Kt×Kt
18	Kt×Kt	B—B1

Virtual resignation, but if 18... Castles 19. R—R1 Q—Kt6 20. Kt—Q2, while if 18... B—B3 19. Kt×B ch. P×Kt 20. R—Q1 Q—K2 21. Q—B3, threatening both 22. B×P and 22. P—B7.

19	R—Q1	Q—K2
20	B—K5	B—Q2
21	Kt—Q6 ch.	Q×Kt
22	P×B ch.	Resigns.

---

15. CARO-KANN DEFENCE

70 WHITE: BILEK—BLACK: BRONSTEIN

Budapest, 1955

1	P—K4	P—QB3
2	P—Q4	P—Q4
3	Kt—QB3	P×P
4	Kt×P	Kt—B3

Perhaps the most controversial line in the Caro-Kann: Black must either submit to a safe but lifeless position after 5... KP×Kt, or accept a dangerously weakened pawn position after 5... KtP×Kt. Many players therefore prefer 4... B—B4.

5	Kt×Kt ch.	KtP×Kt

Naturally Bronstein chooses the second alternative.

6	P—QB3	B—B4
7	Kt—K2	P—KR4

With the idea of avoiding the difficulties facing his QB after the normal 7... P—K3 8. Kt—Kt3 B—Kt3 9. P—KR4 P—KR3 10. P—R5.

8	Kt—B4	P—R5
9	Q—B3	Kt—Q2
10	P—KKt4?	

Just the type of move Black is waiting for with his provocative lay-out. Quiet development (10. B—Q3) might have enabled White to utilize the many weaknesses in the black position.

10	...	P×P e.p.
11	BP×P	P—K4!

If now 12. Kt—K2 B—K3 with the threat of B—Q4 (a threat unaffected by the prior exchange of pawns). With the text reply White achieves that the black bishop has to relinquish the option of playing to K3 before the knight is forced to give way, but his pawn position is now weaker than the opponent's.

12	P—KKt4	B—R2
13	Kt—K2	P×P
14	P×P	

Or 14. Kt×P Kt—K4 15. Q—Kt2 Q—K2 16. B—K2 Castles with a

15. CARO-KANN DEFENCE

tremendous position. After the text White remains with pawn weaknesses everywhere, and the two black bishops have the freedom of the board.

14 ...	B—Kt5 ch.
15 K—B2	

15. B—Q2 would make nonsense of his previous move, which was designed to keep the knight out, because of 15... B×B ch. 16. K×B Kt—K4! 17. Q—K3 Q—Kt3! followed by Castles (Q).

15 ...	Q—K2
16 B—Kt2	Castles (Q)
17 P—QR3?	

He cannot play for an exchange of queens with 17. Q—K3 Kt—K4! (18. P×Kt? KB—B4) and therefore tries to get control of the K-file by making R—K1 possible. However, there is no time for this manoeuvre. A poor best was 17. B—K3, when the black knight would get powerfully into the game by 17... Kt—Kt3—QB5 (or Q4).

17 ...	B—QB4!

A beautiful and far from obvious sacrifice, which shows the power of the black pieces. If now 18. P×B Kt—K4 19. Q—KKt3 R—Q6 20. B—K3 Kt—B5 wins.

18 B—K3	Kt—K4!
19 P×Kt	

If the second offer is refused, Black wins prosaically by 19. Q—Kt3 Kt—Q6 ch. 20. K—B1 B—Q3 21. Q—B3 Kt×P.

19 ...	R—Q6
20 Q×P	Q×Q ch.
21 P×Q	R×B
22 KR—QB1	B—QKt3
23 B—B3	B—K5!
24 B×B	R×B dis. ch.
Resigns.	

If 25. K—B3 R—K6 ch. 26. K—B2 R×KRP ch. If 25. K—B1 R×KRP. A boldly-planned and highly original game.

71 WHITE: HARNIK—BLACK: MIESES

Vienna, 1936

1 P—QB4	P—QB3
2 P—K4	P—Q4
3 KP×P	P×P
4 P—Q4	Kt—QB3
5 Kt—QB3	

By transposition of moves the Panoff Variation has been reached, a fashionable line at the time.

5 ...	P×P
6 P—Q5	Kt—K4
7 Q—Q4	Kt—Q6 ch.
8 B×Kt	P×B
9 Kt—B3	Kt—B3
10 B—Kt5	P—K3!

Stronger than 10... P—KKt3 which, in a famous match game, *Botvinnik-Flohr, 1933*, gave White a clear advantage after 11. B×Kt P×B 12. Castles (K) Q—Kt3 13. KR—K1 ch. K—Q1 14. Q—KR4.

11 B×Kt	Q×B
12 Q×QP	B—Q3

12... B—Q2 is safer, but Mieses allows the check deliberately.

13 Q—Kt5 ch.	B—Q2
14 Q×P	R—QKt1
15 Q×P	R×P
16 Kt—K4!	

Each side combines essential defensive measures with counter-attack. It is because he relied on this move that White went in for the win of the two pawns.

16 ...   **R—K7 ch.?**

Brilliant but inadequate. The winner comments in the *Wiener Schachzeitung* that Black was lost in any case, e.g., 16... B—Kt5 ch. 17. K—B1 Q—B5 18. Q—Q4, but overlooks the reply 18... R×RP! If then 19. Q×P R×R ch. 20. Q×R Q×Kt 21. Q×R ch. K—K2, and Black's two bishops are worth at least the opponent's rook and knight. Or 19. Kt(3)—Q2? R×R ch. 20. Q×R Castles! and Black stands to win. Or 19. R—Kt1 B—Kt4 ch. 20. K—Kt1 R—R5 21. Q×P Q×Kt 22. Q×R ch. K—K2, with dubious complications. If in this line 21. Q—Kt6 B—Q2 22. P—Q6 Castles, and Black is safe.

17 K×R   **B—Kt4 ch.**
18 K—Q1!

The point of White's counterplay. If 18. K—K3? B—B5 mate; if 18. K—Q2 Q—Kt7 ch. with mate to follow in a few moves.

18 ...   **Q×R ch.**
19 K—B2   **B—B4**

Resignation. If 19... Q×R 20. Kt×B ch. leads to mate.

20 Q—Kt8 ch.   **Resigns.**

---

72 WHITE: MORA—BLACK: LANGE

Luxemburg, 1955

1 P—K4	P—QB3
2 P—QB4	P—Q4
3 BP×P	P×P

4 P×P	Kt—KB3
5 Q—R4 ch.	

Proving Black's last move somewhat light-hearted. For now he will have considerable difficulties recovering his pawn: 5... B—Q2 6. Q—Kt3!; or 5... Q—Q2? 6. B—Kt5.

5 ...	QKt—Q2
6 Kt—QB3	P—KKt3
7 P—KR4!	B—Kt2
8 P—R5!	

An ingenious pawn offer to disrupt the black position. Yet Black had to "bite into the sour apple" and play 8... P×P, because, as played, White establishes two horrible tusks on Q5 and KKt5, which ultimately tear Black's game to pieces.

8 ...	Kt×RP
9 P—KKt4	Kt—B3
10 P—Kt5	Kt—R4
11 B—K2	K—B1

At first glance surprising. But without unpinning the knight the black game is completely move-bound, and castling into the open R-file is more than flesh and blood can stand.

12 P—Q4	Kt—Kt3
13 Q—Kt3	B—B4
14 Kt—B3	Q—Kt1

If instead 14... Q—Q3 15. P—R4 with the threat of P—R5. If Black stops this by 15... P—QR4, White plays, as later in the game, Kt—K5, after which Black cannot twice capture on K4 because the QKt would be *en prise*.

15 R—R4!

Stopping 15... Kt—B5. From here on Black's task is hopeless—the loss of time in the opening has been too much.

15 ...	K—Kt1
16 B—K3	Q—Q3
17 Kt—K5	P—K3
18 Kt—B4	Kt×Kt
19 B×Kt	B—B1
20 P×P	P×P
21 P—Q5	P—K4
22 B—B5!	Q×B
23 P—Q6 ch.	Resigns.

On 23... K—Kt2 24. Q×P ch. is the end. A clever and original game even though it is lacking in brilliance.

---

73 WHITE: ESPELI—BLACK: ANDERSEN

Oslo, 1952

1 P—K4	P—QB3
2 P—QB4	P—Q4
3 BP×P	P×P
4 B—Kt5 ch.?	

Merely wasting time and assuring Black an easy development. Theoretically this game is worthless—yet the resultant play is so extraordinary that its absence would be a serious flaw in the collection.

4 ...	B—Q2
5 Q—R4?	

Worser and worser.

5 ...	P×P
6 B×B ch.	Kt×B

7 Q×KP	Kt—B4
8 Q—QB4	

8. Q—B2 would have led to the same denouement. Best in the circumstances was 8. Q—B3 Kt—Q6 ch. 9. K—Q1.

8 ...	Kt—Q6 ch.
9 K—K2	R—B1!
10 Q×Kt	Q×Q ch.
11 K×Q	R×B
12 K—K2	P—KKt3
Resigns.	

So complete a blockade of a whole army by one single unit has never been seen on a chessboard. With his last move Black made sure that his rook could not be driven away by the king after, e.g., 13. P—Q4 B—Kt2 14. K—Q2 B—R3 ch. The continuation could be 15. K—K2 Kt—B3 16. P—KKt3 Castles 17. P—B4 KR—B1; or 17. K—B3 R—Q1 18. K—Kt2 R×P 19. Kt—K2 R×R 20. K×R R—Q8 ch.—and the queen side pieces remain locked in.

---

16. CENTRE COUNTER GAME

74 WHITE: KARAKHAN—BLACK: KAKABADZE

Leningrad, 1957

1 P—K4	P—Q4
2 P×P	Q×P
3 Kt—QB3	Q—QR4
4 P—Q4	Kt—KB3
5 B—Q3	Kt—B3

6 Kt—K2	P—K4
7 P×P	

Clarke, in the *British Chess Magazine*, rightly suggests 7. Castles, with a strong initiative for the pawn: 7... P×P 8. Kt—Kt5 B—QB4 9. B—KB4 Kt—Q4 10. P—QR3. After the text Black should have had no difficulties if he had simply continued with 7... Kt×P.

16. CENTRE COUNTER GAME

7 ...	Kt—KKt5
8 Castles	QKt×P
9 B—Kt5 ch.	

After his insipid opening (5. B—Q3 7. P×P) White is faced with the choice of falling behind in development or surrendering the pair of bishops—an unenviable alternative in so open a position. His choice is audacious but apparently valid.

9 ...	P—B3
10 B—R4	B—K3
11 P—KR3	P—R4

This sacrifice, which constitutes the theme of the game is, in the last resort, incorrect.

12 B—B4	

White prefers to develop. He could have accepted the piece when play might have gone 12. P×Kt P×P 13. Kt—Kt3 (the threat was 13... Kt—B6 ch. 14. P×Kt Q—R4) Q—B2 14. B—B4 Q—K2 15. B×Kt Q—R5 16. R—K1 Q—R7 ch. 17. K—B1 B—B5 ch. 18. Q—Q3! B×Q ch. 19. P×B Castles 20. B—Kt3! and it seems that White keeps the upper hand. He has three minor pieces for queen and pawn, and the black king side pawns are threatened. If then 20... B—Q3 so as to answer 21. B×BP with KR—B1 22. B—K6 ch. K—B2 followed by 23... B×B and 24... Q×Kt, White would continue 21. B×B! R×B 22. B×P R—B1 (or R—B3) 23. QKt—K4.

12 ...	R—Q1
13 Q—K1	B—K2
14 B—QKt3	

And here again White could have accepted the sacrifice: 14. P×Kt P×P 15. Kt—Kt3 Kt—Kt3 16. B—K3 B—B5 17. R—Q1 R×R 18. Q×R B×R 19. K×B! and Black has nothing for his material deficit.

14 ...	P—KKt4
15 B—Q2	Kt—B6 ch.

A very ingenious attempt, which finds an even more ingenious refutation. As Clarke points out, the quiet 15... Q—B2

was better, with a double-edged position after 16. P—B4 P×P 17. B×P Q—Kt3 ch. 18. K—R1. Now for the first time 16. P×Kt could not be played because of 16... P×P 17. Kt—Kt3, B×B 18. RP×B Q—Q3 to be followed by 19... Q—R3.

16 P×Kt	Kt—K4
17 K—Kt2	B×P ch.

Better chances were offered by the alternative 17... Kt×P 18. K×Kt, though the white position seems to hold even then. Clarke gives 18... Q—B4 ch. (the trouble with the preliminary 18... B×P is the intermediate move, 19. Kt—Q5!) 19. Kt—B4! (but not 19. K—Kt2 Q×RP ch. 20. K—Kt1 B—Q3 21. Kt—Kt3 P—R5 22. B×B P×B 23. Q—K4 P×Kt 24. Q—Kt2 P×P ch. 25. R×P B—B4, and if then 26. B×P B×R ch. 27. K×B Q—B4 ch. followed by R—KKt1), P×Kt 20. R—R1 P—R5 21. B×P Q—R4 ch. (either 21... R—KKt1 or R—Q5 are answered with 22. Q—K5!) 22. K—Kt2 R—Kt1 ch. 23. B—Kt3! P×B 24. P×P, etc.

18 K×B	Kt×P
19 Kt—Q5!	

The resource Black overlooked. Although Black wins the white queen with check, he is unable to save his own. This is one of the most ingenious defensive manoeuvres ever seen.

19 ...	P—Kt5 ch.
20 K—Kt3	B—R5 ch.
21 K—Kt2	Kt×Q ch.

16. CENTRE COUNTER GAME

Somewhat better is 21... Q×B! 22. Q×Q Kt×Q 23. R—R1 Kt×B 24. RP×Kt R×Kt 25. R×B R—Q7 with some play for his material deficit.

22 B×Kt	Q—B4
23 B—Kt4	Q—Kt4

Running upon his sword, but 23... Q×Kt ch. 24. B×Q R×B offers no real chance.

24 Kt—B7 ch.	Resigns.

---

17. ALEKHINE'S DEFENCE

75 WHITE: SCHOLTENS—BLACK: VAN OOSTERWIJK-BRUIN

Holland, 1944

1 P—K4	Kt—KB3
2 P—K5	Kt—Q4
3 P—Q4	P—Q3
4 Kt—KB3	B—Kt5
5 B—K2	P—K3
6 Castles	Kt—QB3
7 P—B4	KKt—K2

The openings in which Black tries to entice the white pawns to advance prematurely (*Alekhine Defence, Budapest Gambit a.o.*) had their heyday in the twenties. They are basically unsound if White keeps his head and does not fall in with the opponent's wishes. Thus they are played but rarely today, and even more rarely with success. One only has to look at the congested position of the Black force to understand why this should be so.

8 P×P	Q×P

So as to stop White from playing P—Q5—which, however, cannot be done.

9 Kt—B3	B×Kt

If immediately 9... Castles 10. Kt—KKt5.

10 B×B	Castles
11 Kt—Kt5	

More convincing is 11. P—Q5! Kt—K4 12. B—B4 Kt(2)—Kt3 13. B—Kt3 Q—Kt5 14. B—K2, which gave Unzicker the advantage against Pomar (*Pyrmont, 1951*).

11 ...	Q—Q2
12 B—B4	P—QR3!

Intending to answer 13. Kt×P with Q×P, but White has better.

13 P—Q5!	P×P?

This allows White a most originally conceived attack. But the better 13... P×Kt 14. P×Kt Kt×P 15. P×P! Q×Q 16. B×Q! Kt—Q5 17. P—QR4 would not have been sufficient to equalize.

14 Kt×P	P×P

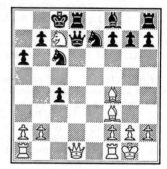

15 Kt—R8!

What a horse! Now Black has to defend against the threat 16. Kt—Kt6 mate and cannot exchange queens.

15 ...	Q—Q5
16 Q—B1	

Threatening both 17. R—Q1 and 17. Q×P! Black's reply is forced, for if 16... P—QKt4? 17. R—Q1 Q—R2 18. R×R ch. K×R (not 18... Kt×R? because of 19. B—K3! Q—Kt1 20. Kt—Kt6 ch. K—B2 21. B—Kt3 ch.) 19. Q—Q2 ch. Q—Q2 20. Q—K3 and wins.

68

17. ALEKHINE'S DEFENCE

16 ...	Q—R2
17 Q×P	R—Q5

The adventurous knight is still taboo, for if 17... Q×Kt 18. B—Kt4 ch. P—B4 19. Q—K6 ch. R—Q2 20. KR—Q1.

18 Q×BP	R×B

Trying to get rid of the principal enemy.

19 Q—K8 ch.	Kt—Q1
20 QR—B1 ch.	Kt—B3
21 B×Kt	B—B4

Or 21... P×B 22. R×P ch. K—Kt2 23. Q—Q7 ch.

22 B—Q7 ch.	K—Kt1
23 Q×R	R—B1
24 Q×R!	Resigns, for if

24... B×Q 25. R—B8 mate.

76 WHITE: BOGOLYUBOV—BLACK: BARNSTEDT

South Baden, 1950

1 P—K4	Kt—KB3
2 P—K5	Kt—Q4
3 P—QB4	Kt—Kt3
4 P—Q4	P—Q3
5 P—B4	P×P
6 BP×P	Kt—B3
7 B—K3	B—B4
8 Kt—QB3	P—K3
9 Kt—B3	Kt—Kt5

The Four Pawns Attack against Alekhine's Defence is still difficult to assess; in this position many different moves have been tried, such as 9... Q—Q2 and 9... B—K2, but the trouble with most of them is that they allow White to play P—Q5 at an inopportune moment. This the text tries to prevent.

10 R—QB1	P—B4
11 B—K2	P×P?

In his anxiety to stop P—Q5 for good, Black develops the opponent. 11... B—K2 should have come first.

12 Kt×P	Q—B2

Attacking QB5 and K4, but White's advantage in development has the usual result—a combination.

13 P—B5!	Kt(Kt3)—Q4

If 13... B×P? 14. Kt×B P×Kt 15. Kt—R4 wins a piece; if 13... Kt—Q2 14. Kt×B P×Kt 15. Kt—Kt5! Q×KP 16. B—Q4 Q—B5 17. R—B4 and wins. The text offers a piece so as to fish in troubled waters—but it is the opponent who does the more lucrative fishing.

14 Kt×B	Q×KP
15 Kt×Kt	Kt×Kt
16 Castles!	P×Kt

For if 16... Kt×B 17. B—Kt5 mate.

17 B—Kt5 ch.	K—Q1
18 B—KB4	Resigns.

Whether the queen goes to K3 or K5, 19. R—K1 spells *finis*.

18. NIMZOVITCH'S DEFENCE

77 WHITE: ROJAHN—BLACK: CZERNIAK

Buenos Aires, 1939

1 P—K4	Kt—QB3

Since the death of Nimzovitch 25 years ago this opening has been a *rarissima avis*. Nor is the present specimen typical: the opening usually lends itself to heavy manoeuvring rather than a fight with yataghans.

2 P—Q4	P—Q4
3 P—K5	B—B4
4 P—KKt4	B—Kt3
5 Kt—KR3	P—K3

18. NIMZOVITCH'S DEFENCE

6 Kt—B4	B—K5
7 R—Kt1	Kt—R3
8 B—K3	B—K2
9 Kt—Q2	B—R5
10 Kt×B	P×Kt
11 B—Kt2	Q—K2

Preparing an indirect defence of the KP. White, relying on his 13th move, allows it—a decision that throws the game into a maelstrom of unfathomable combinations. In retrospect it is easy to say that he should have protected his own pawns by 12. P—QB3 Castles (Q) 13. Q—K2 and only then picked up the KP.

12 B×P	Kt×KP!
13 P—Kt5!	Kt—B5!

A clever rejoinder. Of course, neither 13... B×P? 14. R×B Q×R 15. P×Kt, nor 13... Kt—B4? 14. B×Kt.

14 P×Kt	Kt×B
15 P×P	

Here Alekhine suggests 15. Q—K2! P—KKt4 16. Kt—R5 Kt—Q4 17. B×Kt P×B 18. Kt—B6 ch. K—B1 19. Q×Q ch. K×Q 20. Kt×P ch. K—Q3 21. Kt—B6 with advantage. If here 16... Kt.—B4 17. B×Kt P×B 18. Kt—Kt7 ch. followed by 19. Q×Q ch. and 20. Kt×P ch.

15 ...	B×P ch.!

The point of Black's counterplay. The B is inviolate because otherwise the white queen would fall with check.

16 K—K2	KR—Kt1
17 Q—Q3	B×R
18 Q—Kt5 ch.	

There is no time for 18. R×B Kt—Q4! —White could not capture twice on Q5 because the black KP takes with check.

18 ...	P—B3
19 B×P ch.	K—Q1!
20 B×P	

Black, though a rook ahead, faces a difficult task. To return the rook by 20... Kt—B4 21. Q—R5 ch. Q—B2 22. Q×Q ch. K×Q 23. B×R B×RP 24. Kt—R5 (threatening 25. Kt—B6 R×P 26. Kt—K8 ch.) R×B 25. P—B3 seems insufficient to win. And 20...

R—Kt1, so as to answer 21. Q—R5 ch. Q—B2 22. Q—Kt5 ch. K—K1 23. Kt—R5? with Q×P ch. would be refuted by 23. R×B! after which the winning chances would be with White. With the text Black makes a last winning attempt.

20 ...	Kt×P!
21 Q—R5 ch.	

Here White offered a draw which Black, understandably enough, declined.

21 ...	Q—B2
22 Kt×P ch.!	P×Kt
23 Q—Kt5 ch.	Q—K2

If 23... K—K1 24. Q—R5 ch.; if 23... K—Q2 24. Q—Kt5 ch. The king cannot escape check without interposition.

24 Q—R5 ch.

and Black is forced to accept perpetual check. For if 24... K—K1 25. B—B6 ch. K—B2 26. R—B1 ch. K×P 27. R×B ch. K—R1 28. Q—K5 ch. R—Kt2 29. B×R and wins the ending. And if 24... K—Q2 25. Q—Kt5 ch. K—B2 26. R—QB1 B×QP 27. R×Kt ch. K—Kt1 28. R—B8 ch.! R×R 29. B×KR ch. and the intrepid pawn queens.

In games of this nature it is difficult to say how much the players saw and calculated and how far they relied on instinct and intuition. But whatever the proportion of each—once White allowed 12... Kt×KP, both players unearthed new surprises at virtually every turn, and together they have produced a little masterpiece that will live as long as chess is played.

19. PIRC DEFENCE

78 White: Balogh—Black: Sandor

Budapest, 1956

1 P—K4	P—Q3
2 P—Q4	Kt—KB3
3 Kt—QB3	P—KKt3
4 P—B3	B—Kt2
5 B—K3	P—B3

In a game, *Pedersen-Keller, Helsinki, 1952*, Black tried to play passively and suffered the usual consequences: 5... QKt—Q2 6. Q—Q2 P—KR3 7. Castles P—K4 8. KKt—K2 Q—K2 9. K—Kt1 P—R3 10. P—KKt4 P—Kt3 11. P—KR4 B—Kt2 12. P—Q5 Castles (QR) 13. Kt—B1 K—Kt1 14. P—R4, QR—KB1 15. Kt(B1)—R2 K—B1 16. Kt—Kt4 Kt—QKt1 17. P—Kt5 Kt—Kt1 18. B—R3 ch. K—Q1 19. Kt—B6 ch. B×Kt 20. P×B Q—K1 21. Q×P ch.! Resigns, for if 21... P×Q 22. B×P ch. K—K2 23. Kt—Q5 mate.

6 Q—Q2	QKt—Q2
7 Castles	

It is rather more accurate to delay castling until Black has committed his own king; preferable, therefore, is 7. KKt—K2, and if 7... Q—R4 8. Kt—B1 followed by Kt—Kt3.

7 ...	Q—R4
8 K—Kt1	P—K4

This move has to be undertaken with great caution in the Pirc, for in the long run the resulting weakness of Black's KB3 may be serious. Preferable is the immediate 8... P—QKt4.

9 KKt—K2	Castles
10 P—KKt4	P—QKt4
11 Kt—Kt3	P—Kt5

Better here is 11... Kt—Kt3, threatening ... Kt—B5 and the opening of the QKt file after which White has nothing better than to simplify by 12. Kt—Q5 Q×Q 13. Kt×Kt ch.

12 Kt(B3)—K2	R—Kt1
13 P—KR4	Kt—Kt3

14 Kt—B1	Kt—R5

Threatening 15... Kt—B6 ch.

15 Kt—Kt3	Q—B2
16 B—KR6	B×B

A choice of evils, for otherwise White continues with 17. B×B K×B 18. P—R5.

17 Q×B	P×P
18 Kt—KB5!	B×Kt

Not 18... P×Kt 19. KtP×P Kt—K1 20. R—Kt1 ch.

19 KtP×B	P—Q4
20 P—R5	QP×P

White has a narrow lead in the mutual race to build up a mating attack. If 20... Q—K4 21. B—Q3, while if 20... P—Q6 21. QBP×P Q—K4 22. P—Q4.

21 RP×P	Q—K4
22 P×RP ch.	K—R1

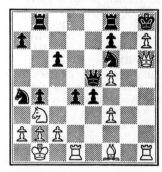

23 B—Kt5!

If at once 23. R—Kt1 Kt×RP and Black can hold on, while now if 23... P×B 24. QR—Kt1 Kt—K1 25. R—Kt8 ch. R×R 26. P×R (Q) ch. K×Q 27. R—Kt1 ch.

23 ...	Kt—Kt5
24 P×Kt	P×B
25 P—B6	Resigns.

A typical Pirc Defence game in which each side goes all out for the attack and the win is a matter of a single tempo.

71

19. PIRC DEFENCE

79 White: Radulescu—Black: Pirc
Balkan Team Tournament, 1946

1 P—K4	P—Q3
2 P—Q4	Kt—KB3
3 Kt—QB3	P—KKt3
4 B—Q3	

In the early days of Pirc's Defence, players with White often used hopefully to expect a quick win; hence this rustic move, after which the bishop soon lacks mobility.

4 ...	B—Kt2
5 KKt—K2	

Also inferior; better is 5. Kt—B3.

5 ...	Castles
6 Castles	QKt—Q2
7 Kt—Kt3	P—K4
8 QKt—K2?	

White continues to hope for a king's side attack, but the sequel shows that he should have played 8. P×P, with a playable, if inferior game.

8 ...	P×P
9 Kt×P	Kt—B4
10 P—QB3	R—K1
11 P—B3	P—Q4!

Justice comes in the form of a counter-attack in the centre which takes advantage of White's disorganized pieces.

12 Kt—Kt3	P×P
13 Kt×Kt	P×B
14 Q×P	P—Kt3
15 Q×Q	

Compare this game with *Sterner-Boleslavsky* (game 51) in which White also tried to escape from positional difficulties by an exchange of queens. But in that case, as here, Black had several positional assets in the ending.

15 ...	R×Q
16 Kt—Kt3	P—B4

Black has the two bishops, White's bishop is bad and his pawn formation immobile, while Black's rook controls the open file and his pawns dominate the centre. What more could a positional player want?

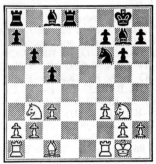

17 B—K3	Kt—Q4
18 KR—Q1	B—QR3
19 B—B2	P—B4
20 P—QR4	B—R3
21 P—R4	B—QB5
22 R—R3	

If 22. Kt—Q2, Kt×P wins a pawn.

22 ...	Kt—K6
23 R×R ch.	R×R
24 P—QR5	

Equally disastrous would be 24. Kt—QR1 R—Q8 ch. 25. K—R2 P—B5 26. Kt—K4 Kt—B8 ch. 27. K—R3 B—K3 ch.

24 ...	Kt—B7
25 Resigns.	

An effective demonstration of an attack without queens.

20. ROBATSCH DEFENCE

80 White: Kilyin—Black:
Gurgenidze
Rostov, 1958

1 P—K4	P—KKt3
2 P—Q4	B—Kt2
3 Kt—QB3	P—QB3

Even in a closed defence a tempo cannot be surrendered lightly; the normal 3... P—Q3 4. Kt—B3 B—Kt5 is sounder.

4 B—QB4	P—QKt4?
5 B—Kt3	P—Kt5

20. ROBATSCH DEFENCE

6 Q—B3!

White correctly meets hyper-hyper-modernism with a dash of nineteenth century red blood; henceforward Black has no chance of achieving a normal development.

6 ...	Kt—B3
7 QKt—K2	Castles
8 P—K5	Kt—K1
9 P—KR4	

A sucker punch if you like; but Black has no adequate defence against it.

9 ...	P—Q4
10 P—R5	P—B3
11 RP×P	BP×P

If 11... RP×P 12. Q—Kt3.

12 Q—R5	Kt—B3
13 Q—R4	KP×P
14 B—R6	B×B
15 Q×B	P—K4
16 Kt—KB3	Q—K2

17 Kt×KP!	B—B4
18 P—KB4	QKt—Q2
19 Kt×BP	Q—K6
20 B×P ch.	Resigns.

81 White: Karaklaic—Black: Robatsch

Smederevska Palanka, 1956

1 P—K4	P—KKt3
2 P—Q4	B—Kt2
3 P—KB4	P—Q3
4 Kt—KB3	Kt—KB3

Later, when Robatsch's system had been more fully worked out, it became clear that Black should delay the development of his KKt and play 4... P—QB4 (5. P × P Q—R4 ch.) here.

5 P—K5!	KKt—Q2
6 B—B4	Kt—Kt3
7 B—Kt3	Kt—R3
8 Castles	P—QB4
9 P—B3	

Black is trying to play a system analogous to the Smyslov variation of the Grunfeld, but the substantial difference here is that White is much better able to support his centre.

9 ...	Castles
10 Kt—Kt5!	

Now Black cannot stabilize the centre, for if 10... P—Q4 11. P—B5 B×BP 12. R×B P×R 13. Q—R5 P—R3 14. Kt—KR3, or if 10... P—R3 11. Kt×P! R×Kt 12. B×R ch. K×B 13. P—B5! in both cases with a winning attack.

10 ...	B—B4
11 P—Kt4!	B×Kt
12 R×B	P—B5
13 B—B2	P×P
14 BP×P	Kt—B2
15 Q—B3	Q—Q2
16 Q—R3	P—KR3
17 Kt—K4	Kt (Kt3)—Q4
18 R—B3	P—B3

Losing quickly, but if 18... K—R2 19. B×P B×B 20. P—Kt5 Q×Q 21. R×Q, followed by R×B.

19 B×P	P×P
20 B×B	K×B
21 Kt—Kt5!	Kt—B3

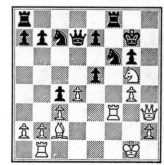

20. ROBATSCH DEFENCE

22 R×Kt!	K×R

If ... P×R, or ... R×R, then 23. Q—R7 ch. wins.

23 R—B1 ch.	K×Kt

24 Q—K3 ch.	Resigns.

White forces mate after 24... K—R5 25. Q—R6 ch. K×P 26. B—Q1 ch. A rousing attack.

21. QUEEN'S GAMBIT

82 WHITE: CASAS—BLACK: PIAZZINI
Buenos Aires, 1952

1 P—QB4	Kt—KB3
2 Kt—QB3	P—K3
3 P—Q4	P—Q4
4 Kt—B3	B—K2
5 B—Kt5	QKt—Q2
6 P—K3	Castles
7 Q—B2	P—B4
8 BP×P	Kt×P
9 Kt×Kt	B×B

Black tries to avoid the isolated QP after the normal 9... P×Kt 10. B×B Q×B, which, while no decisive disadvantage, would create small worries (as, e.g., in the model game, *Flohr-Vidmar, Nottingham, 1936*). He lands in something much worse.

10 P—KR4!	Q—R4 ch.?

So as to have the retreat to Q1 for his bishop. If Black considered White's reply at all, he must no doubt have thought it couldn't do any harm.

11 P—Kt4!	P×P

Prepared to answer 12. Kt×B or 12. P×B, with 12... P—Kt6 ch. 13. Q interposes, Q×Kt.

12 Q×P ch!	K×Q
13 P×B ch.	K—Kt3
14 Kt—K7 mate.	

An extraordinary mating position. From the stylist's point of view it is a pity that the square KR6 is covered twice.

83 WHITE: GEREBEN—BLACK: KOMAROV
Leningrad, 1949

1 P—Q4	P—Q4
2 Kt—KB3	Kt—KB3
3 P—B4	P—K3
4 Kt—B3	QKt—Q2
5 B—Kt5	B—K2
6 P—K3	Castles
7 P×P	

It has been known for ages that the exchange variation is without sting where White has committed himself to an early Kt—KB3. White's lack of precision is due to the fact that he played this game simultaneously with 24 others. It is rare, however, to see a passive simultaneous player make such excellent use of the master's lapse.

7 ...	P×P
8 B—Q3	R—K1
9 Castles	P—B3
10 Q—B2	Kt—B1
11 Kt—K5	Kt—Kt5!

Before White can fortify his knight by P—KB4. White, in his turn, does not mind the following exchanges, because he wants to start the minority attack on the queen side (see move 14).

12 B×B	Q×B
13 Kt×Kt	B×Kt
14 QR—Kt1	Q—Kt4
15 K—R1	

21. QUEEN'S GAMBIT

Waste of time in view of the fact that White needs his knight for defensive purposes in any case. The immediate 15. Kt—K2 would have gained an important tempo.

15 ...	R—K3
16 Kt—K2	R—R3
17 Kt—B4	

Setting an interesting trap: if now 17... Q—R5 18. P—KR3 and if then 18... P—KKt4 19. P—KKt3 traps the queen. Or does it?

17 ...	Q—R5!
18 P—KR3	P—KKt4!
19 P—KKt3	

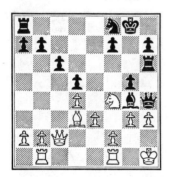

B—B6 ch.!

A sudden change of parts between the trapper and the trapped. If now 20. K—Kt1 Q×P 21. Kt×Q R×Kt and mate cannot be stopped. White tries to provide additional cover for his KR3, but in vain.

20 K—R2	Q×P ch.!
21 Kt×Q	P—Kt5!
Resigns.	

He is a queen up, but cannot stop the threat of 22... R×Kt ch. and 23... R—R8 mate. The winner, a schoolboy, is likely to be the first player to be included in an anthology of chess games on the merit of his performance against a master giving a simultaneous display.

84 White: Ahman—Black: Malmgren

By Correspondence, 1947

1 P—Q4	P—Q4
2 Kt—KB3	Kt—KB3
3 P—B4	P—B3
4 Kt—B3	P—K3
5 P×P	KP×P

Black chooses the Orthodox Exchange variation rather than the Slav; quite correctly in view of the premature development of White's KKt.

6 B—Kt5	B—K2
7 P—K3	QKt—Q2
8 Q—B2	Kt—K5

A surprising pawn sacrifice to disturb White's normal development. It would have been best to decline it by 9. B×B Q×B 10. R—B1, leading back to well-known positions.

9 Kt×Kt	P×Kt
10 Q×KP	Q—R4 ch.
11 K—Q1	P—B3
12 B—KB4	

With the powerful threat, 13. B—Q6. It looks as though Black's sacrifice were quickly to recoil on his own head.

12 ...	Kt—Kt3
13 B—Q6	Kt—Q4
14 B—QB4	

14. B×B Kt×B was necessary, even though Black then threatens to obtain a fine game by 15... B—B4 and 16... Castles (Q).

14 ...   B—B4!

75

A most unpleasant surprise. If now
15. Q×B Kt×P ch. 16. P×Kt Q×Q;
if 15. Q—R4 B×B 16. P—K4 P—KKt4!
17. Q—R5 ch. B—Kt3; and if 15.
P—QKt4 Q—R5 ch. 16. B—Kt3 Q×B
ch. White thus loses at least a piece.

Resigns.

85 WHITE: BORISENKO—BLACK:
KERES

U.S.S.R. Championship, 1955

1	P—Q4	Kt—KB3
2	P—QB4	P—K3
3	Kt—QB3	P—Q4
4	B—Kt5	P—B4

A spirited attempt at avoiding the
passiveness usually associated with the
Orthodox Defence. Opinion as to its
merits has been see-sawing with the
improvements found for either side.

5	P×QP	BP×P
6	Q×P	B—K2
7	P—K4	Kt—B3
8	Q—K3	

At the time this game was played, this
had superseded the previously popular
8. Q—Q2 Kt×KP 9. Kt×Kt P×P 10.
B×B Q×B 11. Q×P Castles 12. P—B3
Kt—Kt5—but now 13. Q—KKt5!
seems to refute Black's play (13... Q×Q
14. Kt×Q Kt—B7 ch. 15. K—Q2
Kt×R 16. B—Q3). This is a suggestion
by Bronstein.

8 ...   Kt—QKt5!

With the idea of answering 9. Castles
with 9... Kt—Kt5; and if then 10. B×B
Kt×Q 11. B×Q Kt×R. For 8...
Kt×QP? see the following game.

9	B—Kt5 ch.	B—Q2
10	B×B ch.	Q×B
11	Q—Q2	P×P
12	B×Kt	B×B

Black is quite unconcerned about his
pawn, for if now 13. Kt×P Kt×Kt
14. P×Kt Castles (K) 15. Kt—K2

KR—Q1 16. R—Q1 QR—B1, followed
by R—B4, and Black regains his pawn
with the superior development.

13	P×P	B×Kt
14	Q×B	Kt×QP!

Most original. If now 15. Q×P
Castles! 16. R—B1 ch. K—Kt1—and
whereas the black king reaches permanent safety on R1, his opposite
number is caught in the centre.

15 Q—K5 ch.   K—B1!

The same idea in a different form.
Since White cannot copy by 16. Castles?
R—B1 ch. 17. K—Kt1 Kt—B6 ch.!
Black's command of the K-file will
become decisive.

16	Kt—K2	R—K1
17	Q—Kt5	P—B3!

If immediately 17... Q—Kt4 18.
Castles (Q)! R×Kt 19. Q—Q8 ch.,
followed by 20. Q×Kt; and if in this
18... R—B1 ch. 19. Kt—B3 Kt×Kt
20. R—Q8 ch. R×R 21. Q×R ch., etc.

18	Q—Q2	Q—Kt4
19	K—B1	K—B2

If 19... Kt—B5 20. R—K1 Kt—Q6 21.
R—Q1 Kt×KtP 22. R—QKt1 Kt—B5
23. R×Q Kt×Q ch. 24. K—K1
followed by 25. R×P. With the text
Black systematically strengthens the
attack against the pinned piece.

20	P—KR4	R—K4
21	R—R3	KR—K1
22	R—K1	Q—B5

21. QUEEN'S GAMBIT

Finally threatening 23... Kt—B5.

23 P—QKt3	Q—KKt5
24 R—Q3	

If 24. P—B3 Kt—K6 ch. 25. Q×Kt Q×R 26. Q×R Q—R8 ch. 27. K—B2 Q×R ch. 28. K×Q R×Q and wins.

24 ...	Kt—B5

Resigns.

86 WHITE: BORISENKO—BLACK: JAROSLAVTSEV

U.S.S.R. Championship, 1957

1 P—Q4	P—Q4
2 P—QB4	P—K3
3 Kt—QB3	Kt—KB3
4 B—Kt5	P—B4
5 P×QP	BP×P
6 Q×P	B—K2
7 P—K4	Kt—B3
8 Q—K3	

In view of Borisenko's defeat by Keres two years before (see game No. 85), it is interesting to speculate how he meant to answer 8... Kt—QKt5.

8 ...	Kt×QP?
9 P×Kt	B×B
10 P—B4	Kt—Kt5
11 Castles	B—K2

The otherwise preferable 11... B—B3 is refuted by 12. B—Kt5 ch. K—B1 13. Q—B5 ch. B—K2 14. P—Q6; or if 12... B—Q2 13. P×P Kt×P ch. 14. K—B2! Kt—Kt5 ch. 15. K—Kt1.

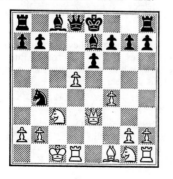

12 Q—Q4!	

Much stronger than 12. P×P Q—B2 13. P×P ch., which allowed Black some counterplay in the game *Taimanov-Prins, Saltsjöbaden, 1952.*

12 ...	Kt×P

If 12... Castles 13. P—Q6 wins a piece.

13 Kt×Kt	P×Kt
14 Q×KtP	B—B3
15 R—K1 ch.	B—K3*

In a game, *Borisenko-Gorfinkel, U.S.S.R., 1955,* Black played the better move 15... K—Q2, and the game ended as follows: 16. Q×P ch. K—Q3 17. B—B4 K—B4 18. B—Kt3 R—B1 19. Q—R5 Q—B2 20. Kt—K2! B—B4 21. Q×B! B×P ch. 22. K×B R×Q 23. R—B1 ch. Resigns.

16 R×B ch.	Resigns.

After 16... P×R, White has only his queen "developed"—yet 17. B—Kt5 ch. immediately finishes the game.

87 WHITE: BOLBOCHAN—BLACK: PACHMAN

Moscow, 1956

1 P—Q4	Kt—KB3
2 P—QB4	P—K3
3 Kt—KB3	P—Q4
4 Kt—B3	P—B4
5 P×QP	Kt×P
6 P—K3	

This move, instead of the formerly popular P—K4, allows White a slight, but lasting initiative.

6 ...	Kt—QB3
7 B—B4	P×P
8 P×P	B—K2
9 Castles	Castles
10 R—K1	Kt×Kt

One would expect Black to develop his queen side pieces with P—QR3

P—QKt4, B—Kt2 and QR—B1. Instead he strengthens his opponent's centre, apparently with the idea of later utilizing the half-open QB-file. He is quickly disillusioned.

11 P×Kt	P—QKt3
12 B—Q3	B—Kt2
13 Q—B2	P—Kt3

It is difficult to decide at this stage whether this or P—KR3 is less weakening. In either case it is easy to be wise after the event.

14 B—KR6	R—K1
15 Q—Q2	R—QB1
16 QR—B1	B—B3
17 Q—B4	Kt—R4?

To invite a white knight to settle on K5 in this type of position is nothing short of suicidal.

18 Kt—K5	Kt—B3
19 Kt—Kt4	B—R5
20 P—Kt3	

White has no objection to "weakening" the KKt3—QKt7 diagonal, since Black will not live to exploit it.

20 ...	B—K2
21 B—B4	R—B2

Overlooking the immediate threat, but Black's position was hopeless whatever he did.

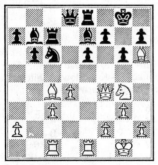

22 Q×P ch.!	Resigns.
If 22... K×Q 23. B×P mate.	

88 WHITE: CHRISTOFFERSEN—BLACK: HARKSEN

By Correspondence, 1915

1 P—Q4	P—Q4
2 P—QB4	P—K3
3 Kt—QB3	P—QB4
4 Kt—B3	Kt—QB3
5 P—K3	Kt—B3
6 B—Q3	B—Q3
7 Castles	Castles
8 P—QR3	P×QP
9 KP×P	P×P
10 B×P	Kt—Q4
11 R—K1	Kt×Kt

The same basic positional error as in the game Bolbochan-Pachman.

12 P×Kt	Q—R4
13 Q—B2	P—K4

It looks as though with this advance Black has solved all opening problems. In fact, however, he is lost.

14 Kt—Kt5!   P—KKt3

15 Kt×RP!

It is almost unbelievable that with all his pieces still to be brought into the attack, White should have such a move at his disposal.

15 ...   K×Kt
16 Q—Q2

Threatening 17. Q—R6 ch. followed by 18. Q×P ch. 16... B—K3 is no defence (17. Q—R6 ch. K—Kt1 18. B×B P×B 19. Q×P ch. K—R1 20.

R—K3) so Black has to protect his KKt3.

16 ...	B—KB4
17 Q—R6 ch.	K—Kt1
18 P—Kt4!	

If now 18... B×KtP 19. Q×P ch. K—R1 20. Q—R6 ch. K—Kt1 21. B—Q3 P—B4 22. B—B4 ch., etc. If 18... B—B7 19. R—K3 to be followed by 20. R—R3. If 18... P×P, so as to return the piece, 19. B—KKt5 B—K2 20. R×B! Kt×R 21. B—B6, etc.

| 18 ... | Q×BP |
| 19 R—K3! | Q×QR |

Or 19... Q×QP 20. P×B Q×B 21. P—B6 Q—Kt5 ch. 22. R—Kt3 Q—Q8 ch. 23. K—Kt2 Q—Q4 ch. 24. R—B3.

20 R—R3	Q×B ch.
21 Q×Q	B×KtP
22 Q—R6!	Resigns.

An elegant finishing touch. If 22... B×R 23. Q×P ch. K—R1 24. Q—R6 ch. K—Kt1 25. B—Q3 P—K5 26. B×P P—B4 27. B—Q5 ch. R—B2 28. Q—Kt6 ch. K—R1 29. B×R B—B5 30. Q—B6 ch. K—R2 31. B—Kt6 ch. K—R3 32. B×P ch. K—R4 33. Q—Kt6 ch. K—R5 34. B×B and mate follows. A long (though absolutely forced) variation given by Brinckmann, which proves the correctness of White's combination.

89 WHITE: TAL—BLACK: MILEV

Munich 1958

1 P—QB4	P—QB4
2 Kt—QB3	Kt—QB3
3 Kt—B3	Kt—B3
4 P—K3	P—K3
5 P—Q4	P—Q4
6 BP×P	KKt×P
7 B—B4	Kt—Kt3

The usual continuation is 7... P×P. The text merely drives the bishop to a better square; and after Black has eliminated it, he remains with a badly weakened pawn position.

| 8 B—Kt5 | P—QR3 |
| 9 B×Kt ch. | P×B |

| 10 Castles | B—Kt2 |
| 11 Kt—K4 | Kt—Q2 |

The convolutions of this knight cost Black the game. He stubbornly refuses to play the natural P×P.

| 12 Q—B2 | Q—Kt3 |
| 13 Kt—K5 | P×P |

Now he has to do it—but meanwhile he has managed to lose the right to castle and his king will soon be exposed to a terrific attack.

14 Kt×Kt	K×Kt
15 P×P	K—K1
16 B—K3	Q—B2
17 P—Q5!	

Opening the K-file with deadly effect (if 17... P—K4 18. P—B4).

| 17 ... | KP×P |

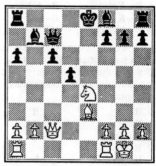

| 18 KR—K1! | K—Q1 |

On accepting the offer of the knight, Black would be faced with 18... P×Kt 19. Q×KP ch. Q—K2 20. Q—QB4! or if 19... B—K2 20. B—B5. As Golombek wittily remarks, Black's only chance would then be to castle in the hope that no one had noticed his king had already moved.

| 19 Q—Kt3 | P—QB4 |

After 19... K—B1 White would "only" win positionally by 20. Kt—B5, B×Kt 21. B×B, followed by 22. R—K7. Now he can finish with a little firework.

| 20 Kt×P! | Resigns. |

For if 20... B×Kt 21. B×B Q×B 22. Q×B R—QB1 23. QR—B1 Q×R 24. Q—K7 mate.

90 WHITE: MIROSHNICHENKO—BLACK:
ANOKHIN

Kirgisian Championship, 1957

1 P—Q4	Kt—KB3
2 P—QB4	P—K3
3 Kt—QB3	P—Q4
4 Kt—B3	P—B4
5 BP×P	KP×P

Obviously Black is not afraid of the Tarrasch Defence. Normally the "Semi-Tarrasch" is expressly designed to avoid this capture in favour of 5... Kt×P. Still, a number of recent games (see, e.g., *Bolbochan-Pachman, No.* 87) have shown that Black has no easy equality even then and that the early advance of the QBP must remain suspect.

6 B—KKt5	B—K3
7 P—K3	B—K2
8 B—Kt5 ch.	KKt—Q2

Better was 8... QKt—Q2; the possible loss of a pawn after 9. B×Kt B×B 10. P×P would only be temporary. He now faces difficulties in completing his development.

9 B×B	Q×B
10 P×P	Q×P
11 Castles	Castles
12 R—B1	Kt—QB3
13 B×Kt	Q×B
14 Kt—Q4	Q—Q3
15 QKt—Kt5	Q—K4
16 Q—Kt3	

Indirectly attacking QKt7 and at the same time protecting K3 so that the black queen can be chivied further and the ultimately victorious advance of the KBP be prepared.

16 ...	Kt—Kt3
17 P—B4	Q—B3
18 Kt—B7	QR—Q1
19 Q—R3	P—QR3

If 19... Kt—B5 Black gets nothing for his pawn after 20. Q×P; for if then 20... Kt×KP 21. KR—K1 to be followed by Kt×B; and if 20... Kt—Q3 21. P—B5! is still possible. Black believes in the good old adage of not giving up

material in an inferior position unless he can free his game by doing so. Now, however, White is poised for the kill.

20 P—B5!	B—B1

Not 20... Kt—B5, because of 21. R×Kt followed by 22. P×B.

21 Kt(Q4)—K6!	Kt—B5

The knight is taboo: 21... P×Kt 22. P×P Q—K4 23. P—K7! The text, however, threatens to force the white queen off her present diagonal so that P—K7 can no longer be played. At the same time, 22. R×Kt could now be answered with 22... P×Kt (23. P×P? Q×R mate).

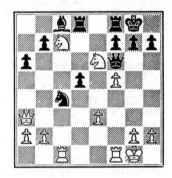

22 Kt×QP!

The pretty point of White's combination. If now 22... R×Kt 23. Q×R mate; or 22... Kt×Q 23. Kt×Q ch. P×Kt 24. Kt×QR, winning the exchange; or 22... Q×Kt 23. P×Q Kt×Q 24. P—K7.

22 ...	Q—K4
23 Kt—K7 ch.	K—R1
24 Kt×QR!	Kt×Q
25 Kt×P ch.	Resigns.

91 WHITE: TOLUSH—BLACK: FURMAN
Moscow, 1957

1 P—Q4	P—Q4
2 P—QB4	P—K3
3 Kt—QB3	P—QB4

4 P×QP	KP×P
5 P—K4	

One of Marshall's gambit lines. *Marshall-Spielmann, Vienna, 1908,* which is generally quoted, continued 5... P×KP 6. P—Q5 P—B4 7. B—Kt5 ch. B—Q2 8. B×B ch. Q×B with advantage to Black. Tolush finds a striking improvement.

5 ...	P×KP
6 P—Q5	P—B4
7 B—KB4!	

Threatening Kt—Kt5 and if, as in the game, Black defends the threat with a developing move, only then B—Kt5 ch. The alternative is for Black to play 7... P—QR3.

7 ...	B—Q3
8 B—Kt5 ch.	K—B2
9 Kt—R3	Kt—KB3
10 B—B4	P—QR3
11 P—QR4	R—K1
12 Q—Q2	Q—K2
13 P—R5	QKt—Q2?

If the advisability of 7... P—QR3 could be argued there is no doubt that 13... P—KR3 was now necessary.

14 Kt—Kt5 ch.	K—Kt3

14... K—Kt1 looks safer at first glance, but there would follow 15. Kt—K6 (threatening 16. Kt—B7 B×Kt 17. P—Q6 ch.) K—R1 16. Kt—B7! B×Kt 17. P—Q6. If then 17.. B×QP 18. B×B Q—Q1 19. B—KB7 would win the exchange, and though Black has at present two pawns for it, his pieces are so badly placed that he won't be able to keep them. And if 17... Q—B1 18. P×B Kt—K4 19. B×Kt R×B 20. Kt—R4! and the advanced BP becomes very unpleasant.

15 Kt—K6	

Threatening 16. B×B Q×B 17. Q—Kt5 ch. so that P—R3 is forced after all.

15 ...	P—R3
16 P—KKt4!	P×P

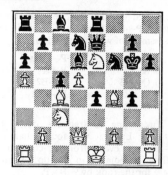

Since 16... Kt×KtP 17. P—R3 followed by R—Kt1 ch. was unplayable, White has succeeded in breaking up the black pawn position. It is amazing how rapidly this leads to the disintegration of the black game.

17 Castles (Q)	Kt—K4
18 B×Kt	B×B
19 Kt×KP!	Kt×Kt
20 Q—B2	Q—B3

So as to answer 21. Q×Kt ch. with Q—B4. But White is in no hurry.

21 KR—K1!	B×P ch.
22 K—Kt1	B×Kt
23 P×B	B—Q5
24 R—Kt1	

If now 24... Q—B4 25. B—Q3 is decisive.

24 ...	K—Kt4
25 R×P ch.!	Resigns.

If 25.. K×R 26. Q×Kt ch. wins.

92 WHITE: SZEKELY—BLACK: CANAL
Budapest, 1933

1 P—Q4	P—Q4
2 P—QB4	P—QB3
3 Kt—QB3	P×P
4 P—K3	

Up to the time of this game it was thought that this recovered the pawn with ease, since 4... P—QKt4 "could not be played". Today the line is continued with 4. P—K4!?, the Canal Gambit, the assessment of which is still dubious.

4 ...	P—QKt4!
5 Kt×P	P×Kt
6 Q—B3	Q—B2
7 Q×R	B—Kt2
8 Q×P	P—K3

Threatening to trap the queen by Kt—B3. Later it was found that 8... P—K4! is even stronger, compelling White immediately to give up a second piece for the rook by 9. B×P.

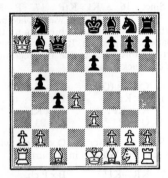

9 P—Q5!	P×P

And not 9... B—B4 because of 10. P—Q6! This little pleasantry would have been impossible after 8... P—K4.

10 Q—Q4	Kt—KB3

For the exchange Black has obtained a strong lead in development and free play for his pieces.

11 Kt—B3	B—Kt5 ch.
12 B—Q2	Kt—B3
13 B×B!	

A clever trap. If now 13... Kt×Q? 14. Kt×Kt White can keep up a permanent blockade of the position on the black squares, and with R+B for the queen he need not lose. But Black is not to be bought off so cheaply.

13 ...	Kt×B!
14 Q—B3	Q—R4
15 Kt—Q2	P—Q5!

A fine vacating sacrifice, opening Q4 for the black pieces.

16 P×P	Kt(B3)—Q4
17 Q—KKt3	Castles
18 K—Q1	Q—R5 ch.
19 P—Kt3	Q—R6
20 P×P	Kt—B6 ch.
21 K—K1	Kt—B7 mate

An unusual mate crowns the theoretically important game.

93 White: VIDMAR—Black:
CHRISTOFFEL

Basle, 1952

1 P—Q4	Kt—KB3
2 P—QB4	P—B3
3 Kt—KB3	P—Q4
4 Kt—B3	P×P
5 P—QR4	B—B4
6 Kt—K5	P—K3
7 P—B3	B—QKt5
8 P—K4	B×P

The Mikenas Sacrifice in the Slav Defence, presumably so-called because it was first played by Cheron against Przepiorka, The Hague, 1928. Chess nomenclature is more bewildering than chess itself!

9 P×B	Kt×P
10 B—Q2!	

Stronger than the formerly popular 10. Q—B3. One of the most fascinating games with this variation is a little-known encounter *Euwe-Alekhine*, played with living pieces at *Amsterdam, 1936*, which went as follows: 10. Q—B3 Q×P 11. Q×P ch. K—Q1 12. B—Kt5 ch. Kt×B 13. Q×KKtP Q—K6 ch. 14. K—Q1 R—B1 15. Kt×P(B4) Q—B5 16. Q×KtP B×Kt 17. P×B Kt—K5 18. Q×R R—B2! 19. K—B2 Q—B7 ch. 20. K—Kt3 R—Kt2 ch.! 21. Q×R Kt—B4 ch. 22. K—R3 Kt×Q, when a draw was agreed.

10 ...	Q×P
11 Kt×Kt	Q×Kt ch.
12 Q—K2	B×B ch.
13 K×B	Q—Q5 ch.

Certainly no improvement on the game, *Smyslov-Reshevsky, The Hague, 1948*: 13... Q—Q4 ch. 14. K—B2, Kt—R3. However, the whole variation is suspect because it is doubtful whether Black's three pawns can be brought forward quickly enough to balance White's extra piece.

14 K—B2   Castles
15 Kt×P   P—QKt4?

A decisive mistake, which bears out the previous note: the pawns are not yet advanceable. 15... Kt—R3 should have been played.

16 Q—K3!   R—Q1?

Losing immediately. He had to exchange queens, but then his previous move would have meant an unnecessary weakening of the position.

17 Q×Q   R×Q
18 P×P   P×P
19 Kt—Kt6!   Resigns.

94 WHITE: PANNO—BLACK: KELLER

Moscow, 1956

1 P—Q4   P—Q4
2 P—QB4   P—QB3
3 Kt—KB3   Kt—KB3
4 Kt—B3   P—K3
5 P—K3   P—QR3
6 B—Q3   P×P
7 B×BP   P—QKt4
8 B—Kt3

Leading to positions known from the Queen's Gambit Accepted. 8. B—Q3 would have been the Meran line.

8 ...   P—B4
9 Castles   B—Kt2
10 Q—K2   QKt—Q2
11 R—Q1   B—K2

So far all the latest theory, but now 11... Q—B2 is preferred. It gives Black a chance to assault the white centre by Kt—B4 before White is ready to occupy the QB-file.

12 P—K4   P×P
13 Kt×QP   Q—B2
14 B—Kt5   Kt—B4

Now this is dubious, because the knight can be pinned. Black should have castled (K), thus lending point to 11... B—K2.

15 QR—B1!

Indirectly protecting both K4 and QKt3, for after 15... Kt×B 16. Kt×Kt the black queen would have no good square (16... Q—Kt3? 17. B—K3).

15 ...   P—Kt5

If now 15... Castles (K) 16. P—K5! Black therefore strikes while the square K5 is still open to him.

16 B×Kt!   P×B

Black cannot relinquish his hold on QB5, for if 16... B×B 17. Kt—R4 B—K2 18. B×P!

17 Kt—R4   Castles (K)

In view of the possibility, Q—K4, this looks safe, but White has seen further.

| 18 B×P! | Q—K4 |

He cannot give the queen for assorted material because on 18... P×B 19. Kt×P Kt×Kt 20. R×Q Kt×R 21. R—Q7 wins further material.

| 19 Kt×Kt | B×Kt |
| 20 B—B5! | |

The point of White's combination. He now threatens 21. Q—Kt4 ch. K—R1 22. Q—R5, so that Black cannot take the knight.

| 20 ... | KR—K1 |
| 21 Q—R5 | B×Kt |

White threatened not only 22. Q×RP ch. but also 22. R×B to be followed by 23. B×P ch.

| 22 R×B! | Q×R |
| 23 R—B7 | Resigns. |

The threat of 24. Q×RP ch. is unanswerable.

95 WHITE: VERA MENCHIK—BLACK: SONJA GRAF

Semmering, 1937

1 P—QB4	P—K3
2 Kt—QB3	P—Q4
3 P—Q4	Kt—KB3
4 Kt—B3	QKt—Q2
5 P—K3	P—B3
6 B—Q3	B—K2

A passive line not in keeping with the previous move, which demands 6... P×P (Meran Defence).

| 7 Castles | Castles |
| 8 P—K4 | |

Perhaps even stronger is the quiet 8. P—QKt3. After the text Black should transpose into the 23rd game *Alekhine-Bogolyubov* (1929 match), by playing 8... P×KP 9. Kt×P P—QKt 3, though even then it is doubtful whether Black can free himself completely.

8 ...	P×KP
9 Kt×P	Kt×Kt(?)
10 B×Kt	Kt—B3

| 11 B—B2 | P—B4 |
| 12 P×P | Q—R4 |

Black is faced with the unpleasant choice of enduring a king side attack or simplifying into an ending that, as a result of her queen side majority, would be very favourable for White.

13 B—K3!

Forcing Black to obstruct his QB4, which would be the best square for the queen.

| 13 ... | B×P |
| 14 B—Q2! | Q—B2 |

If 14... B—Kt5 15. P—QR3 B×B 16. Q×B with much the better game. Black prefers to allow the king side attack, basing her decision on a clever positional trap.

15 B—B3	B—K2
16 Q—K2	P—QKt3
17 Kt—Kt5!	

For if 17. B×Kt B×B 18. Q—K4, which looks deadly, 18... P—Kt3 19. Q×R B—Kt2 20. Q×P R—R1 21. Q×R B×Q; and though 2 R's+P are much more than the queen, White would now have to face two raking bishops.

17 ...	P—Kt3
18 Q—B3	B—Kt2
19 Q—R3	P—KR4
20 QR—Q1!	

Threatening 21. Kt×KP! and at the same time preparing the charming finish.

| 20... | Kt—Kt5 |

21 R—Q7!

Brilliant. Not immediately 21. Q×P? Q×P ch.! 22. Q×Q Kt×Q 23. K×Kt B×Kt. Now, however, the queen sacrifice 22. Q×P P×Q 23. B—R7 mate can no longer be stopped.

21 ... **Resigns.**

Infinitely the best game ever played by a woman.

96 WHITE: JOHANSSON—BLACK: NILSSON

Amsterdam, 1954

1 P—Q4	P—Q4
2 P—QB4	P—K3
3 Kt—KB3	P—QB3
4 Kt—B3	Kt—B3
5 P—K3	QKt—Q2
6 B—Q3	P×P
7 B×BP	P—QKt4
8 B—Q3	B—Kt2

The so-called Neo-Meran Variation which owes a great deal to the research of the British master, Wade. More usual is 8... P—QR3, but the present game shows that Black can put the tempo thus saved to good use.

9 P—K4	P—Kt5
10 P—K5	

This move, which is generally played in the Meran proper, here leads to complications favourable for Black.

10 ...	P×Kt
11 P×Kt	P×KtP
12 P×P	P×R (Q)
13 P×R (Q)	

An original position with four queens on the board so early in the game. The same position was reached in a game, *Rosenberg-Tartakower, Paris, 1954,* which continued: 13... Q—R4 ch. 14. K—K2 B—R3 15. Q×P? (B×B!) Kt—B3 16. Q—KR4 Q(8)×P ch. 17. K—B1 Q(4)—R5 18. Q—K2 Q×Q ch.

19. K×Q Q—B7 ch. Resigns.

13 ...	Q—R4 ch.
14 Kt—Q2	

This allows a pretty finish. Somewhat better was 14. B—Q2 Q×Q ch. 15. K×Q Q×P 16. K—K2, though Black would clearly have the superior game.

14 ...	Q(4)—B6
15 K—K2	Kt—B4!
16 Q×P	Kt×B
17 Q×Kt	Q×Q ch.
18 K×Q	B—R3 ch.
19 K—B2	

Since checks on QB3 or Q4 are quickly fatal, the only alternative is 19. K—K4, when 19... P—B4 ch. 20. K—K5 B—Kt2 ch. 21. K×P B—B1 ch. 22. K—Q6 Q×P ch. 23. K×P Q—Kt3 ch. 24. K—Q5 B—K3 would lead to a pretty mate.

19 ...	Q×P ch.
20 B—Kt2	R—Kt1
21 Q—R1	R×B ch.
22 Q×R	B—Q6 ch.
23 K—B3	B—Kt5 ch.!
Resigns.	

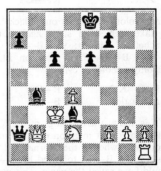

24. K×B costs the queen; 24. Q×B allows mate by Q—B7.

97 WHITE: RETI—BLACK: GRAU

London, 1927

1 P—QB4	P—QB4
2 Kt—KB3	Kt—KB3

3 P—Q4	P—Q4

Leading, by transposition of moves, to the Austrian Defence usually brought about by the sequence 1. P—Q4 P—Q4 2. P—QB4 P—QB4.

4 BP×P	P×P
5 Q×P	Q×P
6 Kt—B3	Q×Q
7 Kt×Q	P—QR3

Black has to lose this move, because after 7... P—K4 8. Kt(4)—Kt5 Kt—R3 9. P—KKt3 his pieces would remain in an unpleasant bind. As a result of his pressure against QKt7, White would soon obtain command of the QB-file.

8 P—KKt3	P—K4
9 Kt—Kt3	

It is strange that Dr. Euwe, when discussing the Austrian Defence in 1951, made no mention of this dangerous move, giving only Kt—B2 and Kt—B3. By threatening later to go to QB5, the knight contributes to the pressure against QKt7.

9 ...	Kt—B3?

As Golombek points out, Black had to take immediate steps against the fianchettoed bishop: 9... B—Q2! 10. B—Kt2 B—B3. From now on Black has only a choice of evils.

10 B—Kt2	B—Q2
11 Castles	B—K2

This allows the exchange of the KKt with subsequent invasion of Q5. But it is doubtful whether the alternative 11... P—R3 12. B—K3 followed by B—B5 would have saved the game. This game strikingly illustrates the difference between qualitative and quantitative development: after the 11th move Black has as many pieces developed as White, but none of them serves any particular purpose, and Black is, in fact, quite lost.

12 B—Kt5	Castles (K)
13 KR—Q1	KR—Q1

Reti disposes of 13... QR—Q1 as follows: 14. B×KKt B×B 15. Kt—B5 B—B1 16. Kt×RP! or 14... P×B 15. Kt—Q5 B—B1 16. QR—B1 and the threat of R×Kt forces material gain.

14 B×KKt	P×B

If 14... B×B 15. Kt—B5 B—B1 16. Kt—Q5, threatening fatally to increase the pressure by R—Q3 and QR—Q1.

15 Kt—Q5	

Threatening both Kt—Kt6 and Kt×B followed by B×P. Thus the reply is forced.

15 ...	QR—Kt1

16 Kt—B5!

The elegant decision. If now 16... B×Kt 17. Kt×P ch. followed by Kt×B —which wins not only a pawn but also the exchange. Meanwhile, both Kt×B ch. and Kt×B are threatened. "Relatively best" was to give a pawn by 16... B—K3 17. Kt×B ch. Kt×Kt 18. B×P R×R ch. 19. R×R B×P 20. R—Q7 K—B1 21. Kt×P.

16 ...	K—B1
17 Kt×BP!	Resigns.

If 17... B×Kt 18. Kt×B ch. winning exchange and pawn. If I had to choose the dozen best miniatures this would be one of them.

22. ALBIN COUNTER GAMBIT

98 WHITE: WOOLVERTON—BLACK: PRITCHARD

London, 1959

1 P—Q4	P—Q4
2 P—QB4	P—K4
3 P×KP	P—Q5
4 Kt—KB3	Kt—QB3
5 P—QR3	KKt—K2
6 P—KKt3	

The logical build-up; the advance of the black QP as always gives White chances on the long white diagonal. The thorn in the flesh, the QP, which is the whole *raison d'etre* of the Albin, has meanwhile to be endured. An attempt to remove it prematurely, by e.g., 6. P—K3 Kt—B4! would give Black a fine game after either 7. B—Q3 P×P or 7. P×P KKt×P.

6 ...	Kt—Kt3
7 B—Kt2	B—Kt5
8 Castles	Q—Q2
9 Q—B2	

A strangely unnatural move, instead of which 9. QKt—Q2 suggested itself. The KP was in no danger yet, for if 9... KKt×P 10. Kt×Kt Kt×Kt 11. B×P—and if 9... B×Kt 10. P×B! KKt×P 11. P—B4, with clear superiority to White in either case.

9 ...	B—K2
10 P—Kt4	R—Q1
11 P—Kt5	QKt×P
12 Kt×Kt	Kt×Kt
13 B—B4?	

If White meant to play for the gain of the QKtP—a logical complement of the king's fianchetto and his 10th and 11th moves—he had to do so now. The unnecessary finesse in the text is designed to threaten B—B6 after the knight has been forced away and the KtP taken.

13 ...	P—Q6!
14 P×P	Kt×QP
15 B×KtP?	

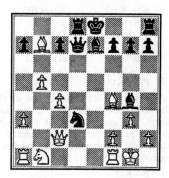

Now this is no longer feasible. 15. B—K3 should have been played.

15 ...	Kt×B!

"You can have her, I don't want her, she's too fat for me!"

16 B—B6

Somewhat better is 16. P×Kt, though after 16... Castles, White's king can hardly be defended.

16 ...	Kt—K7 ch.
17 K—Kt2	

If 17. K—R1 Q×B ch. 18 P×Q B—B6 mate.

17 ...	Q×B ch.
18 P×Q	B—B6 ch.!

Very pretty. After 19. K×B Kt—Q5 ch. Black remains a piece up. So the king takes to his heels—but not for long.

19 K—R3	R—Q3
20 Q—Q2	P—Kt4!
Resigns.	

The double threat of 20... R—R3 mate and P—Kt5 mate cannot be parried.

99 WHITE: SÄMISCH—BLACK: MEDINA

Madrid, 1943

1 P—Q4	P—Q4
2 P—QB4	P—K4
3 P×KP	P—Q5

22. ALBIN COUNTER GAMBIT

4 Kt—KB3	Kt—QB3
5 QKt—Q2	B—K3
6 P—KKt3	Q—Q2
7 B—Kt2	KKt—K2
8 Castles	Kt—Kt3
9 P—QR3	B—K2
10 P—QKt4	Castles (Q)

A surprising decision in view of the advanced state of the white queen side-pawns, but not without its logic—the king helps to defend the threatened queen side, and meanwhile Black has a free hand on the other wing.

11 B—Kt2

White clearly underestimates the potential strength of the black build-up. He had to attack the black king's position immediately by 11. Q—R4 followed by 12. R—Q1.

11 ...	B—R6
12 P—Kt5	QKt×P
13 Q—R4	

If 13. B×P B—B3!

13 ...	B×B!
14 K×B	

White cannot play 14. Q×P because of Q—R6. Nor can he do so at the next move because after 15. Q×P? Kt(Kt3)—R5 ch. 16. P×Kt Q—Kt5 ch., followed by Kt×Kt he would remain without compensation for his piece.

14 ...	Kt×Kt
15 P×Kt	B—B4
16 QR—Q1	Q—B4
17 Kt—Kt3?	

White is still unaware of the fact that Black is ready to mount a quickly decisive attack. He should have nipped it in the bud by 17. Kt—K4.

17 ...	R—Q3!
18 Kt—Q2	

Too late—but there was no defence against the threat of Kt—B5 ch. If, e.g., 18. KR—K1 R—KB3! 19. P—B4 Kt×P ch. 20. P×Kt Q—Kt5 ch. 21. K—B1 R—KR3 wins.

18 ...	Kt—B5 ch.!
19 P×Kt	

19 ...	R—KR3

A clever finishing touch. On 19... R—Kt3 ch. 20. K—R1 White could defend the position. Now, on the other hand, if 20. KR—R1 Q—R6 ch. 21. K—Kt1 R—Kt3 mate; and if 20. K—Kt1 Q—R6 followed by Q×RP mate. Therefore:

Resigns.

---

23. BLACKMAR GAMBIT

100 WHITE: BARTSCH—BLACK: JENNEN

Essen, 1948

1 P—Q4	P—Q4
2 P—K4	P×P
3 Kt—QB3	

Blackmar used to play 3. P—KB3 immediately (compare, e.g., Blackmar-Farrar, 200 *Miniature Games of Chess*, p. 277), but this is refuted out of hand by 3... P—K4. The text is von Popiel's improvement, later taken over by Diemer, who has invested it with many new points.

3 ...	Kt—KB3
4 P—B3	P×P

The Blackmar Gambit Accepted gives White a dangerous initiative. 4... B—B4, chiefly advocated by the masters, H. Müller (Vienna) and H. Wagner (Hamburg) is less dangerous.

5 Q×P

This oversharp line can succeed only against inferior defence. Black should reply 5... Q×P 6. B—K3 Q—KN5! 7. Q—B2 P—K4!, with the threat of B—QKt5 (Euwe). As in many other gambits, Black should aim at returning some of the material gained; otherwise he may easily be swept off the board. The present game is a particularly striking illustration.

5 ...	Q×P
6 B—K3	Q—QKt5?
7 Castles	B—Kt5?

Accentuating his greedy policy. He should have played 7... P—B3 8. R—Q4 Q—R4 with chances of gradually making up his leeway in development.

8 Kt—Kt5!	P—K4

Realizing his danger too late. If Black tries to protect QB2 by 8... Kt—R3, there would follow 9. Q×P Q—K5 (if 9... R—QKt1? 10. Q×R ch.) 10. Q×Kt Q×B ch. 11. K—Kt1 B×R 12. Q—B6 ch. K—Q1 13. Q×P ch. K—K1 14. Kt—Q6 ch. P×Kt 15. B—Kt5 ch.

9 Kt×P ch.	K—K2
10 Q×P!	

As Diemer remarks, two queen sacrifices within 10 moves are likely to constitute a record. If now 10... Q×Q 11. B—B5 mate, and if 10... Q—R4 11. B—B5 ch. Q×B 12. Kt—R6 ch., winning the queen. Black therefore resigned.

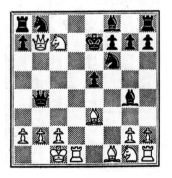

101 WHITE: DIEMER—BLACK:
A. R. FULLER

Hastings, 1957/58

1 P—Q4	Kt—KB3
2 Kt—QB3	P—Q4
3 P—K4	P×P
4 P—B3	P×P
5 Kt×P	P—K3

Entirely different in character from the previous game, this encounter reveals the force of the white attack against solid defence. The drawback of the line chosen is that it leads to a rather passive formation in which great precision is required of Black. Today 5... P—KKt3 is preferred; in this case Black gets his early chances of a counter-attack, as in a match game, *Diemer-Kloss, 1958*, which went: 5... P—KKt3 6. B—QB4 B—Kt2 7. Castles Castles, 8. Q—K1 (White should first safeguard the square Q4) Kt—B3! 9. Q—R4 Kt—KKt5! 10. Kt—K2 Kt×QP 11. Kt—Kt5 Kt×Kt ch. 12. K—R1 P—KR4 13. Kt×P (or 13. R×P Q—Q5! 14. R—B4 ch. Q×B 15. R×Q R—B8 mate) Q—Q5 16. B—Kt3 P—K3 17. P—B3 R×Kt 18. B—K3 R×R ch. 19. R×R Q×B Resigns.

6 B—Kt5	B—K2
7 Q—Q2	Castles
8 B—Q3	QKt—Q2
9 Q—B4	P—QKt3?

The cause of all future difficulties, this move allows the exchange of the black-squared bishop and later enables White to gain a deadly tempo (move 20). Black should have completed his development with 9... R—K1 10... Kt—B1 and 11... B—Q2.

10 Q—R4

Threatening 11. B×P ch.

10 ...	R—K1
11 Kt—K5	Kt—B1
12 Kt—B6!	Q—Q3
13 Kt×B ch.	Q×Kt
14 Castles (K)	Kt—Kt3
15 B×Kt	BP×B

(if RP×B 16. R×Kt!)

16 Kt—K4	R—B1
17 B×Kt	P×B
18 R×P	R×R
19 Kt×R ch.	K—R1
20 Q—K4	

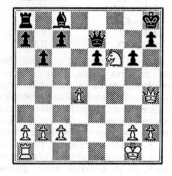

The decisive gain of time. It is remarkable that the bloodletting in the previous moves has in no way weakened the force of the white attack.

20 ...	R—Kt1
21 R—KB1	B—Kt2
22 Q—K5	Q—Q3?

Overlooking the pretty finish, but the game is hopeless. If 22... Q—Kt2 23. P—B4 (threatening P—Q5 P×P Kt—K8!), virtually forcing Black to weaken his position still further by 23... P—KR3 and only then 24. Q×KP.

23 Kt—K8 ch.!	Resigns.

For is 23... Q×Q 24. R—B8 mate. A problem-like coup, with line obstruction and model mate.

24. STAUNTON GAMBIT

102 WHITE: BARDA—BLACK: ROSSOLIMO

Hastings, 1949/50

1 P—Q4	P—KB4
2 P—K4	P×P
3 Kt—QB3	Kt—KB3
4 B—KKt5	Kt—B3
5 P—B3	P—K4!

An interesting innovation by Rossolimo. In the other main line, beginning with 4. P—B3, the move led to a speedy black win in the game *Toran v. Canal, Venice, 1953*, which went as follows: 4. P—B3 Kt—B3 5. P×P P—K4 6. P×P QKt×P 7. Kt—B3 P—Q3 8. B—KB4 B—KKt5 9. B×P P×B 10. Q×Q ch. R×Q 11. Kt×P B—Kt5 12. B—Q3 B—KR4 13. Castles Castles 14. QR—K1, QR—K1 15. Kt—B3 Kt—Kt5 16. Kt—Q4? R×R ch. 17. B×R B—B4 18. Kt—K2 R×P 19. P—B3 Kt—K4 Resigns.

6 P—Q5	Kt—Q5
7 P×P	B—K2
8 B—QB4	

Parrying the threat 8... Kt×QP, for after 9. B×B Kt×B 10. Q—R5 ch.

Kt—K3 11. Castles (Q) the open diagonal would be worth more than the pawn. Yet for all its ingenuity the move should have been replaced by the cautious 8. B—K3.

8 ...	P—Q3
9 KKt—K2	Kt—Kt5!

A most surprising conception, which exploits the weakness of the square K6. If now 10. B×B, Q×B 11. Kt×Kt Kt—K6! 12. B—Kt5 ch. K—Q1 13. Q—Q2 P×Kt with a fine game.

10 Kt×Kt	B×B
11 B—Kt5 ch.	

This meets with an ingenious refutation, but if 11. Kt—B5 B×Kt 12. P×B Kt—K6!—if then 13. Q—R5 ch., K—B1 and White still cannot protect everything.

11 ...	P—B3!
12 Kt×P	

12. P×P Castles! 13. P×P B×P 14. Q×Kt P×Kt 15. B—B4 ch., K—R1 would certainly be no improvement.

12 ...	P×Kt
13 B×P ch.	K—K2!

The point of the combination. Now Black retains his piece, for if 14. B×R Q—Kt3 15. Q—K2 B—R3 16. Q×Kt Q—K6 ch. 17. Kt—K2 Q—Q7 ch. 18. K—B2 R—B1 ch. wins. Whereas the "developed" black king is perfectly safe, his white colleague is suddenly in the firing line of all black pieces. There followed: 14. Castles R—QKt1 15. Q—K2 Q—Kt3 ch. 16. K—R1 Q—K6 17. R—B3 Q×Q 18. Kt×Q R×P 19. QR—KB1 Kt—B3 20. R—QR3 P—QR3 21. Kt—Kt3 B—Q7 22. P—B3 B—K6 23. Kt—B5 ch. B×Kt 24. P×B KR—QKt1 Resigns.

103 WHITE: EDGAR—BLACK: LOTT

By Correspondence, 1955

1 P—Q4	P—KB4
2 P—K4	P×P
3 Kt—QB3	Kt—KB3
4 B—KKt5	P—K3

This, too, is a perfectly playable defence against the Staunton Gambit, but not with the continuation chosen by Black.

5 B×Kt	Q×B
6 Kt×P	Q—Kt3?

Here the queen will be exposed to multiple attacks, Correct is 6... Q—K2 to be followed by the queen's fianchetto and Castles (Q).

7 B—Q3!	Q×P
8 Q—R5 ch.	P—Kt3

On a king move, the simple 9. Kt—Kt3 gives White an overwhelming edge in development. 8... Q—Kt3 would lose the queen by a knight check. After the text White gives up virtually his whole force to catch the black king in a mating net.

9 Q—K5	Q×R
10 Q×R	Q×Kt ch.
11 K—Q2	Q×R
12 Kt—B6 ch.	K—K2

If 12... K—B2 13. Q—Kt8 ch. K×Kt 14. Q×B ch. K—Kt4 15. P—B4 ch. K—Kt5 16. Q—R6 Q—KKt8 17. Q—Kt5 ch. K—R6 18. B—B1 ch.! Q×B 19. Q—Kt3 mate.

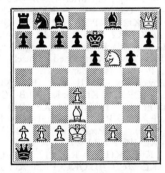

13 Kt—Q5 ch.!   P×Kt

The alternatives are no better: if 13... K—B2 14. Q×P ch. B—Kt2 15. Q×P ch. K—B1 16. Kt—B6 B×Kt 17. Q×B ch. K—Kt1 18. B—Kt6 with unanswerable mate; if 13... K—Q3 14. Q×B ch. K×Kt 15. Q—B5 mate; if 13... K—K1 14. Q×P×Kt 15. B×P ch. K—Q1 16. Q—R4 ch. B—K2 17. Q—R8 ch. B—B1 18. Q×B mate.

14 Q×P ch.	K—Q3
15 Q×KtP ch.	K—K2
16 Q—Kt5 ch.	K—B2
17 B—Kt6 ch.	K—Kt1
18 Q—B6!	

A quiet move followed by some skilful

24. STAUNTON GAMBIT

king's manoeuvring, and Black is helpless.

18 ...	B—Kt5 ch.
19 P—B3	Q×P ch.

20 K—Q1!	Q—R8 ch.
21 K—K2	Q—Kt7 ch.
22 K—B3	Q×QBP ch.
23 K—Kt2	Resigns.

25. OLD INDIAN DEFENCE

104 WHITE: KORCHNOI—BLACK: ZILBER
Russian Team Championship, 1958

1 P—Q4	Kt—KB3
2 P—QB4	P—Q3
3 Kt—QB3	P—K4
4 Kt—B3	

In a game, *Dr. Meyer-Schmid, Correspondence, 1948,* White closed the centre by 4. P—Q5, but after 4... B—K2 5. P—K4, Castles 6. P—KKt3 P—B3! 7. B—Kt2 P×P 8. BP×P P—QR4 9. KKt—K2 Kt—R3 10. Castles, Kt—B4, Black had fully equalized. White now overreached himself by 11. P—B4? (sounder is 11. P—KR3, followed by 12. B—K3) P—QKt4! 12. P—QR3 Q—Kt3 13. K—R1 B—Q2! (but not 13... P—Kt5 14. RP×P Q×P 15. P×P P×P 16. P—Q6 R—Q1 17. Kt—Q5) 14. P×P P×P 15. B—K3 P—Kt5 16. P×P P×P 17. R×R R×R 18. Kt—QKt1 Q—R3 19. Kt—Q2 B—Kt5 20. B—B3 QKt×P! 21. Kt×Kt B×B ch. 22. R×B Kt×Kt 23. K—Kt2 R—Q1 24. B—B1 R×P! 25. Q—K1 (if 25. Q×R Q×Kt ch. wins) Q—B5; White resigns—a trifle premature, but he has no compensation for the two pawns minus.

4 ...	QKt—Q2
5 P—KKt3	P—B3
6 P—K4	Q—R4

A time-wasting expedition; better is 6... B—K2.

7 Q—B2	P×P
8 Kt×P	Kt—K4
9 P—B4	Kt—Kt3
10 B—K3	P—R4

His best chance is to reconcile himself to loss of the centre and play 10... B—K2.

11 P—KR3	B—Q2
12 Castles	Castles
13 Kt—Kt3	Q—B2
14 Q—B2	P—B4
15 B—Kt2	B—K2

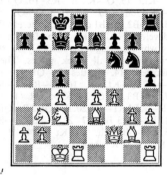

16 P—K5!

The surprising feature of this game is that the decision does not come through White's grip on Q5, but by means of an entirely different break-through.

16 ...	P×P
17 P—B5	Kt—B1
18 B×P	B×B
19 Kt×B	B—B3
20 R×R ch.	K×R
21 R—Q1 ch.	Kt (B1)—Q2
22 Kt×Kt	Kt×Kt
23 P—B6!	B×B

There is nothing to be done, for if 23... P×P 24. Q×P ch., or if 23... P—KKt3 24. B×B P×B 25. Kt—K4 K—B1 26. Kt—Q6 ch.

24 P×P	R—Kt1
25 Q×BP	Resigns.

92

105 WHITE: DONNER—BLACK: EUWE

Match, 1955

1 Kt—KB3	Kt—KB3
2 P—B4	P—KKt3
3 P—KKt3	B—Kt2
4 B—Kt2	Castles
5 P—Q4	P—Q3
6 Castles	QKt—Q2
7 Q—B2	

After the normal 7. Kt—B3 P—K4 8. P—K4 P—B3 9. R—K1, a game *Smyslov-Plater, Moscow, 1947*, continued 9... Q—B2 (more active is 9... P×P 10. Kt×P R—K1) 10. P—KR3 P×P 11. Kt×P Kt—Kt3 12. P—Kt3 R—K1 13. B—Kt5 P—QR4 14. Q—Q2 P—R5 15. QR—Q1 P×P 16. P×P QKt—Q2 17. B—R6 B—R1 18. Kt—B5! Kt—B4 19. Kt×P R—K2 20. P—QKt4 Kt—K3 21. P—B5 P—Kt3 22. P—K5 Kt—Q2 23. B×P! Resigns, for if 23... Q×B 24. Kt—Q5.

7 ...	P—K4
8 R—Q1	R—K1
9 Kt—B3	P—B3
10 P—K4	Q—B2

The counter-attack on the queen's wing is strategically doubtful; a better line is 10... P×P 11. Kt×P Q—K2 12. P—KR3 Kt—B4 13. R—K1 Kt—Kt5 (*Cuderman-Matanovic, Yugoslav Championship, 1958*).

11 P—KR3	P—QKt4
12 P—B5!	QP×P
13 P×KP	

The point of White strategy; he breaks the black centre and prepares for an eventual advance of his KP.

13 ...	QKt×P
14 Kt×Kt	Q×Kt
15 P—B4?	

Much better is 15. B—B4 Q—R4 16. P—KKt4 Q—R5 (the sacrifice at KKt5 is now much less promising than in the game) 17. B—Kt3 Q—Kt4 18. P—B4, and White wins. If Black avoids this variation by 15... Q—K3 then 16. R—Q6 Q—B5 17. B—B1 Q—Kt5 18. R×P is good for White.

15 ...	Q—R4
16 P—K5	

Now if 16. P—KKt4 B×P 17. P×B Kt×KtP 18. B—B3 B—Q5 ch. 19. R×B P×R and Black wins. If in this line 18. P—K5 Q—R7 ch. 19. K—B1 B×P 20. P×B R×P 21. B—K4 R—B4 ch.! 22. B×R Q—R8 ch. 23. K—K2 Q—Kt7 ch. 24. K—K1 Q—Kt8 ch. 25. K—K2 Q—B7 ch. 26. K—Q3 P—B5 ch. 27. K—K4 R—K1 ch., followed by mate.

16 ...   B×P!

Much better than 16... B—B4 17. Q—B2 P—Kt5 18. P×Kt P×Kt 19. P—KKt4.

17 P×Kt	B×P
18 Kt—K4	R×Kt

Not 18... B—Q5 ch.? 19. R×B, but 18... B—Kt2 19. Kt—B2 B×B 20. K×B R—K7 is also good.

19 B×R	R—K1
20 B—K3	B—B4
21 Q×P	

Losing quickly. White could still put

up a good fight by 21. B×B R×B 22. Q—B2 B—Q5 23. R×B P×R 24. B—B8, although after 24... Q—Q4 Black's attack remains very strong.

21 ...	R×B
22 R—Q2	Q—B6
23 Resigns.	

If 23. B—B2 B—R6 24. B—K1 R×B ch. 25. R×R Q×P ch. and wins.

106 WHITE: RAVINSKY—BLACK: BRONSTEIN

Moscow, 1953

1 P—Q4	Kt—KB3
2 P—QB4	P—Q3
3 Kt—QB3	P—KKt3
4 P—KKt3	B—Kt2
5 B—Kt2	Castles
6 P—K4	P—K4
7 P—Q5	

Twenty years ago White always handled the King's Indian by the method of this and the next move; the present game illustrates why this plan has been abandoned.

7 ...	P—B4
8 KKt—K2	

Better is 8. P×P e.p., P×P 9. KKt—K2, followed soon by P—QKt4-5 in order to gain control of Q5.

8 ...	QKt—Q2
9 Castles	Kt—R4
10 B—Q2	P—B4
11 P—B3	

Here White seriously underestimates the threat to his king; much better is 11. P×P P×P 12. P—B4.

11 ...	P—QR3
12 P—QR3	P—B5
13 P—KKt4	Kt (R4)—B3
14 B—K1	P—KR4
15 P—Kt5	Kt—Kt5!

The key to the attack; if instead 15... Kt—R2 16. P—KR4, White is safe.

16 P×Kt	P×P
17 P—KR4	

There is no effective defence, for if 17. Kt×P P×Kt 18. Q×P Kt—K4 followed by ... P—B6.

17 ...	P×P e.p.
18 B×P	Q×P ch.
19 K—R1	K—B2
20 R—B3	R—R1

21 Kt—KKt1	Kt—B3
22 P—Kt4	P×P
23 P×P	B×B
24 Kt×B	

Equally hopeless is 24. R×B R×R ch. 25. Kt×R R—R1 26. Q—B3 Q—R3 27. K—Kt2 P—KKt4.

24 ...	Q—Kt5
25 Q—Q3	Kt—R2
26 Resigns.	

107 WHITE: OREN—BLACK: DYNER

Tel Aviv, 1952

1 P—Q4	Kt—KB3
2 P—QB4	P—KKt3
3 P—KKt3	B—Kt2
4 B—Kt2	P—B4
5 P—Q5	Castles
6 P—K4	P—Q3
7 Kt—K2	KKt—Q2
8 Castles	P—QKt4
9 P×P	P—QR3
10 P×P	Kt×P
11 QKt—B3	R—Kt1
12 P—Kt3	Kt—Kt5
13 B—Kt2	Kt—K4
14 Kt—R4	Kt (Kt5)—Q6

Black's pawn sacrifice has not turned out too well, which explains why he plunges into unfavourable complications rather than continuing solidly with 14... B—Q2.

15 B—QB3	B—QR3
16 P—B4	Kt—KKt5
17 B×B!	K×B

If 17... Kt—K6 18. Q—Q2 Kt×R 19. Q—B3! Kt—K6 20. B—R6 P—B3 21. B×R Q×B 22. B—B3, and White retains a sound extra pawn.

18 R—B3	P—B5
19 P×P	R—Kt5
20 R×Kt	B×P

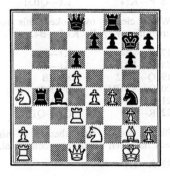

21 R—R3

This is not quite the best, although it suffices to win after a fascinating combinative sequence. Both 21. R—Q4 B×Kt and 21. R—Q2 Kt—K6 would favour Black, but White could win comfortably enough by 21. R—QB3 R×Kt 22. Q—Q4 ch.

21 ...   Q—R4

Now Black threatens 22... B×Kt 23. Q×B R×Kt 24. R×R Q×R 25. Q×Kt Q—Q5 ch.

22 B—B3!

Not 22. Kt (K2)—B3? Q—R2 ch. nor 22. Kt—Q4 Q—R2 nor 22. Q—Q4 ch. P—B3 23. Kt (K2)—B3 B—Kt6! nor finally 22. R—B1 B×Kt 23. Q×B Q—R2 ch.

22 ...   B—Kt6

This looks decisive, but it is defeated by a last minute resource reminiscent of a Western; however, after 22... B×Kt 23. Q×B R×Kt 24. R×R Q×R 25. Q—Kt2 ch. Kt—B3 26. R—Q1, White's extra pawn should eventually decide matters.

| 23 R×B | Q—R2 ch. |
| 24 Kt—Kt6! | Resigns. |

For if 24... Q×Kt ch. White has the wonderful resource 25. Q—Q4 ch.! winning a piece in all variations.

108 WHITE: WALLIS—BLACK: HORSEMAN

Nottingham, 1954

1 Kt—KB3	Kt—KB3
2 P—B4	P—Q3
3 P—Q4	QKt—Q2
4 Kt—B3	P—K4
5 P—K4	P—B3
6 B—K2	P—KKt3
7 Castles	B—Kt2
8 P—KR3	

A quiet system of development which carries a concealed punch.

8 ...	Castles
9 B—Kt5	P×P
10 Kt×P	Kt—B4
11 B—B3	R—K1
12 R—K1	Q—Kt3?

Up to here Black has played well, but the simple 12... Kt—K3 13. Kt×Kt B×Kt would now have been much better, and would have easily equalized.

13 Kt—Kt3	B—K3
14 P—K5	Kt×Kt
15 KP×Kt	Kt×R
16 P×B	B×BP
17 Q×Kt	R×R ch.
18 Q×R	Q×P
19 B—R6	B—K3
20 Kt—K4	P—Q4

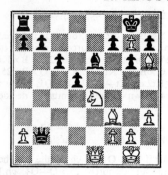

| 21 Q—Kt4! | Q—R8 ch. |
| 22 B—Q1! | Resigns. |

Mate is inevitable after 22... Q × B ch. 23. K—R2.

---

109 WHITE: TARASOV—BLACK: BUSLAEV

Tiflis, 1956

1 P—Q4	Kt—KB3
2 P—QB4	P—KKt3
3 Kt—QB3	B—Kt2
4 P—K4	P—Q3
5 P—B3	Castles
6 B—K3	P—B3

There are many short games available in which Black defends badly against the 5. P—B3 system; a typical example is a game, *Rabar-Znosko-Borovsky, Lucerne, 1949.* which continued 6... QKt—Q2 7. Q—Q2 P—B4 8. P—Q5 R—K1 9. P—KKt4 Kt—B1 10. B—R6 B—R1 11. P—KR4 Kt (B3)—Q2 12. P—R5 Q—R4 13. P × P RP × P 14. R—B1 Kt—B3 15. Q—R2 Kt (B1)—R2 16. B—K2 Q—Kt3 17. R—B2 P—K4 18. Kt—R3 B—Kt2 19. Kt—KKt5, Kt × Kt 20. B × B Kt (B3)—R2 21. B—B6! Resigns.

| 7 Q—Q2 | P—QR3 |
| 8 Castles |

White commits himself a little too early; sounder is the immediate 8. P—KR4.

| 8 ... | P—QKt4! |
| 9 B—R6 | Q—R4 |
| 10 P—KR4 |

And here 10. K—Kt1 is better.

10 ...	P—Kt5
11 Kt—Kt1	P—B4
12 B × B	K × B
13 P—K5

Too optimistic; he could still obtain reasonable attacking chances by 13. P—Q5, Q × P 14. P—Kt4.

13 ...	P × KP
14 P × KP	Kt—R4
15 Kt—K2	Q × P
16 P—Kt4	Kt—QB3!

White clearly overlooked this resource; if now 17. P × Kt B—B4.

17 Kt—B4	Kt—Kt6
18 R—Kt1	Kt—Q5
19 Q—KB2	Kt × B
20 Q × Kt (B1)	B—K3
21 Kt × B ch.	P × Kt
22 R—Kt3	QR—Q1

Black's steady strengthening of his attack has been admirably economical.

23 R—K1

| 23 ... | Q—Kt6! |
| 24 Resigns. |

If 24. Q—B2 Q × BP ch., while if 24. R—Kt2 Black has a pretty mate by 24... Q—B7 ch. 25. R × Q Kt—Kt6.

110 WHITE: SZUKSZTA—BLACK: TAL

Uppsala, 1956

1 P—Q4	Kt—KB3
2 P—QB4	P—KKt3
3 Kt—QB3	B—Kt2
4 P—K4	P—Q3
5 P—B3	Castles
6 B—K3	P—K4
7 KKt—K2	P—B3
8 Q—Kt3	P×P

To open the centre before White has the chance to castle.

9 Kt×P	P—Q4
10 BP×P	P×P
11 P×P	Kt—B3

A lapse, since White could have got the better game a couple of moves later; an inversion of moves with 11... R—K1; leads to the same position on move 14. If, after 11... Kt—B3 White replies 12. Kt×Kt P×Kt 13. P×P R—K1 14. K—B2 R×B 15. K×R B—R3 ch. 16. P—B4 Q—K2 ch. 17. K—B2, Kt—Kt5 ch. and wins.

12 P×Kt	R—K1
13 K—B2	

Falling into the trap. White could have refuted Black's incorrect order of moves by 13. Castles R×B 14. Kt—B2.

13 ...	R×B
14 R—Q1	

If 14. K×R B—R3 ch. 15. P—B4 Kt—Kt5 ch. 16. K—K4 Kt—B7 ch. 17. K—K3 B×P ch. 18. K×B Q×Kt ch. 19. K—B3 B—Kt5 ch. 20. K—Kt3 Q—K6 ch. 21. K—R4 P—Kt4 mate. Now, however, the whole attack is apparently refuted, since both 15. K×R and 15. P×P are threatened.

(See diagram.)

14 ...	Kt—Kt5 ch.
15 P×Kt	B×Kt
16 R×B	Q×R
17 Q—Q5	R—K7 db. ch.!

Black must have foreseen this splendid finish before beginning his combination.

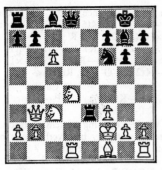

18 K×R	B×P ch.
19 K—K1	R—K1 ch.
20 B—K2	R×B ch.
21 Resigns.	

Despite his sacrifices, Black is materially to the good after 21. Kt×R Q×Q. The extraordinary feature of this game is that it was played as a "lightning" encounter with clocks, each side having five minutes for all his moves. Black in fact made every move almost instantaneously.

111 WHITE: SMOLLNY—BLACK: ASAFOV

Leningrad, 1956

1 P—Q4	Kt—KB3
2 P—QB4	P—KKt3
3 Kt—QB3	B—Kt2
4 P—K4	P—Q3
5 B—K2	

Another, similar idea is 5. B—Kt5 P—B4 6. P—Q5 Castles 7. B—Q3. A game, *Bisguier-Baker, New York, 1958,* continued 7... P—QR3? (correct is the central counter-attack 7... P—K3) 8. P—B4 P—Kt4 (and here he should take measures against White's P—K5 by 8... Kt—K1 9. Kt—B3 B—Kt5) 9. Kt—B3 QKt—Q2 10. Castles R—Kt1 11. P—K5 Kt—K1 12. Q—K2 P—B3 13. P—K6 Kt—Kt3 14. P—B5! P×B 15. Kt×KKtP P—R3 (if 15... P×QBP 16. B—K4 keeps the bishop on its attacking diagonal 16. Kt—B7 Q—B2 17. P×KKtP P×P 18. B—K4, Kt—B3 19. Q—Q2 R×Kt (otherwise 20. Kt×P

26. KING'S INDIAN DEFENCE

ch., wins at once) 20. KtP×R ch.
K—B1 21. B—Kt6 B—Kt2 22. R×Kt!
B×R (if 22... P×R 23. P—K7 ch.
Q×P 24. R—K1 Kt—B1 25. R×Q
Kt×R 26. B—R5) 23. Q×P ch.
B—Kt2 24. Q—R7, Resigns.

5 . . .	Castles
6 B—Kt5	P—B4
7 P—Q5	P—QR3

White's opening system, introduced into master play by Averbakh, is best met by the counter-attack 7... P—K3 8. Kt—B3 P—KR3 9. B—Q2 P×P 10. KP×P B—B4 11. Castles Kt—K5.

8 P—QR4	Q—R4
9 B—Q2	Q—B2

Further loss of time; 9... P—K3 is still correct.

10 P—KKt4	P—K3
11 P—Kt5	Kt—K1
12 P—R4	P×P?

This helps the white attack. 12... P—B4, although opening lines when Black is still underdeveloped, is the only way to achieve some counterplay.

13 Kt×P	Q—Q1
14 P—KR5	Kt—QB3
15 P×P	RP×P
16 Q—Kt3	

Preparing to bring the queen to the KR file.

16 . . .	Kt—Q5
17 Q—Kt3!	Kt—B7 ch.
18 K—Q1	Kt×R
19 Q—R4	P—B3
20 Q—R7 ch.	K—B2

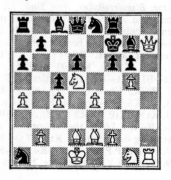

21 Q×P ch.!	K×Q
22 B—R5 ch.	K—R2
23 B—B7 dis. ch.	B—R3
24 P—Kt6 ch.	Resigns.

112 White: Darga—Black: Toran

Luxemburg, 1955

1 P—Q4	Kt—KB3
2 P—QB4	P—KKt3
3 Kt—QB3	B—Kt2
4 P—K4	P—Q3

A seemingly innocent transposition of moves 4... Castles 5. P—B4 P—B4? was severely punished in a training game *Keres-Geller, Russia, 1952*: 6. P—K5 Kt—K1 7. P×P Q—R4 8. B—Q2 Q×BP 9. Kt—Q5 Kt—QB3 10. Kt—KB3 (threatening P—QKt4) P—QR3 11. B—K3 Q—R4 ch. 12. K—B2 (now the queen is threatened by B—Kt6) P—QKt4 13. P—QR4 R—Kt1 14. RP×P Q—Q1 15. P×Kt P×P 16. Kt—Kt6 Resigns.

5 B—K2

In the early days of the Four Pawns Attack White used to play 5. P—B4 P—B4 6. Kt—B3 P×P 7. Kt×P Kt—B3; but then comes 8. Kt—B2 Kt—Q2 9. B—K2 Kt—B4 10. B—B3 B×Kt ch. 11. P×B Q—R4 (*Teschner-Gligoric, Helsinki, 1952*).

5 . . .	Castles
6 P—B4	P—B4
7 Kt—B3	P×P
8 Kt×P	Kt—B3
9 Kt—B2	Kt—Q2

Black's idea of exchanging off White's QKt so as to weaken his pawns is fundamentally faulty, since the absence of his own KB is more vital. Sounder is 9... B—K3 10. Castles R—B1 11. B—K3 P—QR3 12. R—B1 Q—R4 13. K—R1 P—QKt4.

10 Castles	Kt—B4
11 B—B3	B×Kt
12 P×B	Q—R4

Black is trying to carry out the same

plan as did Gligoric against Teschner but the fact that here he has already castled is an important difference in White's favour. Much better is 12... P—B4.

13 P—B5	Q×BP

No better is 13... P×P 14. P×P B×P 15. B×Kt B×Kt 16. Q×B P×B 17. B—R6 KR—K1 18. Q—B5 P—B3 19. Q—Kt4 ch. K—B2 20. R×P ch. P×R 21. Q—Kt7 ch. K—K3 22. R—K1 ch. K—B4 23. P—Kt4 mate.

14 B—R6	R—K1
15 Kt—K3	Q—Q5
16 Q—K1	Kt—Q2?

After this timid move White has full control of the board. A tougher defence is 16... Kt—Q6 17. Q—Kt3 K—R1.

17 R—Q1	Q—Kt3
18 K—R1	Kt—B3
19 B—Kt5	Kt—K4
20 Q—R4	K—Kt2
21 B—K2	

Preparing the decisive action on the KB file.

21 ...	Kt (K4)—Q2
22 Kt—Q5	Kt×Kt

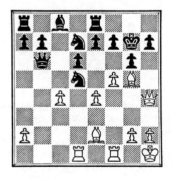

23 P×P!	Resigns.

For if 23... BP×P 24. R—B7 ch. K×R 25. Q×P ch. K—K3 26. B—Kt4 ch. K—K4 27. R×Kt ch. K×P 28. B—B3 mate, while if 23... Kt (Q4)—B3 24. R×Kt Kt×R 25. B×Kt ch. P×B 26. Q×RP ch.

113 WHITE: DARGA—BLACK: WADE
Moscow, 1956

1 Kt—KB3	Kt—KB3
2 P—KKt3	P—KKt3
3 B—Kt2	B—Kt2
4 Castles	Castles
5 P—B4	P—B4
6 Kt—B3	Kt—B3
7 P—Q4	P—Q3
8 P×P	P×P
9 B—B4	B—K3

The simplest way to take the sting out of this exchange variation against the Yugoslav line of the King's Indian, is 9... Kt—Q5 10. B—K5 Kt—B3 11. B—B4 Kt—Q5. No less than three Yugoslav championship games between Udovcic and Gligoric ended in a draw by repetition in this way!

10 Kt—K5	Kt×Kt

And here 10... Kt—KR4 is better.

11 B×Kt	Kt—Q2
12 B×B	K×B
13 B×P	R—QKt1
14 B—Q5	B×B
15 Q×B	R×P
16 KR—Q1	Q—R4

Black sidesteps pin No. 1.

17 QR—B1	Kt—B3
18 Q—K5	

Pin No. 2, and a more serious one. White threatens P—Kt4-5.

18 ...	R—Q1
19 Kt—Q5	R—Q7
20 P—Kt4	P—KR3
21 P—KR4	K—Kt1
22 Kt×P ch.	K—R2

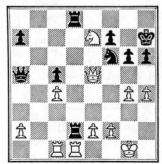

23 Q×Kt!

Indicating that pin No. 3—that of the knight at Q5—was illusory.

23 ...   R×R ch.
24 R×R   Resigns.

For if 24... R×R ch. 25. K—Kt2, and Black has no defence against 26. Q×BP ch., followed by mate.

114 WHITE: FREEMAN—BLACK: MEDNIS

New York, 1955

1 P—Q4	Kt—KB3
2 P—QB4	P—KKt3
3 Kt—QB3	B—Kt2
4 P—KKt3	Castles
5 B—Kt2	P—Q3
6 Kt—B3	Kt—B3
7 P—K4	

A familiar mistake, since Black now obtains excellent play on the central black squares. After the natural 7. Castles, Black can either reply 7... P—K4 or with the Simagin move 7... B—Kt5; or finally with Panno's 7... P—QR3. An illustration of this last system is a game, *Mühlberg-Averbakh, Dresden, 1956*, which continued 8. P—KR3 R—Kt1 9. B—K3? (better 9. P—K4 P—QKt4 10. P—K5!) P—QKt4 10. Kt—Q2 B—Q2 11. P×P P×P 12. P—R3 P—K4 13. P×P QKt×P 14. P—B4? (better 14. P—Kt3) Kt—B5! 15. Kt×Kt P×Kt 16. Q—Q2 P—Q4! 17. P—QR4 (if 17. Kt×P Kt×Kt 18. Q×Kt B×KtP 19. QR—Q1 B—R5, and Black's QBP is very dangerous) Q—K2 18. P—R5 P—B4 19. B×QP? (losing immediately, but even after 19. B—B2 P—Q5 Black's centre is irresistible) R×P! 20. Q×R Q×B ch. 21. K—R2 Kt×B 22. Kt×Kt Q—K3 23. Resigns, for if 23. Q—Q2 Q×RP ch. wins easily.

7 ...   B—Kt5
8 P—KR3   B×Kt
9 B×B   Kt—Q2

Still stronger is 9... P—K4 10. P—Q5

Kt—Q5 11. B—Kt2 Kt—Q2, followed by ... P—KB4.

10 B—K3   Kt—R4
11 Q—R4?

For here White could retain approximate equality by 11. B—K2 Kt—Kt3 12. P—Kt3 P—QB4 13. QR—B1.

11 ...	P—QB4
12 P—Q5	P—QR3
13 B—Q2	Kt—K4
14 B—K2	Kt (R4)×P!
15 B×Kt	P—QKt4
16 B×P	P×B
17 Q—B2	P—Kt5
18 Kt—Q1	Kt—B6 ch.
19 K—B1	R×P!
20 R—QKt1	

If 20. R×R P—Kt6 21. Q×KtP Kt×B ch. wins the queen.

20 ...   Q—R4
21 K—Kt2   P—Kt6!

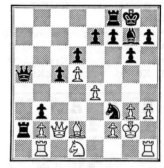

22 Resigns.

Although Black's queen, knight, and QKtP are all en prise, White can capture none of them. If 22. K×Kt P×Q 23. B×Q P×R (Q). If 22. Q×KtP Kt×B; while if 22. B×Q P×Q 23. R—QB1 P×Kt (Q) 24. KR×Q R×B.

115 WHITE: ROJAHN—BLACK: ANGOS

Munich, 1958

1 P—QB4	Kt—KB3
2 P—KKt3	P—KKt3
3 B—Kt2	B—Kt2

4 Kt—QB3	P—Q3
5 Kt—B3	KKt—Q2

An experiment which Black is unlikely to repeat.

6 P—Q4	Castles
7 B—Kt5	P—QB4

7... P—KB3 8. B—K3 P—K4 gives more counter-chances.

8 Castles	Kt—QB3
9 P×P	Kt×P
10 Q—Q2	B—K3
11 B—R6	B×B

A little better is 11... B×P, although after 12. B×B K×B 13. Kt—Q4 Kt—K3 14. Kt×QKt P×Kt 15. P—Kt3 B—R3 16. B×P, White's queen's-side majority should eventually tell.

12 Q×B	P—B3
13 P—Kt3	B—B2
14 KR—Q1	Kt—K3
15 B—R3	Q—R4
16 Kt—Q5	Kt—B2
17 Kt—K3	Kt—K4

Going off at a tangent: 17... P—Q4 would still keep a reasonable hold on the centre.

18 Kt—Q4	Kt—K1

19 Kt—K6	B×Kt
20 B×B ch.	Kt—B2
21 R—Q5!	Q—B6

Expecting to gain the necessary tempo for ... P—B4 and ... Q—Kt2 but ...

22 R—KR5!

Probably the most beautiful move in all the 1,300 games in the 1958 world team championship. After 22... Q×R ch. 23. K—Kt2 P×R, the quiet 24. Kt—B5 leaves Black helpless against 25. Kt×P ch. and 26. Q×R mate, for if 24... Kt—B2 25. Q—Kt7 mate.

22 ...	Resigns.

27. GRÜNFELD DEFENCE

116 WHITE: GRUBER—BLACK: BOZIC
Skopje, 1950

1 P—QB4	Kt—KB3
2 Kt—KB3	P—KKt3
3 Kt—B3	P—Q4
4 P—Q4	B—Kt2
5 P—K3	

5. Q—Kt3 is in high esteem at the moment after a game in the 1958 world title match between Smyslov and Botvinnik, which continued 5... P×P 6. Q×BP Castles 7. P—K4 B—Kt5 8. B—K3 KKt—Q2 9. R—Q1 Kt—Kt3 10. Q—Kt3 Kt—B3 11. P—Q5 Kt—K4 12. B—K2 Kt×Kt ch. 13. P×Kt B—R4 14. P—KR4 Q—Q2 (preferable is 14... Q—B1, to guard the QKtP and provide a retreat square for the knight) 15. P—R4 P—R4 16. Kt—Kt5 Kt—B1 17. B—Q4 Kt—Q3 (and here 17... B×B 18. Kt×B Kt—Kt3 19. B—Kt5 Q—Q3 is better) 18. B×B K×B 19. Kt—Q4 K—Kt1 20. R—KKt1 Q—R6 21. Q—K3 P—QB4 22. P×P e.p. P×P 23. Q—Kt5 P—QB4 24. Kt—B6 Resigns.

5 ...	Castles
6 Q—Kt3	P×P
7 B×P	QKt—Q2
8 Kt—KKt5	

Recommended by Fine as good for White, but the simpler 8. P—K4 is preferable.

8 ...	P—K3
9 B×P!?	

This leads to almost unfathomable complications, but White has no real choice after his last move.

9 ...	P×B
10 Kt×KP	Q—K2
11 Kt×P dis. ch.	K—R1
12 Kt×R	Kt—Kt5
13 P—KR3	

Also suggested by Fine, but in view of the outcome of this game 13. Kt—Q1 is better.

13 ...	Kt×BP
14 R—B1	Q—R5
15 K—K2	Kt—B4!

| 16 P×Kt | B—Kt5 ch.! |
| 17 P×B | |

If White declines the sacrifice by 17. K—Q2 Black wins by R—Q1 ch. 18. Kt—Q5 Kt—K5 ch. 19. K—B2 Kt×P 20. Q—Kt5 B—B4 ch. 21. R×B Q—K5 ch. 22. K—Q1 P×R 23. Kt (R8)—B7 Kt—K3.

| 17 ... | Q×P ch. |
| 18 K—Q2 | Q×P |

Better than 18... R—Q1 ch. 19. Kt—Q5 Kt—K5 ch. 20. K—B2.

19 R×Kt

Or 19. R—K1, Kt—K5 db. ch. 20. K—Q1 B×Kt, followed by 21... R—Q1 ch.

19 ...	R×R ch.
20 K—Q3	Q—B8 ch.
21 K—K4	R—Q7!
22 Q—Q5	

Despair, for if 22. B×R Q—B4 mate.

22 ...	Q—Kt7 ch.
23 K—B4	R—B7 ch.
24 Resigns.	

117 White: Kiarner—Black: Rozhdestvensky

Estonia, 1958

1 P—Q4	Kt—KB3
2 P—QB4	P—KKt3
3 Kt—QB3	P—Q4
4 Kt—B3	

An interesting idea is 4. B—B4 B—Kt2 5. Q—R4 ch., after which a game, *Padevsky-Korchnoi, Uppsala, 1956*, continued 5... B—Q2 (better 5... P—B3 6. B×Kt R×B 7. Q×P B—K3 with more than enough compensation for the sacrificed pawn); 6. Q—Kt3 B—B3 7. P—K4! P×BP 8. KB×P Castles 9. P—Q5 P—QKt4 10. P×B P×B 11. Q—Kt7 Kt×KP 12. R—Q1 Q—B1 13. Q×R? (White could win by 13. Kt×Kt Q—K3 14. Q×R Q×Kt ch. 15. Kt—K2 Kt×P 16. Q—Kt7 R—Kt1 17. Q×BP R×P 18. R—Q8 ch. B—B1 19. Castles) B×Kt ch. 14. P×B Kt×P (B6) 15. B—R6 Q—K3 ch. 16. K—B1 Kt×R 17. B×R Q—B4 18. Kt—B3 Q—Kt8 19. Q—Kt7 Kt—K6 db. ch. 20. Resigns. A good player is never so dangerous as when in a lost position.

4 ...	B—Kt2
5 B—B4	P—B3
6 P—K3	Castles
7 P—KR3	Q—Kt3
8 Q—Q2	Kt—K5
9 Kt×Kt	P×Kt
10 Kt—Kt5	

White could retain a sound positional advantage by 10. P—B5 Q—Q1 11. Kt—K5, followed by B—B4 and Castles KR, as pointed out by Clarke in the *British Chess Magazine*. Instead, White prefers a course which involves great risks for both players.

| 10 ... | P—QB4 |
| 11 Castles | Kt—B3 |

12 P×P   Q—R3

Much stronger than 12... Q×P 13. Kt×KP.

13 P—R3   B—B4
14 P—KKt4   QR—Q1
15 Q—B2   R×R ch.
16 Q×R   R—Q1
17 Q—B2   Q—R4

This is not quite adequate. Clarke recommends 17... Kt—Kt5! 18. Q—Kt1 (if 18. P×Kt Q—R8 ch. 19. Q—Kt1 R—Q8 ch.) Kt—Q6 ch. 19. B×Kt R×B 20. P×B Q×P ch. 21. Q—B2 Q—R7 22. Q—Kt1 Q—B5 ch., with a draw.

18 B—K2   Kt—Kt5

19 B—B7

An extraordinarily complex position. White could also capture the knight immediately by 19. P×Kt Q—R8 ch. 20. Q—Kt1 B×P ch. 21. K—B2, Q—R6 22. Q×B R—Q7 ch. 23. K×R Q×Q ch. 24. K—K1 Q×P ch. 25. K—B1 B—Q2 26. P—R4 (not 26. Kt×KP Q—Kt8 ch.), with a very obscure position.

19 ...   Q—R3

But not 19... Q×B 20. P×Kt, and White is safe.

20 R—Q1

White evidently distrusts a similar variation to that given in the note to his nineteenth move, and so makes an ingenious effort at a swindle which succeeds.

20 ...   Kt×Q
21 R×R ch.   B—B1
22 P×B   Q—QB3
23 B—B4   Kt—K8?

Overlooking an unexpected coup. He could put up a very good fight by 23... P—KR3 24. Kt×BP K×Kt 25. P×P ch. Q×P 26. K×Kt Q—Kt7, when Black has the better chances.

24 Kt—K6!   Resigns.

After 24... P×Kt 25. B—R6 White forces mate.

118 WHITE: SZABO—BLACK: OLAFSSON
Dallas, 1957

1 P—Q4   Kt—KB3
2 P—QB4   P—KKt3
3 P—KKt3   B—Kt2

If Black aims for dull equality by 3... P—B3 (4. B—Kt2 P—Q4), White can cross his plans by 4. P—Q5 P×P 5. P×P Q—R4 ch. 6. Kt—B3 Kt—K5 7. Q—Q4 Kt×Kt 8. B—Q2! Q×QP 9. Q×Kt Kt—B3 10. Q×R Kt—Q5 11. R—B1 Q×R 12. Q×Kt Q×Kt 13. Q×P! Resigns (*Feuerstein-Bennett, New York, 1955*). An entertaining little skirmish.

4 B—Kt2   P—Q4
5 P×P   Kt×P
6 P—K4   Kt—Kt5
7 P—Q5

But not 7. Q—R4 ch. QKt—B3 8. P—Q5 P—QKt4, with advantage to Black.

7 ...   P—QB3
8 Kt—K2

8. P—QR3 Q—R4! is weaker.

8 ...   P×P
9 P×P   B—B4

10 Q—R4 ch.?

A manoeuvre which this game completely refutes. The safe line is 10. Castles Castles 11. QKt—B3 QKt—R3.

10 ...   QKt—B3
11 Castles

27. GRÜNFELD DEFENCE

If 11. QKt—B3 B—B7 12. P—Kt3 P—QKt4 favours Black, while if 11. P×Kt? Kt—B7 ch. 12. K—B1 Q—Q8 mate.

11 ...	B—B7
12 Q—R3	Kt×QP
13 Q—B5	B×Kt
14 B×Kt	

White mistakenly thinks that he is improving on an earlier game in which 14. R×B P—K3 15. Kt—B3 Q—Kt3 gave Black a favourable ending.

14 ...	B—B4
15 B—Kt5	

White's hope is to hold Black's king in the centre; his better alternative, to regain the pawn at once by 15. B×Kt ch.

15 ...	QR—B1
16 KR—K1	Castles
17 Kt—B3	P—KR3
18 B—K3	

18. B×KP Kt×B 19. Q×Kt B×Kt loses a piece.

18 ...	Kt—R4
19 Q×RP	

White still hopes to emerge unscathed after 19... B×Kt 20. KR—Q1.

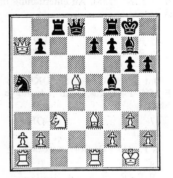

19 ...	R×Kt!
20 KR—Q1	

For if 20. P×R Q×B 21. QR—Q1 Q—B6.

20 ...	R—Q6
21 R×R	B×R

22 B—Kt2	B—R3
23 B—Kt6	

The last hope. If 23... Q—Q7 24. B×Kt Q×B 25. B×P recovering the piece.

23 ...	Q—Q3!

A pretty final stroke. If 24. B×Kt B—Q5 wins the queen.

24 Resigns.

119 WHITE: TARTAKOWER—BLACK: STUMPERS

Baarn, 1947

1 Kt—KB3	Kt—KB3
2 P—KKt3	P—KKt3
3 P—B4	B—Kt2
4 P—Q4	Castles
5 B—Kt2	P—Q4
6 P×P	Kt×P
7 Castles	P—QB3

Although less aggressive than the normal 7... P—QB4 or 7... Kt—Kt3, this move is nevertheless quite playable.

8 P—K4

More accurate is 8. KKt—Q2 Kt—R3 9. Kt—Kt3 QKt—B2 10. B—Q2 Kt—Kt4 11. P—K3, with greater centre control for White.

8 ...	Kt—Kt3
9 P—KR3	B—K3
10 Kt—R3	Kt—R3
11 Kt—B2	Kt—B2

From now on Black seems overawed by his famous opponent and falls into the common error in such situations of playing too conservatively. He could obtain quite good counterplay by 11... Q—B1 12. K—R2 R—Q1.

12 K—R2	B—B5
13 R—K1	Kt—K3
14 P—Kt3	B—QR3
15 R—QKt1	

A little bit of psychology; Black thinks that his best reply 15... P—QB4, is somehow prevented and so misses his last opportunity of playing it.

27. GRÜNFELD DEFENCE

15 ...	Q—Q3?
16 B—K3	Kt—Q2
17 P—K5	Q—B2
18 Kt—Kt4	Q—R4

Black is utterly baffled by his opponent's hypermodern manoeuvring; he could still hold on by 18... Kt—Kt1, although that is not a move which anyone would care to make even in a closed position.

19 Q—Q2

Threatening 20. Kt×P.

19 ...	KR—K1
20 Kt×B	Q×Kt
21 B—B1	Q—R6
22 P—QKt4	Kt—B2

If 22... P—QR4 White would still keep the queen hemmed in by 23. P—Kt5.

23 Kt—Kt5	Kt—Kt3
24 Kt—K4	Resigns.

A very pretty finishing touch. Black cannot prevent the loss of his queen by 25. R—Kt3 Q—R5 26. Kt—B5, or 26. Kt—B3.

28. BENONI DEFENCE

120 White: Naylor—Black: Wade

Whitby, 1958

1 Kt—KB3	P—KKt3
2 P—Q4	B—Kt2
3 P—K4	P—QB4
4 P—Q5	

If 4. P×P Q—R4 ch.

4 ...	P—Q3
5 Kt—B3	Kt—KB3
6 B—KB4	

Sounder is 6. B—K2, when a game, *Smyslov-Schmid, Helsinki, 1952,* illustrates how White can dominate the centre with his knights: 6... Castles 7. Castles Kt—R3 8. Kt—Q2 Kt—B2 9. P—QR4 P—Kt3 10. Kt—B4 B—QR3 11. B—B4 R—Kt1 12. P—QKt3 Kt—Q2 12. Q—Q2 P—B4 13. QR—Q1 P×P 14. Kt×KP R—B4 15. B—Kt4 R×P 16. B—K6 ch. Kt×B 17. Q×R Kt—B1 18. Kt—Kt5 B—Kt2 19. Kt×Kt Q—B1 20. Kt×QP! P×Kt 21. Q×QP Q×Kt 22. Q×Q ch. Resigns.

6 ...	Castles
7 Q—Q2	P—QR3
8 P—QR4	Q—R4

Again threatening ... P—QKt4.

9 R—R3	Q—Kt5
10 R—Kt3	Kt×KP!

A very deep sacrifice, the point of which is that Black obtains not only enough material for the queen, but also command of the centre.

11 Q—K3

Not 11. Q—K2 Kt×Kt.

11 ...	Kt×Kt
12 R×Q	Kt×QP
13 Q—K4	Kt×R
14 Q×KP	QKt—B3
15 Q—Kt5	

White's king would be still more exposed after 15. Q×QP Kt×P ch. 16. K—K2 B—Kt5.

15 ...	Kt×P ch.
16 K—Q2	Kt (B7)—Q5
17 Kt×Kt	Kt×Kt

18 Q—Kt3

No better is 18. B×QP P—R3 19. Q—R4 Kt—B4, followed by 20... R—Q1.

18 . . .	B—K3
19 B—Q3	Kt—Kt6 ch.
20 K—B2	P—B5
21 B—K2	Kt—Q5 ch.
22 K—Q2	P—Q4

At last Black has got his centre pawns going and White's next blunder only hastens the end; otherwise Black would play ... Kt—B4, and advance all his queen's side pawns.

23 B—K5?	Kt—B4
24 Q—B4?	

If 24. Q—QB3 P—Q5 25. Q—R5 P—Kt3 wins a piece.

24 . . .	B—R3
25 Resigns.	

121 WHITE: AVERBAKH—BLACK: TOLUSH

Training Game, 1952

1 P—Q4	Kt—KB3
2 P—QB4	P—B4
3 P—Q5	P—K3
4 Kt—QB3	P×P
5 P×P	P—Q3
6 P—K4	

A good, although little used system is

6. Kt—B3 P—KKt3 7. B—Kt5 B—Kt2 8. P—K4 Castles? (better is 8... B—Kt5 9. B—K2 B×Kt, so as to maintain a hold on the central black squares) 9. B—K2 P—KR3 10. B—R4 B—Kt5 11. Kt—Q2 B×B 12. Q×B P—R3 13. P—R4 R—K1 14. Castles KR QKt—Q2 15. P—B4 Q—B2 16. QR—K1 QR—B1 17. Kt—B4 Kt—Kt3 18. P—K5! P×P (no better are 18... KKt×P 19. Kt×P Kt×BP 20. Q—B3, or 18... Kt×Kt 19. Q×Kt P×P 20. P×P R×P 21. B—Kt3) 19. P—Q6 Q—B3 20. B×Kt, B×B 21. Kt×Kt QR—Q1 22. Kt (Kt6)—Q5, Resigns. (*Bobotsov-Mühlberg, Varna, 1957.*)

6 . . .	P—KKt3
7 B—K2	B—Kt2
8 Kt—B3	Castles
9 Castles	R—K1
10 Q—B2	P—QR3

A more promising system is 10... Kt—R3, followed by ... Kt—B2.

11 P—QR4	QKt—Q2
12 B—KB4	Q—B2
13 Kt—Q2	Kt—K4
14 P—R3	Kt (B3)—Q2
15 B—K3	

This shows up the basic disadvantage of Black's system of development; his knight cannot be permanently maintained on K4, and once it is driven away, he has to defend a completely passive position.

15 . . .	P—B3
16 P—B4	Kt—B2
17 B—B2	P—B4

Superficially, this looks a good freeing move; but Black should instead content himself with 17... Kt—B1.

18 P×P	B×Kt
19 P×P	P×P
20 P×B	R×B
21 Q×P ch.	K—B1
22 QR—K1	R×R

If 22... R×Kt 23. B—R4, and Black cannot avoid a winning attack based on R—K8 ch., or B—K7 ch.

23 R×R

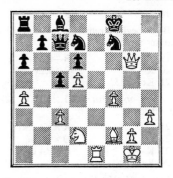

23 ...	Kt—Kt3
24 R—K8 ch.	K×R
25 Q—Kt8 ch.	Resigns.

For if 25... K—K2 26. B—R4 ch. K—Q2 27. Q×Kt mate.

122 WHITE: SHAPOSHNIKOV—BLACK: BASTRIKOV

White Russia, 1954

1 P—Q4	Kt—KB3
2 P—QB4	P—B4
3 P—Q5	P—QKt4

The Volga Gambit, which has some surprise value, but is not really sound.

| 4 P×P | P—K3 |

A more promising line is 4... P—KKt3 which gives White real chances of going wrong, for instance 5. Kt—QB3 B—KKt2 6. P—K4 P—Q3 7. Kt—B3 Castles 8. B—K2 (inferior is 8. P—KR3 P—QR3 9. B—K2? P×P 10. B×P Kt×KP! 11. Kt×Kt Q—R4 ch. 12. Kt—B3, B×Kt ch. 13. P×B Q×B 14. Kt—Q2 Q—Q6 15. Q—B3 Q×Q 16. Kt×Q B—R3 17. B—R6 R—K1 18. Kt—Q2 Kt—Q2 19. B—B4 Kt—Kt3 20. B—K3 Kt×P 21. P—QB4 Kt×B 22. P×Kt KR—Kt1 23. K—Q1 R—Kt5 24. QR—B1 B—Kt2 25. Resigns; *Matchett-O'Kelly, Bognor, 1956*) P—QR3 9. Castles? (White could save an important tempo by 9. P×P) P×P 10. B×P Q—Kt3 11. Kt—Q2 B—QR3 12. Kt—B4 Q—Kt2

13. B×B Q×B 14. Q—K2? (White runs into trouble after this self-pin; much better is 14. Kt—K3) QKt—Q2 15. B—K3 KR—Kt1 16. QR—Kt1 Kt—K1 17. KR—K1 B×Kt 18. P×B R×R 19. Resigns, for if 19. R×R Kt—K4 wins a piece. (*Van Scheltinga-Opocensky, Buenos Aires, 1939*).

5 Kt—QB3	P×P
6 Kt×P	B—Kt2
7 P—K4	

The best answer, returning the pawn so as to develop rapidly.

| 7 ... | Kt×P |
| 8 B—KB4 | Q—R4 ch. |

Normal development no longer works, for if 8... P—Q3 9. B—B4 B—K2 10. Q—K2, and Black is in great difficulty.

| 9 P—Kt4 | P×P |
| 10 B—B4 | |

But not 10. Kt—B7 ch. K—Q1 11. Kt×R P—Kt6 dis. ch. and Black wins.

10 ...	P—Kt6 dis. ch.
11 K—B1	P—Kt7
12 R—Kt1	B—Q3
13 Q—Q4	

Far stronger than 13. B×B Kt—Q7 ch. 14. K—K2 Kt×R 15. Q×Kt B×Kt 16. B×B Q×P ch. 17. K—K1 Q×B.

13 ...	Castles
14 Q×Kt	B×B
15 Kt—K7 ch. ?	

Having obtained a winning position, Black begins to slip. Correct is 15. Q×B B×Kt 16. B×B Q×P ch. 17. Q—B4 Q×Q ch. 18. B×Q R—B1 19. B—Q3.

| 15 ... | K—R1 |
| 16 Q×KB? | |

After this a won game suddenly becomes a loss. Correct is 16. Q×QB Q—B6 17. Q—K4 Q—B8 ch. 18. K—K2 Q—Q7 ch. 19. K—B3, as Clarke points out in the *British Chess Magazine*.

| 16 ... | Q—B6 |

28. BENONI DEFENCE

17 Kt—B3   R—K1
18 Q×P

18 ...   Kt—R3!

Black begins a remarkable and decisive counter-attack.

19 P×Kt   B—K5
20 K—K2   B—Kt3
21 Kt—Kt5

A last hope, for if 21... B×Q 22. Kt×B mate.

21 ...   R×Kt ch.!
22 Q×R   Q×B ch.
23 K—B3   B—R4 ch.
24 Resigns.

For if 24. K—K3 R—K1, wins the queen, and if 24. K—Kt3, Q—Kt5 mate.

29. QUEEN'S INDIAN DEFENCE

123 WHITE: UHLMANN—BLACK: BALANEL

Erfurt, 1955

1 P—Q4   Kt—KB3
2 Kt—KB3   P—QKt3
3 P—KKt3   B—Kt2
4 B—Kt2   P—B4
5 Castles   P—K3

This game more than any other shows the fatal effect of confusing different variations. Black's subsequent play, right up to his 11th move, is modelled on the so-called Marienbad System, which continues 5... P×P 6. Kt×P B×B 7. K×B P—Kt3 8. P—QB4 Q—B1 9. P—Kt3 B—Kt2 10. Kt—QB3 Q—Kt2 ch., with an even game. The text-move, however, does not at all fit into this system, as will be seen seven moves later.

6 P—B4   P×QP
7 Kt×P   B×B
8 K×B   Q—B1
9 P—Kt3   B—K2
10 B—Kt2   P—Q4?
11 P×P   Q—Kt2

This was the idea. It looks as though Black will regain his pawn with an even

game, but he has overlooked a deadly intermediate move.

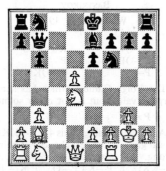

12 P—K4!   Kt×KP

Or 12... P×P 13. Kt—B5 Castles 14. P—K5! with a tremendous attack. In this line 14. Kt×B ch.? would be an error because of 14... Q×Kt 15. B—R3 Q×P ch. 16. P—B3 Q—K4!

13 P—B3!   Kt—KB3
14 P×P   Castles
15 Kt—B5

Now threatening 16. Kt×B ch. Q×Kt 17. B—R3. Black's answer is an immediately decisive error, but after, e.g., 15... Kt—B3 White would be a

108

pawn to the good with much the better position.

15 ...   R—Q1?
16 P×P ch.   K×P

Or 16... K—B1 17. Q×R ch. B×Q 18. B—R3 ch. K×P 19. Kt—Q6 ch., etc.

17. Q×R   Resigns.

124 WHITE: UHLMANN—BLACK: SMYSLOV

Moscow, 1956

1 P—Q4   Kt—KB3
2 P—QB4   P—K3
3 Kt—KB3   P—QKt3
4 P—KKt3   B—R3

A rarely-played alternative to 4... B—Kt2. Instead of contesting control of his K5 as in the normal Queen's Indian, Black here directs his forces against QB5. The present game illustrates this basic idea to perfection.

5 P—Kt3   P—Q4
6 B—KKt2   B—Kt5 ch.

For the time being, the QBP protects itself, since 6... P×P would be answered very strongly with 7. Kt—K5. But White immediately starts worrying about the pawn and, instead of retaining the option just outlined, opens the long diagonal for "safety's sake".

7 KKt—Q2?

Much stronger was 7. B—Q2.

7 ...   P—B4
8 QP×P   KB×P
9 B—Kt2   Castles
10 Castles   Kt—B3
11 Kt—QB3

White will find that he cannot conveniently pester the black-squared bishop from QR4. He should therefore have delayed the text-move and played 11. P—QR3 so as to threaten P—QKt4-Kt5.

11 ...   R—B1
12 P×P

He tears out the eye that annoys him —but in doing so opens the K-file and the B-diagonal. Nor is 12. Kt—R4, B—Kt5 13. P×P much better—it avoids the immediate tactical onslaught, but the strategic problems facing him remain much the same. It seems to us White should have tried to defend the BP by 12. R—B1 and, if necessary, Kt (3)—Kt1, keeping the position closed at all costs.

12 ...   P×P
13 Kt—R4?

This is met by a beautiful combination

13 ...   Kt—Q5!
14 Kt—QB3

Back home, for if 14. R—K1 Kt—B7! winning the exchange (15. Q×Kt B×P ch.). And if White concedes the pair of bishops by 14. B×Kt B×B 15. R—Kt1, he can still not save his material after 15... Q—K2; for if then 16. R—K1 B×P ch. 17. K×B Kt—Kt5 ch., etc., as in the following note; or 16. B—B3 (obstructing the knight's best square), Q—R6 with the threat of P—QKt4.

14 ...   Q—K2
15 R—K1

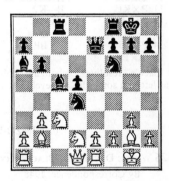

15 ...   Kt—B7!

A brilliant denouement, against which White is helpless. If now 16. Q×Kt B×P ch. 17. K×B (if 17. K—R1 B×R 18. R×B P—Q5) Kt—Kt5 ch., and White has the choice between mate abroad and mate at home:

18. K—B3 Q—B3 ch.! 19. K×Kt R—B5 ch. 20. Kt×R, B—B1 ch. and mate next move. 18. K—Kt1 Q—K6 ch. 19. K—R1 Kt—B7 ch. and mate in three by means of Philidor's Legacy.

16 R—KB1   Kt×R
17 Q×Kt   KR—Q1
18 B—KB3   B—R6
    Resigns.

He is not only the exchange down, but has no reasonable defence against P—Q5 followed by the entry of the rook on QB7.

125 WHITE: SOULTANBÉIEFF—BLACK: DUBYNA

Liège, 1953

1 P—Q4   Kt—KB3
2 P—QB4   P—K3
3 Kt—KB3   P—QKt3
4 P—K3   B—Kt2
5 B—Q3   B—K5
6 Kt—B3   B—Kt5
7 Q—B2   B×B
8 Q×B   P—Q4
9 P×P   Kt×P
10 Castles Kt×Kt
11 P×Kt   B—K2
12 Kt—K5   Castles
13 P—KB4   P—QB4
14 P—B5   P×BP
15 Q×P

Black's resolute exchanging policy has left him somewhat undeveloped. He

cannot now make good the deficiency by, say, 15... Kt—R3 because of 16. Kt×P Q—K1 17. Q—Q3, which would lose a pawn. He must therefore play 15... Q—K1 which, by taking the pressure off the QP, gives White the chance to play P—K4, greatly increasing the mobility of his pieces. Disliking this prospect, Black finds a strong-looking move which, however, loses immediately.

15 ...   Q—Q4?

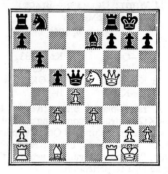

16 Kt—Kt6!

If now 16... Q×Q 17. Kt×B ch. wins a piece, therefore:

16 ...   Q—Kt2
17 Q—Q5!

The same motif a second time. Black tries to counter with:

17 ...   Kt—B3
18 Q×Kt!

And now the third! Black resigns.

30. NIMZO-INDIAN DEFENCE

126 WHITE: DYCKHOFF—BLACK: KOCH

By Correspondence, 1948

1 P—Q4   Kt—KB3
2 P—QB4   P—K3
3 Kt—QB3   B—Kt5
4 P—K3

The Rubinstein variation, today the most popular line of the defence.

4 ...   Castles
5 B—Q3   P—B4
6 Kt—B3   Kt—B3
7 Castles   P—Q4
8 P—QR3   B×Kt
9 P×B   P—QKt3
10 Kt—K5!

A very strong move, which had been discarded as the result of a game

Landau-Keres, Kemeri, 1937, in which White, after 10... Kt×Kt 11. P×Kt Kt—Q2 12. P—B4 P×P 13. B×P B—Kt2 played 14. B—Q3?, allowing Black an immediate initiative by 14... P—B5! 15. B×P Q—B2 16. Q—K2 QR—B1.

10 ...	Kt×Kt
11 P×Kt	Kt—Q2
12 P—B4	P×P
13 B×P	B—Kt2
14 Q—K2!	

Retaining the white bishop in its strong position, preparing an eventual king side attack with P—K4 and P—KB5, threatening to occupy the queen's file and keeping square QR6 under control so that Black cannot think of getting counterplay by P—QR3, which is always answered with P—QR4

14 ...   Q—B2

In retrospect, 14... Q—K2 (stopping the white bishop from reaching KR4 and giving support to K3) was preferable but it was difficult to see at this stage that the counter-attack against White's foremost KP would be ineffectual.

15 B—Q2!   QR—Q1

If 15... B—Q4, White exchanges and then builds up a king side attack by B—K1, P—KKt4, B—Kt3 and P—B5. Black wants to retake on his Q4 with a rook . . .

16 B—K1	Kt—Kt1
17 B—R4	R—Q2
18 P—K4	

But doesn't get the chance!

18 ...   Kt—B3
19 P—B5!

The KP protects itself, for if now 19... Q×P 20. P×P P×P 21. B—Kt3, followed by 22. B×P ch.; or 19... Kt×P 20. P×P etc. Finally, if 19... R—K1 20. P×P P×P 21. Q—Kt4 Kt×P 22. B×P ch. K—R1 23. Q—R5 and the black rooks cannot protect each other while 23... P—Kt3 would be refuted by 24. B—B6 ch.

19 ...	Kt—Q1
20 B—KKt3	

Threatening R—B4—R4.

20 ...	Q—B1
21 R—B4	P×P
22 P×P	B—Q4
23 P—K6!	

The conquest of K6 logically rounds off the wonderful strategic achievement. If now 23... P×P 24. P×P Kt×P 25. Q×Kt ch.! B×Q 26. B×B ch., and no matter how Black replies, he remains with a decisive disadvantage in material. Therefore:

Resigns.

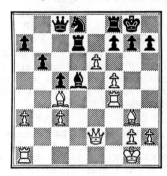

127 WHITE: GELLER—BLACK:
GOLOMBEK

Budapest, 1952

1 P—Q4	Kt—KB3
2 P—QB4	P—K3
3 Kt—QB3	B—Kt5
4 P—K3	P—B4
5 P—QR3	P×P
6 P×B	P×Kt
7 Kt—B3	

In harmony with his ferocious attacking style, Geller turns the opening into a gambit. Golombek accepts in order to see what would happen, for 7... Castles, followed by P—Q4 was perfectly safe.

7 ...	P×P
8 B×P	P—Q4

9 P—B5   P—QKt 3

But this, as Golombek himself observes, is dangerous with the king still in the centre. One would have expected 9... Castles.

10 B—Kt5 ch.   B—Q2

11 B×B ch.   KKt×B

Forced, for if 11... QKt×B 12. P—B6 would cripple the black game, As played Black only succeeds in holding his QB3 square by discovering an amazing combination.

12 Q—B2

Before he can play B×P, he must make sure of square QB6.

12 ...   Kt—QB3!

13 B×P   Kt×KtP

14 Q—Kt1   R—KKt1

If 14... Kt×P? 15. Castles R—Kt1 16. Q×P wins. Black must give the exchange and the resultant position is far too open to give the knights any chance against the rooks.

15 P—B6   Kt×P

And here 15... Kt—B4 is refuted by 16. Q×P R×B 17. Q×R Kt—B7 ch. 18. K—K2 Kt×R 19. Kt—K5 Q—K2 20. R×Kt Castles 21. Kt×P R—B1 22. R×P!

16 Q×RP

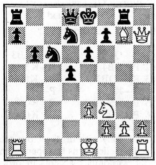

16 ...   Kt—B3!

17 B×Kt   Q×B

18 Q×R ch.   K—Q2!

Not 18... K—K2 19. Q—Kt5. But now both White's queen and rook are attacked, and the following clever "zwischenzug" is met—by a clever "zwischenzug".

19 Kt—K5 ch!   Kt×Kt

Not 19... Q×Kt 20. Q×P ch. and wins.

20 Q×R   Kt—B6 ch.!

Sacrificing the one knight he has for the two rooks ensures the draw. The theme comes out most clearly after 21. K—K2 Q—Kt7 ch. 22. K×Kt Q—B3 ch., when Black gets his perpetual without regaining any material. In the game there followed:

21 P×Kt   Q×R ch.

22 K—K2   Q—Kt7 ch.

and draws by perpetual check.

If 23. K—B1 Q—Kt8 ch. 24. K—Kt2 Q—Kt3 ch., etc. One of the select coterie of drawn games that gained a special prize for both contestants (other examples were *Mieses-Pillsbury, Vienna, 1903, Gunsberg-Przepiorka, San Remo, 1911, Ulvestad-Reinfeld, Ventnor City, 1939*).

---

128 White: Uhlmann—Black: Botvinnik

Munich, 1958

1 P—Q4   P—K3

2 P—QB4   Kt—KB3

3 Kt—QB3   B—Kt5

4 P—K3   P—QKt3

5 B—Q3   B—Kt2

6 Kt—B3   Kt—K5

7 Castles

The tacit offer of a draw: 7... B×Kt 8. P×B Kt×QBP 9. Q—B2 B×Kt 10. P×B Q—Kt4 ch. 11. K—R1 Q—R4 12. R—KKt1 Q×P ch. 13. R—Kt2 P—KB4 14. Q×Kt Q—Q8 ch. 15. R—Kt1 Q—B6 ch., as Botvinnik points out in his notes to the game.

7 ...   P—KB4

8 Q—B2   B×Kt

| 9 P×B | Castles |
| 10 R—Kt1 | |

As Botvinnik himself remarks, this new move gains point only from the fact that Black tries to block the white pawns. Since 11. P—B5 was no threat, Black should have continued with 10... R—B3—R3. As played, he will have to worry about the weakness of his QKt3.

| 10 ... | P—B4 |
| 11 P—QR4! | |

Since Black cannot play Kt—QB3, he cannot very well stop the further advance of this pawn.

| 11 ... | Q—B2 |
| 12 P—R5! | P—Q3 |

It would be very dangerous in Black's present state of undress to capture the pawn. The black queen would then be tied to the bishop so that White could work up a dangerous king side attack by some such sequence as Kt—K1, P—B3, P—K4 and P—K5!

13 Kt—Q2?

Now the weakness of Black's QKt3 works as a boomerang: White overplays his hand. He first had to play 13. P×P.

13 ...	Kt×Kt
14 B×Kt	Kt—Q2
15 R—Kt2	

In the belief that he approaches his end. He does—and 15. P×KtP was therefore necessary though Black could now capture with the knight.

| 15 ... | P×RP! |

Threatening 16... Kt—Kt3 followed by P—R5.

| 16 R—R1 | Kt—Kt3 |
| 17 R×P | |

This is the position White played for —and it is one that is hopelessly lost for him. Of course, if now 17... Kt×P 18. B×Kt Q×R 19. R×B, but Black has a diabolical intermediate move.

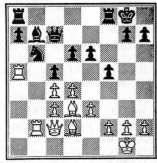

| 17 ... | B—K5! |

Leaving White no defence against Kt×P.

| 18 B×B | P×B |
| 19 Q—Kt3 | |

Or 19. Q×P Kt×P 20. Q×P ch. Q—B2 and wins.

19 ...	Kt×P
20 Q×Kt	Q×R
21 Q×P ch.	K—R1
22 R—R2	Q—B2
23 Q×KP?	

Allowing an immediate decision, but the game was hopeless.

| 23 ... | Q—B2 |
| Resigns. | |

129 WHITE: GONZALEZ—BLACK: PERRINE

By Correspondence, 1943

1 P—Q4	Kt—KB3
2 P—QB4	P—K3
3 Kt—QB3	B—Kt5
4 Q—B2	Kt—B3

The Zurich, or Milner-Barry variation, which aims at an early P—K4 and subsequent control of square Q5. By playing P—K4 at his 7th move, White helps Black in attaining his objects.

5 Kt—B3	P—Q3
6 B—Kt5	Castles
7 P—K4	P—K4

8 P—Q5	Kt—Q5
9 Q—Q3	P—KR3
10 B—R4?	

It was bad to allow the black knight to go to Q5. It is worse to permit it to stay there. 10. B—Q2! would have avoided what follows.

10 ...	P—KKt4!
11 B—Kt3	Kt×KP!

For if 12. Q×Kt (K4) B—KB4 13. Q—K3 Kt—B7 ch. wins the queen; and if White first exchanges knights and then plays Q×Kt R—K1 still wins the queen.

12 Kt×Kt	P×Kt
13 Q×P	R—K1

If now 14. B—K2 B—KB4 15. Castles (K) Kt×B 16. RP×Kt B×Kt followed by R×B wins a piece. Therefore White has to castle on the other side—and that's no pleasure.

14 Castles	Kt×Kt
15 P×Kt	B—R6 ch.

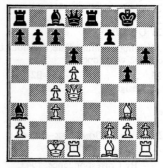

16 K—B2

Forced, for if 16. K—Kt1 B—B4 ch. 17. K—R1 B—B7 traps the rook. White's trouble is that here as well as in the game continuation he cannot ward off the bishop's check by B—Q3, because then B—B4 would again catch the queen.

16 ...	B—B4 ch.
17 K—Kt3	P—B4!

Bringing his queen into the attack with gain of tempo—if 18. P×P e.p. B—B4 followed by Q—Kt3 ch.

18 Q—Q2	Q—R4
19 B—Q3	

At last the white queen is safely *behind* this bishop. But the position has deteriorated too much by now.

19 ...	P—Kt4!
20 P×P	

He had to stop Q—R5 mate—a threat that dominates the rest of the game.

20 ...	B×B
21 Q×B	P—B5 ch.!
22 Q×P	

Again, if 22. K×P Q—R5 mate.

22 ...	QR—B1
23 Q—Q3	R—K5!

If now 24. Q×R R×P mate.

24 K—B2	R(5)—QB5
Resigns.	

130 WHITE:MAKARCZYK—BLACK: SLIWA

Warsaw, 1952

1 P—Q4	Kt—KB3
2 P—QB4	P—K3
3 Kt—QB3	B—Kt5
4 Q—B2	Kt—B3
5 Kt—B3	P—Q3

A different idea is 5... P—Q4, as in a game, *Gerusel-Lombardy, Toronto, 1957*: 6. P—QR3 B×Kt ch. 7. Q×B Kt—K5 8. Q—B2 P—K4! 9. P×KP B—B4 10. Q—R4 Castles 11. B—K3? (P—K3!) P—Q5 12. R—Q1 P×B! 13. R×Q P×P ch. 14. K—Q1 KR×R ch. 15. K—B1 P—QR3! 16. Q—Kt3 Kt—B4 17. Q—B3 Kt—R4 18. P—K4 Kt (R4) —Kt6 ch. Resigns.

6 P—QR3	B×Kt ch.
7 Q×B	Castles
8 P—KKt3	P—K4!
9 P×P	

Very dangerous, as the sequel shows. In a game, *Kotov-Denker, Groningen, 1946*, the identical pawn offer was disregarded, and after 9. B—Kt2 R—K1 10. P—Q5 the game transposed into a frequently-seen line, in which the rook on K1 is not serving any particular purpose.

9 ...	P×P
10 Kt×P	Kt×Kt
11 Q×Kt	R—K1
12 Q—B3	Kt—K5
13 Q—K3	

White tries to avoid the difficulties arising from Kt—B4, but has no convenient means of doing so. If, instead of the text 13. Q—B3 B—Q2 14. B—Kt2 B—B3 15. R—KKt1 Q—Q5 and he is completely paralysed (if 16. P—K3 Kt—B6! 17. Q—R5 P—KKt3).

13 ...	B—Kt5!

The beginning of a deep combination. White has no means of avoiding it, because his KB is tied to the defence of the KP.

14 P—R3

14 ...	Q—Q2!
15 B—Q2	

If 15. P×B QR—Q1 16. Q—Q3 Q—R5 17. P—Kt3 Q—R4 ch. wins.

15 ...	QR—Q1
16 B—B3	

The alternatives: (a) 16. R—Q1 B—B6! 17. R—KKt1 (the bishop cannot be captured either way because of 17... Kt×B) 17... P—QKt3 18. B—Kt2 Kt×Kt (if 19. R×Kt Q×Kt R×P ch. 20. Q×R Q×R ch. 21. Q×Q R×Q mate) 19... R×Q 20. R×Q R×P ch. followed by 21... R×R and wins. (b) 16. Castles B—B4 17. B—Kt2 Q—R5, and

the attack against QB7 and QB5 cannot be parried.

16 ...	Kt×B
17 Q×Kt	B—B6
18 R—KKt1	R—K5!

Gaining an important tempo.

19 P—Kt3	R—Q5
20 Q—B1	R—Q7!

Now White has no useful move left: except for pawn moves and QR—Kt1—R1 he is in complete zugzwang.

21 P—KKt4	Q—Q5
22 R—Kt1	R—Q8 ch.!
Resigns.	

If 23. Q×R Q—B6 ch. and mate next move. A magnificent game—one of the finest in this collection.

131 WHITE: NAVAROVSZKY—BLACK: FLORIAN

Budapest, 1955

1 P—Q4	Kt—KB3
2 P—QB4	P—K3
3 Kt—QB3	B—Kt5
4 Q—B2	Kt—B3
5 P—K3	Castles
6 B—Q3	

White should first play 6. P—QR3 to force the black bishop to declare itself. After the inaccurate text move, Black prepares a surprising retreat where the bishop does not interfere with the other black pieces.

6 ...	R—K1!
7 B—Q2	B—B1!
8 P—QR3	P—QR4
9 Castles	

A most unfortunate "temporizing" move! Florian himself says that White did not want to commit himself too early how to develop his KKt—for if 9. Kt—B3 P—Q3 (to be followed by 10... P—K4) and if 9. Kt—K2 P—Q4! because now 9... P—Q3 could be answered with 10. P—B4. But to commit his king is certainly much worse!

9 ...	P—Q4!

10 Kt—B3	B—Q2
11 P—K4	Kt—QKt5!

Since White cannot keep the piece thus offered no matter how he plays, it was best to decline it immediately and play 12. Q—Kt1, reconciling himself to the loss of the pair of bishops.

12 P×Kt?	P×P
13 Kt—QKt1	

No better is 13. BP×P P×Kt 14. B×P P×P 15. P—K5 P—KKt3! and Black's knight is taboo because of 16. P×Kt R—R8 ch. 17. K—Q2 B—R3 ch., but a little better was the attempt to keep the position closed by 13. P—K5 P×Kt 14. B×P P×P 15. B×P.

13 . . .	P—Kt6!
14 Q—B3	

For if 14. Q×P B—R5, Black first wins the exchange and then regains the piece by P×KP.

14 . . .	P×KP
15 B—K2	P×Kt
16 B×P	R—R8!

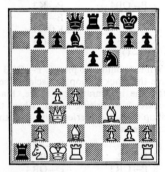

17 B—B4

Trying to stop the threatened 17... P—K4, followed by 18... B—KB4. However:

17 . . .	P—K4!
18 P×P	B—KB4

Black plays it all the same. The mating threat on Kt8 breaks all resistance.

19 R×Q	R×R
20 B—Q5	R×Kt ch.
21 K—Q2	Kt—K5 ch.

22 K—K3	Kt×Q
Resigns.	

Black remains a rook and minor piece to the good.

132
Munich, 1936

1 P—Q4	Kt—KB3
2 P—QB4	P—K3
3 Kt—QB3	B—Kt5
4 Q—B2	P—B4
5 P×P	Kt—B3
6 Kt—B3	B×P
7 B—Kt5	Kt—Q5?

A fatal loss of time, which meets with terrible punishment. 7... P—QKt3 is normally played in this position.

8 Kt×Kt	B×Kt
9 P—K4!	B×Kt ch.

If 9... P—Q3 10. R—Q1 with advantage. After the text Black's moves are virtually forced. Not having castled yet, he cannot answer 10. Q×B with Kt×P because of 11. Q×P, and thus has to look on helplessly while his whole force is crippled by one bishop.

10 Q×B	Castles
11 P—K5	Kt—K5
12 B×Q	Kt×Q
13 B—K7!	R—K1
14 B—R3	Kt—R5

13... Kt—K5 14. P—B3 Kt—Kt4 15. P—KR4 loses the knight.

15 P—QKt3	Kt—Kt3
16 B—Q6!	

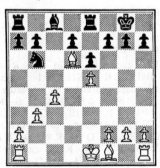

This completes the blockade. White threatens to win a piece at once by P—QR4—R5, so that Black's next move is still forced. The rest is a mopping-up requiring no further notes.

16 ...	P—QR4
17 B—B7	R—R3
18 P—B5	Kt—Q4
19 B×R	Kt×B
20 B—B4	P—QKt3
21 P×P	Kt—R1
22 Castles (Q)	Kt×P
23 R—Q6	Resigns.

Were it not for game No. *73* (*Espeli-Andersen*) this one-man blockade would be unique in the annals of chess.

133 WHITE: TOTH—BLACK: NAJDORF

Mar del Plata, 1956

1 P—Q4	Kt—KB3
2 P—QB4	P—K3
3 Kt—QB3	B—Kt5
4 B—Kt5	

A continuation which, after initial successes, has had serious setbacks and is rarely seen today.

4 ...	P—KR3
5 B—R4	P—B4
6 P—Q5	P×P

Also possible is 6... P—QKt4 (*Korchnoi-Durasevic*, Game No. *134*).

| 7 P×P | P—Q3 |

Modern opening theory has unearthed a number of possibilities of sacrificing the queen for assorted timber early in the opening. Thus Bronstein, against Spassky, at Amsterdam, 1956, as Black played 1. P—Q4 Kt—KB3 2. P—QB4 P—KKt3 3. Kt—QB3 B—Kt2 4. P—K4 P—Q3 5. P—B3 P—K4 6. P—Q5 Kt—R4 7. B—K3 Kt—R3 8. Q—Q2 Q—R5 ch. 9. P—Kt3 Kt×P 10. Q—KB2 Kt×B 11. Q×Q Kt×B 12. K—B2 Kt×BP, an idea which since then has been copied in several games. Or Tal, as Black against Bobotsov, Varna, 1958, played 1. P—Q4 Kt—KB3

2. P—QB4 P—KKt3 3. Kt—QB3 B—Kt2 4. P—K4 P—Q3 5. P—B3 Castles 6. KKt—K2 P—B4 7. B—K3 QKt—Q2 8. Q—Q2 P—QR3 9. Castles Q—R4 10. K—Kt1 P—QKt4! and now answered 11. Kt—Q5 with 11... Kt×Kt! 12. Q×Q Kt×B 13. R—B1 Kt×BP.

Sämisch points out that a similar possibility exists in the present position. Instead of 7... P—Q3 Black could have played 7... Kt×P 8. B×Q Kt×Kt 9. Q—Kt3 Kt—K5 ch. 10. K—Q1 Kt×P ch. 11. K—B2 K×B. White would probably do best to give up a pawn and decline the sacrifice by 8. Q×Kt Q×B 9. Q—K5 ch.

8 P—B3	Castles
9 P—K4	QKt—Q2
10 Kt—R3	Kt—K4
11 Kt—B2	Kt—Kt3
12 B—Kt3	Kt—R4

The play of the black knights to get control of the black squares on the king side is very elegant indeed.

| 13 Kt—Q3 | Kt×B |
| 14 P×Kt | P—B4! |

Opening up the weakened position.

15 P×P	B×Kt ch.
16 P×B	B×P
17 B—K2	Q—Kt4
18 K—B2	

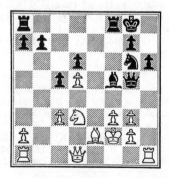

A sad necessity. If 18. P—Kt4 B×Kt and White has the unpleasant choice between 19. B×B QR—K1 ch. and 19. Q×B Kt—B5.

18 ...   QR—K1
19 Q—QB1

If, trying to stop the check on K6
19. P—B4 B×Kt 20. Q×B R×P ch.
21. P×R Kt×P wins. Or 20. B×B
Kt×P 21. P×Kt Q×BP ch. 22. K—Kt1
(22. Q—B3 Q—Q7 ch.) Q—B7 ch.
23. K—R2 R—B5 wins.

19 ...   R×B ch.!
20 K×R   R—K1 ch.
21 K—B2   B×Kt
Resigns.

After 21. Q×Q R—K7 ch. 22.
K—Kt1 P×Q, White is material down
and his position is hopeless.

134 WHITE: KORCHNOI—BLACK:
DURASEVIC

Belgrade, 1956

1 P—Q4	Kt—KB3
2 P—QB4	P—K3
3 Kt—QB3	B—Kt5
4 B—Kt5	P—B4
5 P—Q5	P—KR3
6 B—R4	P—QKt4

If Black tries to shake off the pressure
of White's QB immediately by 6...
P—KKt4 there could follow 7. B—Kt3
Kt—K5 8. Q—B2 Q—B3 9. R—B1
P×P 10. P×P Q—Q5 11. R—B1
B×Kt ch. 12. P×B Q×P ch. 13. Q×Q
Kt×Q 14. B—K5 Kt×R 15. B×R and
wins.

7 P—K4

But this is too ambitious, and it is
instructive to see how Black tears the
proud White centre to pieces. White can
get a promising game by 7. R—B1
P×BP 8. P—K4 P—Kt4 9. B—Kt3
Kt×P 10. B×P Q—B3 11. Kt—K2
(*Guimard-Medina, Mar del Plata, 1953.*)

7 ...   P—Q3
8 Q—B2   Castles
9 P×KP   Kt—B3!

A clever idea. After 10. P×P ch.

R×P Black would have essentially the
same threats as in the game, but in
addition the K-file would be open and
Kt×P a nasty threat.

10 Kt—B3   B×P
11 P×P

White has to hit at something all the
time, otherwise Black plays P—KKt4-
Kt5 followed by Kt—Q5. However,
even the hitting proves inadequate.

11 ...   Kt—Q5
12 Kt×Kt   P×Kt
13 P—QR3   B—R4
14 P—QKt4   P—Kt4
15 B—Kt3   R—B1!

This is the trouble. In trying to keep
the black pieces occupied White had to
open the QB-file.

16 P×B   R×Kt
17 Q—Q2

If 17. Q—Kt2 R—Kt6 18. Q—Q2
Kt×P White can no longer interpose on
QKt4—not that it helps much.

17 ...   Kt×P
18 Q×P   Q×P
19 Q—Kt4   Q×Q
20 P×Q

There follows a queenless middle game
in which most of the developed White
pieces have disappeared.

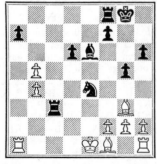

20 ...   R—K1

Stopping the natural developing move
21. B—K2 (21... Kt×B followed by 22...

30. NIMZO-INDIAN DEFENCE

B—B5), and threatening 21... B—Kt6 to be followed by Kt × B dis. ch.

21 P—B3   R—K6 ch.!

Now the king can no longer escape via KB2.

22 K—Q1	B—Kt6 ch.
23 K—B1	R—B1 ch.
24 K—Kt2	R—B7 ch.
25 K—R3	R—Q7
Resigns.	

31. BUDAPEST DEFENCE

135 White: Deutgen—Black: Schmid

Celle, 1948

1 P—Q4	Kt—KB3
2 P—QB4	P—K4
3 P×P	Kt—K5

The Fajarowicz variation, which by now has virtually disappeared, because the simple move 4. P—QR3! (*Donner-Persitz, Cheltenham, 1953*) kills all potential attacking chances.

4 Kt—QB3	B—Kt5
5 Q—B2	P—Q4
6 P×P e.p.	B—KB4
7 Q—Kt3?	

White had the better game even in the line chosen, but the timid text is a serious error. He had to brazen it out with 7. B—Q2! B×Kt 8. B×B Kt—Kt6? 9. P—K4! B×P 10. B—Q3 B×B 11. Q×B Kt×R 12. B×P R—Kt1 13. Q—K4 ch. K—Q2 14. Castles, and the white attack wins through.

7 ...	Kt—QB3
8 Kt—B3	Q×P
9 P—K3	Castles (Q)
10 B—K2	Q—Kt3!

It is not surprising that Black has a win in view of his enormous edge in development, but the winning move comes as a surprise, nevertheless. Black now threatens to win the queen by 11... Kt—B4 and if White prepares a retreat by 11. B—Q2 Kt × B 12. Kt × Kt B—B7!

11 Kt—R4	Q—B3
12 Kt×B	Q×Kt

And now the double threat of mate to the king (Q×P) and the queen (Kt—B4) is unanswerable

13 Castles	Kt—B4
Resigns.	

32. ENGLISH OPENING

136 White: Schmid—Black: Muth

Bamberg, 1949

1 P—QB4	P—K4
2 Kt—QB3	Kt—KB3
3 Kt—B3	Kt—B3
4 P—K4	

An unusual idea favoured by Nimzo-vitch. White surrenders control of his Q4 so as to make sure of occupying Q5.

4 ...	B—B4
5 Kt×P	Kt×Kt
6 P—Q4	B—Q3?

The genesis of Black's later troubles: 6... B—Kt5 7. P×Kt Kt×P is the way to equalize.

7 P—B5	B×P
8 P×Kt	Kt—Kt1
9 Q—Kt4	K—B1
10 Q—Kt3	P—Q3

11 B—KKt5	Q—K1
12 P×P	B×P
13 B—KB4	B—QKt5
14 Castles	

With such an enormous advantage in development, White can afford to treat the game on Morphy-like principles.

14 ...	B×Kt
15 Q×B	B—K3
16 B—K2	Kt—K2

If 16... Q—R5 17. Q×P B×P (if 17... R—QB1 18. R—Q8 ch.) 18. R—Q8 ch. R×R 19. Q×R ch. Q—K1 20. B—Q6 ch.

| 17 R—Q2! | P—KB3 |

Now if 17... Q—R5 18. B—KR6 R—KKt1 19. KR—Q1 Kt—B3 20. Q—B5 ch. K—K1 21. B—QKt5 Q×KP 22. R—K2 Q×P 23. B—Kt5.

| 18 KR—Q1 | Q—R5 |
| 19 B—R5! | Kt—B3 |

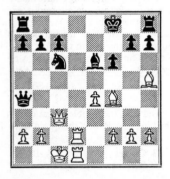

20 B×P

It is a pity that White here misses the chance for a finish analogous to the famous Torre-Lasker game: 20. R—Q7! B×R 21. R×B Q×RP 22. Q×P ch.! P×Q 23. B—R6 ch. K—Kt1 24. R—Kt7 ch. K—B1 25. R×BP dis. ch. K—Kt1 26. R—Kt7 ch. K—B1 27. R×KtP dis. ch. K—Kt1 28. R—Kt7 ch. K—B1 29. R×QRP dis. ch. K—Kt1 30. B—B7 ch.! and wins.

| 20 ... | Q×KP |

If 20... Q×RP, then not 21. Q—B5

ch. K—Kt1 22. Q×Kt? Q—R8 ch. 23. K—B2 Q×R ch., but 21. B—Q6 ch. followed by 23. B—R3.

| 21 P—QKt3! | |

Threatening 22. R—K2 Q—B4 23. P—KKt4.

| 21 ... | Q—B4 |
| 22 P—KKt4 | Q—K5 |

Or 22... Q—QKt4 23. R—Q6! and wins.

| 23 P—B3 | Resigns. |

The queen hunt ends unexpectedly in mid-board, for if 23... Q—Kt5 24. B—Q6 ch.

137 WHITE: FILIP—BLACK: BENI

Prague, 1956

| 1 P—QB4 | P—K4 |

A semi-symmetrical line beginning with 1... P—QB4 is also playable. A game, *Najdorf-Botvinnik, Moscow, 1956*, continued 2. P—KKt3 P—KKt3 3. B—Kt2 B—Kt2 4. Kt—KB3 Kt—QB3 5. Castles P—Q3 6. P—Q3 Kt—R3 7. Kt—B3 Castles 8. R—Kt1 R—Kt1 9. P—QR3 P—Kt3 10. P—QKt4 B—Kt2 11. P—Kt5 Kt—R4 12. P—K4 B×Kt 13. B×Kt B—Kt2 14. B×B K×B 15. Kt—R4 P—K3 16. P—B4 P—B3 17. Q—Kt4 B—B1 18. P—B5 P—K4 19. Kt×P P×Kt 20. Q×P ch. K—R1 21. Q—R6 ch., drawn by perpetual check.

2 Kt—QB3	P—Q3
3 P—KKt3	P—KKt3
4 B—Kt2	B—Kt2
5 Kt—B3	Kt—K2

Against the normal 5... Kt—KB3 Black probably feared Filip's favourite system 6. P—Q3, followed by a general queen's side advance.

| 6 Castles | P—QB3 |

This constitutes a serious weakening of his Q3. 6... Castles, followed by ... P—KB4 is sounder.

7	P—Q4	Castles
8	P×P	P×P
9	B—Kt5	P—B3
10	B—K3	Kt—R3
11	Q×Q	R×Q
12	QR—Q1	B—K3
13	P—Kt3	P—Kt3
14	B—B1	Kt—KB4

This natural move is the decisive mistake. Far stronger is 14... Kt—Kt5 and if 15. B—QR3 P—QR4.

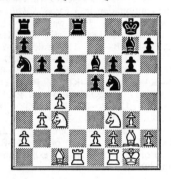

15 Kt—KR4!

This fine and unexpected move would never occur to most players—but White's doubled KRP is of far less consequence than Black's weak QBP.

15	...	Kt×Kt
16	P×Kt	R×R

If 16... B—Q2 17. R×B R×R 18. B×P wins a sound pawn.

17	R×R	R—QB1
18	R—Q6	K—B2

An ingenious attempt to solve his difficulties by tactical means which meets with an inspired refutation.

19	B×P	B—B1
20	R×B	

Very neat. If 20... K×R 21. B—Kt7, while if 20... Kt—B4 21. R—K8, but Black is not yet finished.

20	...	Kt—B2
21	B—Q7	R—Q1
22	R×P ch.	

A variation on the same theme as two moves previously.

22	...	K—Kt2
23	B—KR3	B—Kt5

A last hope; if 24. Kt—Q5 R×Kt, but White's reply ends all resistance.

24	R—B6	Resigns.

138 WHITE: NEY—BLACK:
SHAMKOVITCH
Russian Team Championship, 1956

1	P—QB4	Kt—KB3
2	Kt—QB3	P—Q4
3	P×P	Kt×P
4	Kt—B3	

In an earlier game, *Shaposnikov-Shamkovitch, Correspondence, 1953,* White made an interesting pawn sacrifice 4. P—K4 Kt—Kt5 5. P—Q4 Q×P 6. Q—K2. Black now continued passively with 6... P—QB3 7. P—B4 P—QKt3? (better 7... P—KKt3) 8. Kt—B3 Q—Q1 9. Q—KB2 P—K3 10. B—K3 Kt—Q6 ch. 11. B×Kt Q×B 12. R—Q1 Q—B5 13. Kt—K5 Q—R3 14. Q—Kt3 Kt—Q2 15. P—B5 P—B3 16. Kt×P Q—Kt2 17. Kt—Q8! K×Kt 18. P×P K—K1 19. P×Kt ch. B×P 20. Castles K—B2 21. Kt—Q5 B—Kt4 22. Kt—B7 B—R5 23. Q—K5 Resigns; for if 23... B×R 24. Q—K6 ch. K—Kt3 25. Kt×R Q×Kt 26. R×B B—B4 27. Q—Kt4 ch. K—B2 28. R—Q7 ch. B—K2 29. P—K5 P×P 30. Q—B5 ch. K—K1 31. Q—K6, and wins.

4	...	P—KKt3
5	P—KR4	

A typically Russian idea, in which White poses novel problems to his opponent in the very opening. If in reply 5... P—KR4 White can develop a minor piece at KKt5, while if 5... B—Kt2 6. P—R5.

5	...	P—KR3
6	P—K3	B—Kt2

32. ENGLISH OPENING

7 B—B4	Kt—Kt3
8 B—Kt3	P—QB4
9 Kt—K4?	

Overlooking the reply: better is 9. P—Q4 P×P 10. Kt×P Kt—B3, with equality.

9 ...	P—B5
10 B×P	Kt×B
11 Q—R4 ch.	Kt—B3
12 Q×Kt	B—B4

In return for the pawn sacrifice Black has the two bishops, the more active pieces, and a gaping hole at White's Q3.

| 13 Kt—B5 | R—QB1 |
| 14 P—KKt4 | |

If 14. Kt×P Q—Kt3 15. Kt—B5 Kt—Kt5, while if 14. P—Q4 P—Kt3.

| 14 ... | P—QKt4! |

Stronger than 14... B—Q2 15. Q—K4 Now if 15. Q—B4 B—Q6, White's king is trapped in the centre.

15 Q×P	B×KKtP
16 Kt—R2	B—B4
17 P—K4	

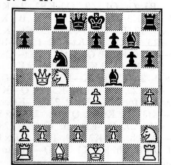

| 17 ... | Castles! |

Black chooses the quickest way to win. Less clear is 17... B—R6 18. Q—Kt3 B—Kt7 19. R—KKt1.

18 P×B	Q—Q4
19 Castles	P×P
20 P—Q3	Kt—Q5
21 Resigns.	

Black wins the queen or mates by ...Kt—K7.

---

139 WHITE: BARSHAUSKAS—BLACK: CHESNAUSKAS

Lithuanian Championship, 1955

1 P—QB4	Kt—KB3
2 Kt—QB3	P—K3
3 P—K4	P—Q4

After 3... P—QB4 4. P—K5 Kt—Kt1 5. Kt—B3 Kt—QB3 6. P—Q4 P×P White can make an interesting pawn sacrifice by 7. Kt×P Kt×P 8. B—B4. The continuation in a game, *Sokolsky-Roizman, Minsk, 1958*, was 8... P—B3 9. Q—R4 B—Q3? (better 9... Kt—Kt3) 10. B—Kt3 B—Kt1 11. Castles K—B2 12. B—K2 Kt—K2 13. P—B5 Kt(K2)—B3 14. Kt×P! K×Kt 15. P—B4 R—K1 (if 15... Kt—Kt3 16. P—B5 ch. K×P 17. Q—Kt4 mate) 16. P×Kt Kt×P 17. B—R5 P—KKt3 18. Q—Kt3 ch. K—B4 19. KR—B1 ch. K—Kt4 20. Kt—K4 ch. K×B 21. B×Kt Resigns because of 22. Q—R3 mate or 22. Kt×P ch. An exhilarating king hunt.

| 4 P—K5 | KKt—Q2 |

Losing time in development; better is 4... P—Q5 5. P×Kt P×Kt 6. KtP×P Q×P 7. P—Q4 P—B4 8. Kt—B3 P—KR3 9. B—K2 P×P 10. P×P B—Kt5 ch.

5 P—Q4	P×P
6 B×P	Kt—Kt3
7 B—Kt3	P—QB4
8 Kt—B3	Kt—B3
9 B—K3	P×P
10 Kt×P	Kt×P

Acceptance of White's pawn sacrifice increases White's lead in mobility. Better is 10... Kt×Kt 11. B×Kt B—Q2 with no serious positional weaknesses.

| 11 Q—R5 | Q—B3 |
| 12 Kt—K4 | Kt—Q6 ch. |

For the next few moves Black strives to save himself by tactical means, but such a plan must be unsound in view of White's plus in development.

| 13 K—Q2 | Q—K4 |
| 14 Kt—KKt5 | P—Kt3 |

15	Q—B3	P—B3
16	K×Kt	P×Kt
17	KR—K1	B—B4

Black is already desperate, but after 17... B—K2 18. QR—Q1 Black is still in great danger. Clarke in the *British Chess Magazine* gives the variation 18... R—B1 19. Q—R3 P—KR4 20. KB×P P—Kt5 21. Q—Kt3 Q×Q 22. RP×Q, with great advantage to White.

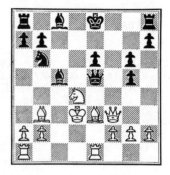

18 Kt×P?

White's one hesitancy in an otherwise well conducted attack; correct is 18. B×KP B×B 19. Kt×B, and Black's exposed king is powerless.

18	...	B×Kt
19	B×QB	R—Q1 ch.?

Clarke points out the difficult drawing chance of 19... R—KB1 20. B—B7 ch. R×B 21. B×B R×Q ch. 22. P×R R—Q1 ch. 23. K—B2 R—Q4 24. R×Q ch. R×R, with an equal ending.

20	K—B2	R—KB1
21	B—B7 ch.!	K—Q2

The difference is that after 21... R×B 22. B×B R×Q is not check so that White can play 23. R×Q ch., winning a rook.

22	Q×P ch.	Q—B2
23	B—K6 ch.	Resigns.

For if 23... K—Q3 24. Q×Q ch. wins a piece.

140 White: Botvinnik—Black: Sherbakov

Russian Championship, 1955

1	P—QB4	Kt—KB3
2	Kt—QB3	P—KKt3
3	P—KKt3	B—Kt2
4	B—Kt2	Castles
5	P—K4	P—Q3
6	KKt—K2	P—K4

Giving White a focal point for his later attack by P—KB4. Better is 6... P—B4, followed by ... Kt—B3 and ... Kt—K1—B2—K3—Q5, a manoeuvre suggested by Taimanov.

7	Castles	QKt—Q2
8	P—Q3	Kt—B4
9	P—B4	P—B3

Black could still obtain reasonable counterplay by 9... B—Kt5 10. P—KR3 B×Kt 11. Kt×B P×P 12. P×P Q—K2.

10	P—KR3	Kt—K3
11	P—B5	Kt—Q5
12	P—KKt4	

The dark side of Black's P—K4 is that the further advance of White's pawn storm threatens to incarcerate the black bishop by P—Kt5 and P—B6.

12	...	Kt—K1
13	B—K3	P—QR3
14	Q—Q2	P—QKt4
15	B—Kt5	

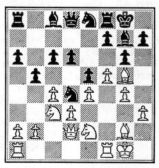

| 15 | ... | B—B3? |

Henceforward White has matters all

32. ENGLISH OPENING

his own way; Black's last hope of putting up a reasonable resistance is 15... P—B3 16. B—K3 P—Kt5 17. Kt—Q1 P—B4 18. B×Kt BP×B 19. Q×P B—R3, as suggested by Chistiakov in the tournament book.

16 B×B	Kt×B
17 Kt×Kt	P×Kt
18 Kt—K2	Q—Kt3
19 QBP×P!	

Depriving Black of his last chance of a look-in by ... P×P.

19 ...	RP×P
20 Q—R6	B—Q2
21 P—Kt5	Kt—R4
22 Kt—B4	Kt—Kt2
23 P—B6	Resigns.

For if 23... Kt—K1 24. Kt—Q5! P×Kt 25. R—B4, followed by 26. R—R4, with unavoidable mate.

33. PETROSIAN SYSTEM

141 White: Perez—Black: Bouwmeester

Vevey, 1958

1 P—K4	P—QB4
2 Kt—KB3	P—K3
3 P—Q3	P—Q4
4 QKt—Q2	P—KKt3
5 P—KKt3	B—Kt2
6 B—Kt2	Kt—K2
7 Castles	QKt—B3
8 R—K1	Q—B2?

White is playing a King's Indian Defence in reverse, a system popularized by the Russian grandmaster, Petrosian. Against Black defences played by White with a move in hand, extra care is necessary because of White's surplus tempo. Here, Black errs by delaying castling. Correct is 8... Castles 9. P—K5 Q—B2 10. Q—K2 P—B3.

The Petrosian system can also be reached from the French Defence after 1. P—K4 P—K3 2. P—Q3 P—Q4 3. Kt—Q2 P—QB4 4. P—KKt3, or by an immediate king's fianchetto. Here is an example (*Ufimtsev-Grushevsky, Alma Ata, 1958*): 1. Kt—KB3 Kt—KB3 2. P—KKt3 P—Q4 3. B—Kt2 P—K3 4. Castles B—K2 5. P—Q3 Castles 6. QKt—Q2 P—B4 7. P—K4 Kt—B3 8. P—B3 P—QKt3 9. R—K1 B—Kt2 10. P—K5 Kt—Q2 11. Kt—B1 Q—B2 (the fianchettoing of Black's QB is a bad idea against the Petrosian System because it makes it difficult for Black to

hit back in the centre with ... P—B3) 12. B—B4 P—QKt4 13. P—KR4 KR—K1 14. Kt (B1)—R2 Kt—B1 15. P—R5 QR—Q1 16. Kt—Kt4 P—Q5 17. Kt—Kt5 P×P 18. P×P Kt—Kt1 19. Kt—B6 ch. B×Kt 20. P×B P—K4 21. P×P P×B 22. P×Kt (Q) ch. R×Q 23. B×B Resigns, for if 23... Q×B 24. Q—Kt4 K—R1 25. Q×P P—B4 26. Kt—K6, winning easily.

9 P×P!

A powerful move which disorganizes Black's position. If now 9... P×P 10. Kt—Kt3 P—Kt3 11. B—B4 Q—Q2 12. P—B4.

9 ...	Kt×P
10 Kt—Kt3	Q—K2

Or 10... P—Kt3 11. P—B4 Kt (Q4)—K2 12. B—B4, followed by P—Q4, with great advantage for White.

11 Kt—Kt5   Kt—Kt3

No better is 11... Kt—B2 12. Kt—K4 Kt—R3 13. B—Kt5 P—B3 14. B—K3, winning a pawn.

12 Kt—K4	P—B5
13 P×P	Kt×P
14 Q—K2	

White makes every tempo count. If 14... Kt×P 15. P—QR4, followed by 16. P—QB3, and the knight is trapped.

14 ...	Kt—Q3
15 Kt×Kt ch.	Q×Kt

16 B—B4	Q—K2
17 QR—Q1	B—Q2
18 B—Q6	

Now the king is securely fixed in the centre.

18 ...	Q—B3
19 Kt—B5	Kt—Q5

If 19... Castles 20. Kt×P K×Kt 21. Q—Kt5 ch. and wins.

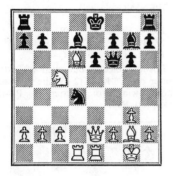

20 R×Kt!
The quickest and neatest way to force the win.

20 ...	Q×R
21 R—Q1	Q×P
22 Kt×B	R—QB1

Or 22... K×Kt 23. B—K5 dis. ch., winning the queen.

23 Kt—B5   Resigns.

Black has no defence to the triple threat of 24. B×P 24. Kt—R4, followed by 25. Q—Kt5 ch. and 24. Kt×KP.

142 White: Fischer—Black: Dr. Lapiken

Oklahoma, 1956

1 Kt—KB3	Kt—KB3
2 P—KKt3	P—Q4
3 B—Kt2	B—B4
4 Castles	P—K3
5 P—Q3	P—B3
6 QKt—Q2	Kt—R3

In this opening, White sometimes aims for Q—K1, followed by P—K4, and

... Kt—R3 is an idea of Smyslov's to answer Q—K1 by ... Kt—QKt5.

7 P—QR3	Kt—B4
8 P—B4	P—QKt4

This move is much too optimistic and is the direct cause of Black's defeat. Correct is 8... P—QR4, preventing 9. P—QKt4 and threatening 9... P—R5.

9 Kt—Q4

Taking immediate advantage of Black's mistake, White either wins a pawn or obtains the two bishops in an open position.

9 ...	Q—Q2
10 Kt×B	P×Kt
11 Kt—Kt3	

This astute move envisages a variation in which White's bishops dominate the board: 11... KtP×P 12. P×P P×P 13. Q×Q ch. K×Q 14. R—Q1 ch. K—B2 15. B—B4 ch., with an overwhelming position.

11 ...	P—KR3
12 B—K3	Kt—K3
13 Kt—Q4	P—Kt3
14 Q—Kt3	

The correct method of exploiting an advantage in development is to proceed as far as possible by direct threats, in this case 15. P×KtP. Black cannot win a piece by 14... QP×P 15. P×P Kt×Kt 16. B×Kt Q×B because of 17. B×P ch.

14 ...   R—QKt1

33. PETROSIAN SYSTEM

15 Kt×QBP

An excellent combination which breaks open the position and completely destroys Black's defence.

15 ...   Q×Kt
16 P×QP   Kt—B4
17 Q—B3   Q—Q3

Or 17... Q—Kt3 18. P—QKt4.

18 B×Kt   Q×B
19 Q×Kt   Resigns.

For if 19... R—Kt1 20. Q—K5 ch. Fischer was only thirteen at the time of this game, and his clear-cut method of exploiting Black's mistakes foreshadows the world master which he became two years later.

34. CATALAN OPENING

143 WHITE: OLAFSSON—BLACK:
           VAN SCHELTINGA
           Beverwijk, 1959

1 P—QB4   P—K3
2 P—KKt3   P—Q4
3 B—Kt2   P—QB3
4 Q—B2   P×P
5 Q×BP   P—K4

An interesting idea; although Black's KP has taken two moves to reach the fourth rank, he now develops his QB with gain of time.

6 Kt—KB3   B—Q3
7 Castles   Q—K2
8 P—K4

"Sacrificing" his Q4 square so as to obtain more scope for his pieces.

8 ...   B—K3
9 Q—B2   P—QB4
10 Kt—B3   Kt—KB3
11 Kt—KR4

White's plan is now clear: he intends to occupy the white squares in the centre.

11 ...   Castles
12 Kt—B5   Q—Q2
13 P—Q3   Kt—B3
14 B—Kt5   Kt—Q5

Here and at the next move Black goes badly wrong. He has two better continuations: 14... Kt—K1, and 14... B×Kt 15. P×B Q×P 16. P—B4 P×P 17. B×P B×B 18. R×B Q—Q2, when White has less compensation for his pawn than in the game.

15 Q—Q2   Kt×Kt?

Almost a fatal blunder. Black might still hold on by 15... B×Kt 16. P×B Kt×P 17. B—R3 KR—Q1.

16 P×Kt   B×BP
17 B×Kt   P×B
18 Kt—Q5   Q—Q1

Losing quickly, but even after the better 18... K—Kt2 White's attack should win through after 19. P—B4 P×P 20. P×P.

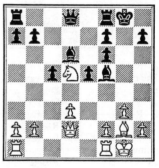

19 P—KKt4

An elegant refutation of Black's last move. If 19... B×KtP 20. Q—R6 B—K2 21. Kt×P ch. B×Kt 22. B—K4.

19 ...   B—Kt3
20 P—KR4   P—KR4

Otherwise 21. P—R5 wins a piece.

21 P×P   B—R2

If 21... B×RP 22. Q—R6 B—Kt3 23. P—R5 and wins.

22 Q—R6   B—K2
23 B—K4   P—B4
24 K—R2   Resigns.

There is no way of preventing the mating attack beginning with 25. R—Kt1 ch.

35. KING'S FIANCHETTO OPENING

144 WHITE: LARSEN—BLACK: OLAFSSON

Beverwijk, 1959

1 P—KKt3	P—K4
2 B—Kt2	P—Q4
3 P—QKt4	

A doubtful gambit; better is 3. P—QB4.

3 ...	B×P
4 P—QB4	B—K3
5 B—Kt2	Kt—QB3
6 P—B4	

White is continuing on the theme of gaining scope for his bishops, but much more important is the weakening of his pawn formation. Better is 6. Kt—KB3.

6 ...	KKt—K2
7 Kt—KB3	P—Q5

The correct method of dealing with almost all gambits; Black returns the pawn in order to pass over to the attack himself.

8 Kt×KP	Kt×Kt
9 P×Kt	Castles
10 Q—B2	

If 10. Q—R4 B—QB4 11. Q—Kt5 P—QKt3! 12. B×R Q×B, and the ruined position of White's king's side gives Black more than enough compensation for the sacrificed exchange.

10 ...	Kt—Kt3
11 B×KtP	R—Kt1
12 B—K4	

If 12. Q—K4 B×P 13. B×P R×B 14. Q×R Q×B.

12 ...	P—KB4!

Strategically the game is already decided, for if 13. P×P e.p. Q×P 14. B—KB3 Kt—K4, with an overwhelming attack, but now Black systematically prepares an irruption by ... P—B5.

13 B—Q3	Kt×P
14 Castles	B—B4
15 B—R3	Q—Q3
16 B×B	Q×B
17 Q—B1	

Hoping to be able to complete his development by 18. Kt—R3, followed by Kt—B2, but Black's attack comes much too quickly.

17 ...	P—B5
18 P×P	Kt×B
19 P×Kt	B—R6
20 R—B3	Q—KR4
21 R—Kt3	R×P
22 Kt—R3	QR—KB1
23 Kt—B2	Q—KB4
24 Resigns.	

The final position forms a neat geometrical tableau.

36. RETI OPENING

145 WHITE: BRAUN—BLACK: FUCHS

Kienbaum, 1958

1 P—KKt3	P—Q4
2 B—Kt2	P—K4
3 P—QB4	P—Q5

4 P—Q3	P—QB4
5 Kt—KB3	Kt—QB3
6 Castles	B—K2

Another strong continuation against White's passive opening plan is 6... Kt—B3 7. Kt—R3 B—K2 8. Kt—B2

127

Castles 9. B—Q2 Kt—K1 10. P—QR3
P—QR4 11. P—QKt4 P—B4 12.
P—Kt5 P—K5 13. P×Kt P×Kt
14. B×P Q—B2 15. P×P B×P 16.
B×B Q×B 17. P—QR4 R—R3 18.
R—Kt1 Q—Q2 19. Kt—K1 P—B5
20. B×BP R×B! 21. P×R Q—R6
22. P—B5 R—R3 23. Kt—B3 B—Q3
24. Resigns (*Lloyd-Gray, Cambridge,
1959*). An effective finish.

7 P—K3	B—Kt5
8 P—KR3	B—B4
9 P×P	KP×P
10 B—B4?	

White hopes for 10... Kt—B3 11.
Kt—K5, with advantage, but the
accurate move here is 10. R—K1
Kt—B3 11. B—B4.

10 ...	P—KKt4!
11 B—B1	

A sorry retreat, but if 11. B—K5
P—B3, wins a piece.

11 ...	P—KR4
12 Q—K2	

A quiet continuation like 12. R—K1
P—B3 13. Kt—R3 Q—Q2 14. K—R2
Castles, followed by ... Kt—R3 and
... Kt—Kt5 ch., gives Black a winning
attack.

12 ...	P—B3
13 Kt×KtP	P×Kt
14 B×Kt ch.	P×B
15 Q—K5	

The idea of White's counter-combina-
tion; but although he now wins material,
Black's attack becomes very strong
because of the exchange of White's
important KB.

15 ...	Q—Q2
16 Q×R	Castles
17 Q×RP	B×QP
18 Q—Kt4?	

Losing quickly, White had to play
18. B×P Q—B4 19. P—KR4 B×P
with a difficult position.

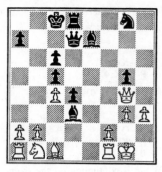

18 ...	B—B4!
19 Q—B3	R—B1
20 Q—R3	B×P
21 R—Q1	

If he sacrifices the exchange by 21.
Kt—Q2, Black does not take it at once,
but plays first 21... Q—B4.

21 ...	Q—B4
22 Q—R6 ch.	

There is no defence, for if 22. P—B3
Q—B7, or 22. R—Q2 Q—K5; in either
case with unavoidable mate.

22 ...	K—Kt1
23 Q×P	Q×P ch.
24 K—R1	B—B1!
25 Resigns.	

For if 25. Q—Kt5 ch. comes the
deadly counter-check 25... B—Kt2 ch.

146 WHITE: HANNINEN—BLACK: SZABO
Wageningen, 1957

1 Kt—KB3	Kt—KB3
2 P—QKt3	P—KKt3
3 B—Kt2	B—Kt2
4 P—Kt3	P—Q3
5 B—Kt2	P—K4
6 P—Q3	Castles
7 Castles	P—B4

Indicating that Black, intending to
concentrate on a king's side attack, is
ready to abandon his own Q4 square to
White in order to prevent White himself
playing P—Q4.

8 P—B4	Kt—R4
9 Q—Q2	Kt—QB3
10 Kt—B3	P—KR3

So as to play ... P—B4 without permitting 11. Kt—KKt5.

| 11 Kt—Q5 | P—B4 |
| 12 P—QR3 | |

Unnecessary, for White could show up the weak side of his opponent's over-sharp play by 12. P—QKt4 P×P 13. Kt×KtP Kt×Kt 14. Q×Kt P—B5 15. B—QR3 R—B3 16. Kt—Q2.

12 ...	P—B5
13 P—QKt4	Kt—Q5
14 Kt×Kt	BP×Kt
15 P—Kt5	B—K3
16 P—QR4	Q—Q2
17 B—QR3	QR—Q1
18 P—R5	

Up to here, with the exception of the inaccuracy on move 12, White has continued logically with his own queen's side offensive, but here he overlooks a trap. Much better is 18. P—Kt6 RP×P 19. Kt×KtP Q—KB2 20. P—B5, when Black is tied down to defence.

| 18 ... | B—R6 |

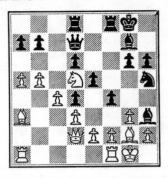

19 B×P
19. P—Kt6 is still better.

| 19 ... | B×B! |

The refutation.

| 20 B×R | Q—R6 |
| 21 B×B | P—B6 |

The point of the combination; Black threatens both 21... B×R and 21... B—R8.

22 P×P	B×P
23 Kt—K3	K×B
24 Q—Kt4	R—Q2
25 R—R2	Kt—B3
26 Resigns.	

There is no defence to 26... Kt—Kt5.

37. RETI DUTCH AND RETI STAUNTON GAMBIT

147 WHITE: ZIMMERMANN—BLACK:
WALTHER

Zurich, 1955

| 1 Kt—KB3 | P—KB4 |
| 2 P—KKt3 | |

For the gambit continuation, 2. P—K4 see the following game.

2 ...	Kt—KB3
3 B—Kt2	P—KKt3
4 P—B4	

This move, which allows the black KB a long diagonal, is always suspect in the so-called Leningrad variation characterized by Black's king's fianchetto. Strangely enough, throughout the following part of the game, White does nothing to stop Black's black-squared preponderance (P—K3 and P—Q4).

4 ...	B—Kt2
5 Kt—B3	Castles
6 Castles	P—B4
7 P—Q3	P—Q3
8 B—Q2	Kt—R4
9 Q—B1	

Resolutely refusing to play P—K3.

| 9 ... | P—B5! |

A positional sacrifice increasing the power of his KR and QB.

10 P×P	Kt—QB3
11 Kt—K4	B—R3
12 Kt (K4)—Kt5	

Why he does not even now play P—K3 is a mystery. After the text move "the fun starts in earnest".

12 ...	B—Kt5
13 P—KR3	B×Kt (Kt4)!
14 P×KB	

For whether 14. Kt×B Kt—Q5 or 14. P×QB Kt×P, the threat against his KP greatly incommodates White. The text, on the other hand, allows a "positional" sacrifice on his KB3.

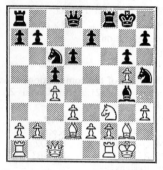

14 ...	B×Kt
15 B×B	R×B!
16 P×R	Kt—Q5
17 Q—Q1	Q—Q2
18 K—Kt2	R—KB1
19 P—B4	R×P!

Knights are more valuable than rooks in this game. The finish is a classic attack with queen and two knights, the latter being shed in the course of it.

20 B×R	Kt×B ch.
21 K—Kt3	Q×P ch.
22 K×Kt	Kt—K3 ch.
23 K—K4	Kt×P ch.
24 K—B4	P—K4 ch.!

The fifth and last sacrifice. Now Black's queen and king finish the job by themselves.

25 K×Kt	K—Kt2!
Resigns.	

The whole white force cannot stop mate by P—R3.

---

148 WHITE: ROBATSCH—BLACK: WEGHOFER

Kapfenberg, 1955

1 Kt—KB3	P—KB4
2 P—K4	P×P
3 Kt—Kt5	Kt—KB3
4 P—Q3	P—K4

This, or P—Q4, are the recognized replies to this original and dangerous gambit. After 4... P×P, on the other hand, White gets an attack that is probably irresistible.

5 P×P	P—Q4?

P—K4 or P—Q4, but not both! With this move Black starts a wild attack with totally inadequate means and soon pays the penalty.

6 P×P	Q×P
7 B—Q2	B—QB4
8 Kt—QB3	Q—Q5
9 Q—K2	Kt—Kt5

All in the same style.

10 KKt—K4	B—Kt3
11 P—KR3	Kt—KB3
12 Kt×Kt ch.	P×Kt
13 Q—R5 ch.	

The result of Black's fantastic ideas is that he is totally undeveloped, which enables White to take over the attack immediately.

13 ...	K—K2
14 Castles	B—K3
15 B—KKt5!	

37. RETI DUTCH AND RETI STAUNTON GAMBIT

15 ...   Q—QKt5

Running into a mate. The only chance to prolong the game consisted in 15... Q×R ch., followed by P×B, but this desperate remedy would have cost too many pawns.

16	P—R3	Q—R4
17	B×P ch.!	K×B
18	Kt—K4 ch.	Resigns.

For 18... K—Kt2 would have led to 19. Q—Kt5 ch. K—B2 20. Q—B6 ch. and 21. R—Q8 mate.

38. BIRD'S OPENING

149 WHITE: LAABER—BLACK: HÖGBORG
By Correspondence, 1954/55

1	P—KB4	P—Q4
2	P—K3	Kt—KB3
3	Kt—KB3	P—B4
4	P—QKt3	P—K3
5	B—Kt2	B—Q3

As in the famous game, *Lasker-Bauer, Amsterdam, 1889*, and later played by Lasker himself (against Tartakower, at Nottingham, 1936). However, White's move in the present game, 6. Kt—K5 (keeping B—Kt5 in reserve against Kt—B3) is a significant improvement over the older 6. B—Q3. Laaber is probably right in his remark that the black KB should be developed to K2 or KKt2.

6	Kt—K5	Castles
7	B—Q3	Kt—K5

To stop 8. Q—B3, after which White, in full control of both K4 and K5, would already threaten a king side-attack by P—KKt4-Kt5.

8	B×Kt	P×B
9	Q—Kt4	P—B4?

After this move Black will be in permanent difficulties, largely because his QB will be completely shut out of the game. 9... P—B3! should have been played.

10	Q—R3	R—B3
11	Kt—R3	R—R3
12	Q—Kt3	B—K2

An ingenious attempt at displacing the white queen and thus relieving the attack on his KKt2, which finds a surprising refutation.

| 13 | Kt—B7! | B—R5 |

Of course not 13... K×Kt 14. Q×P ch. The text looks very strong, for if now 14. Kt×Q B×Q ch., and White cannot recapture and would then lose the knight errant.

14	Kt×R ch.!	K—B1
15	B×P ch.	K—K1
16	Kt—B4	B×Q ch.
17	P×B	

White's sacrifice of the queen—for rook, knight and pawn—has been purely positional. He has no direct attack, but his pieces are so powerfully placed that Black soon runs out of moves.

17	...	Kt—B3
18	Castles (Q)	Q—Q2
19	B—B6	P—Kt4
20	Kt—K5	Kt×Kt
21	B×Kt	Resigns.

At first glance a surprising decision, but White threatens both 22. P—Q3 and 22. Kt—Kt8. If 21... Q—B3 22. P—Q3 P×P 23. R×P Q×P 24. R—R5 Q×P 25. R—Kt5 Q—K8 ch. 26. K—Kt2 B—Kt2 27. R—Kt8 ch. K—K2 28. R—Kt7 ch. K—K1 29. B—B6 (variation by Laaber).

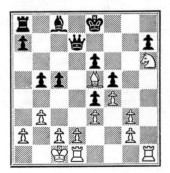

39. ORANG OUTANG OPENING

150 WHITE: SOKOLSKY—BLACK:
STRUGATSCH

White Russia, 1958

1 P—QKt4

One may—or may not—like the name "Orang Outang Opening", but it is surely nonsensical simply to ignore it and call this the "Polish Opening" as M.C.O. and some other British writers are doing. The Polish Defence consists of the moves 1. P—Q4 Kt—KB3 2. K5—KB3 P—QKt4 (as, e.g., in *Torre-Dus Chotimirsky, Moscow, 1925*) and is an ambitious attempt to stop White from reaching the Q4—QB4 set-up after he has first played Kt—KB3. Thus 1. P—QKt4 is by no means a Polish Defence with colours reversed. To call it the Polish Opening is as logical as to call 1. P—K4 the Budapest Opening.

1 ...	P—K4
2 B—Kt2	P—KB3
3 P—K4	B×P
4 B—B4	Kt—B3?

Apparently with a view to kicking the bishop off his strong diagonal (see Black's 7th move), otherwise this move, which makes the logical P—Q4 more difficult, is hard to understand. A game, *Tartakower-Colle* (*Bartfeld, 1926*) continued 4... Kt—K2 5. P—B4 P—Q4! 6. P×QP P×P 7. Q—B3 B—Q3 8. Kt—K2 Kt—Kt3 9. P—Q4 Q—K2 and Black obtained an even game.

5 P—B4	P×P

Now, when P—Q4 can no longer be played, this is quite wrong and allows White a terrific attack.

6 Kt—KR3	KKt—K2
7 Kt×P	Kt—R4?

7... P—Q4, while necessary to stop immediate disaster, is no longer sufficient to give Black a playable game, e.g.,

8. P×P Kt—R4 9. B—Q3 Castles 10. Q—R5 P—KKt3 11. B×KtP P×B 12. Kt×P P×Kt (not 12... Q—K1 13. Q—R8 ch., followed by 14. Q—R7 mate) 13. Q×P ch. K—R1 14. Castles and wins.

8 B×P!

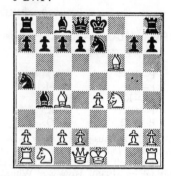

Very original. If now 8... P×B 9. Q—R5 ch. or 8... Kt×B 9. B×P, followed by 10. Q—R5 ch.

8 ...	R—B1
9 Kt—R5!	Kt×B

Now, if 9... P×B' 10. Kt—Kt7 mate, and if 9... R×B 10. Kt×R ch. P×Kt 11. Q—R5 ch. Kt—Kt3 12. B—Kt8 and Black has no means of saving the pinned knight.

10 Kt×P ch.	K—B2
11 Castles	K—Kt1
12 Q—R5	R×B
13 R×R	Kt—Kt3
14 R×Kt!	P×R
15 Q×P	K—R1

Or 15... Kt—K4 16. Q—Kt3 Q—B3 17. Kt—R5 ch. Q—Kt3 18. Q×Kt and White remains two pawns up

16 Kt—K8!	Q—K2
17 Kt—B6	Resigns.

If 17... Q—Kt2 18. Q—R5 ch. Not a profound game, but an original one.

APPENDIX

RUY LOPEZ

151 WHITE: WADE—BLACK: MARDLE

Bognor, 1960

1 P—K4	P—K4
2 Kt—KB3	Kt—QB3
3 B—Kt5	P—QR3
4 B—R4	Kt—B3
5 Castles	Kt×P
6 P—Q4	P—QKt4
7 B—Kt3	P—Q4
8 P×P	B—K3
9 P—B3	B—QB4
10 Q—Q3	

The Motzko variation, which at least has the merit of being less analysed than 10. QKt—Q2 Castles 11. B—B2 Kt×KBP or 11... P—KB4.

10 ...	P—B3

An awkward innovation to meet for the first time. The "book" here is 10... Kt—K2 or 10... Castles.

11 P×P	Q×P
12 B×P	

Into the lion's den; later analysis showed that the pawn is too hot to take and that White should decline it by 12. B—K3.

12 ...	Castles QR
13 B×B ch.	Q×B
14 Q—K2	

Choosing the wrong retreat square, since here he falls into a pin on the king's file. 14. Q—B2 is necessary.

14 ...	KR—K1
15 B—K3	

Losing by force; but equally after 15. QKt—Q2 Kt×KBP! 16. Q×Q ch. R×Q 17. R×Kt R—K7 18. Kt—Q4 Kt×Kt! Black wins material.

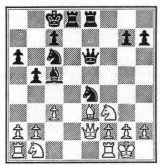

15 ...	Kt×KBP!
16 R×Kt	Q×B
17 Q×Q	R—Q8 ch.!
Resigns.	

After 18. Kt—K1 R×Kt ch. 19. Q×R R×Q is mate.

152 WHITE: BECHER—BLACK:
ACHENBACH

Heidelberg, 1960

1 P—K4	P—K4
2 Kt—KB3	Kt—QB3
3 B—Kt5	P—QR3
4 B×Kt	

Lasker's old favourite, which is rarely seen in modern tournaments; the sting of White's king's side majority can be undermined by Black's useful pair of bishops.

4 ...	QP×B
5 Kt—B3	P—B3
6 P—Q4	P×P
7 Kt×P	B—Q3

Black wrongly steers clear of the ending after 7... P—QB4 8. Kt(Q4)—K2 Q×Q ch. 9. Kt×Q B—K3 10. B—K3 Castles 11. Kt(Q1)—B3. True, he must

133

then be careful not to allow the exchange of the black-squared bishops, e.g. 11... B—Q3 12. Castles QR Kt—K2 13. B—B4! (*O'Kelly-Milev, Bucharest 1953*), but a more gradual mobilization by 11... P—QKt3 12. Castles Kt—K2 13. KR—Q1 R—K1 14. P—B3 P— KKt4 15. K—B2 B—Kt2 (*Seitz-Unzicker, Madrid 1957*), gives Black prospects of increasing his control of the board by steady encroachment.

8 B—K3   Q—K2

Upon the more natural 8... Kt—K2 White obtains useful play on the black squares by 9. Q—R5 ch. P—Kt3 10. Q—R6 (Unzicker).

9 Q—Q3   B—Q2
10 Castles QR   Castles
11 Kt—Kt3

White has a useful surplus of pieces on the queen's side in preparation for the coming attack.

11 ...   P—KR4

Preparing to develop the king's knight.

12 Kt—R4   Kt—R3
13 Kt(R4)—B5

Threatening to begin combining with 14. Kt×KtP K×Kt 15. Kt—R5 ch., followed by 16. Q×P.

13 ...   B×Kt
14 B×B   Q—K4
15 P—B3

White has eliminated Black's positional trump of the two bishops, and in view of the somewhat better situation of his minor pieces has established an advantage. This would not have amounted to much after 15... B—K3, but Black is deceived by the discovered attack on the queen into aiming for higher stakes.

15 ...   B—R6
16 Q—K3

Better than 16. Q—K2 Q—Kt4 ch.

16 ...   B×P
17 KR—Kt1   Q×RP

Black seems to have out-combined his opponent, for if 18. Q—B2 Q—B5 ch.

19. B—K3 R×R ch.   20. K×R (20. R×R Q×BP) Q—Q3 ch. and the bishop escapes, while if White interpolates 18. R×R ch. R×R 19. Q—B2 Q—B5 ch. 20. B—K3 Q×BP! (21. R×B Q—Q8 mate).

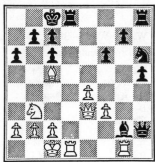

18 B—B8!

An incisive desperado move which not only anticipates the consolidation of Black's king's position by ...K—Kt1 or ...P—QKt3 but directly threatens 19. B×P. Black's reply is hopeless, but the other alternatives all lead to a quick mate:

If 18... QR×B 19. Q—R7.

If 18... KR×B 19. Q—R7 R—Q3 20. Q—R8 ch. K—Q2 21. Q×R.

If 18... Kt—B2 19. Q—R7 Kt—Q3 20. Kt—B5.

If 18... B×P 19. Q—R7 R×R ch. 20. R×R B×R 21. Q—R8 ch. K—Q2 22. Kt—B5 mate.

18 ...   R—Q3
19 B×R   P×B
20 R—Q2   Resigns.

153 WHITE: GIPSLIS—BLACK: SPASSKY
Riga, 1959

1 P—K4   P—K4
2 Kt—KB3   Kt—QB3
3 B—Kt5   Kt—B3
4 Castles   B—B4

As Spassky mischievously comments in his notes in the tournament bulletin, there is expectation that this variation will be disposed of every time it is played, but "we who choose this defence are still awaiting the refutation".

5 P—B3	Castles
6 P—Q4	B—Kt3
7 P×P	

Probably White's soundest line is 7. R—K1 P—Q3 8. P—KR3 Kt—K2 9. Q—Q3 (an idea of Matanovic's). The other attempt at a direct refutation is 7. B×Kt KtP×B 8. Kt×P Kt×P 9. R—K1, but a game *Karaklaic-O'Kelly, Bognor 1960*, showed that Black has nothing to fear after 9... Kt—Q3 (the pin after 9... Kt-B3 10. B—Kt5 cannot be tolerated) 10. B—B4 P—QR4 11. P—B4 P—B3 12. P—B5 P×Kt 13. B×P Kt—B5 14. P×B Kt×P (Kt3) 15. Kt—B3 P—Q3.

7 ...	KKt×P
8 Q—Q5	Kt—B4
9 B—Kt5	Q—K1

Better than the self-pin 9... Kt—K2.

10 QKt—Q2?

An obvious developing move, but it enables Black to embarrass the white queen. Sounder here is 10. Kt—R3.

| 10 ... | P—Q3 |

Already Black threatens 11... B—K3.

| 11 P×P | B—K3 |
| 12 B×Kt | |

White would lose quickly after 12. P—Q7 Q—Kt1 13. P—Q8(Q) R×Q.

| 12 ... | P×B |
| 13 Q—Q4 | |

Setting a couple of deep traps, but Black threads his way through the complications and reaches a clearly winning position. After the preferable 13. P—Q7 P×Q 14. P×Q(Q) KR×Q 15. Kt—Q4 B—Q2 Black would have a nice pair of bishops for the ending, but White could still fight.

| 13 ... | P—B3 |

White was hoping for 13... Kt—Kt6 14. Q—KR4 Kt×R 15. B—K7 Kt—B7

16. Q—K4 with promising counter-chances.

14 QR—K1

The best hope, for if the bishop moves Black really can play 14... Kt—Kt6.

| 14 ... | Q—Kt3 |

Avoiding the second trap. Gipslis had prepared the variation 14... P×B 15. Kt×P Q—Kt3 16. Kt×B Kt×Kt 17. Q—QB4 QR—K1 18. P—Q7 R—K2 19. Kt—B3! and Black is in a tangle.

| . 15 B—R4 | B—Q4 |
| 16 R—K2 | |

The only decent defence to the threatened 16... Kt—Q6.

| 16 ... | Kt—K5 |
| 17 Q—Q3 | |

Or 17. Q—R4 Kt×Kt 18. R×Kt B×Kt.

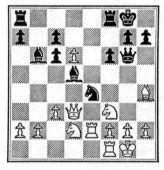

| 17 ... | Kt—Kt6 |

A typical desperado combination based on the unprotected white queen.

| 18 Q—R6 | Kt×R |

The rest is simple.

19 K×Kt	P×P
20 B—Kt3	KR—K1
21 B×P	R×R
22 Q×R	R—K1

Resigns.

If 23. Q—Q1 Q—Q6 ch. 24. K—Kt1 B×Kt; or 23. Q—R6 Q—B7 24. K—Kt1 B×Kt 25. Kt×B Q—Q8 ch. Spassky's elegant play illustrates the importance of retaining an attack rather than prematurely grabbing material.

KING'S GAMBIT

154 WHITE: MILNER-BARRY—BLACK: HAYGARTH

York, 1959

1 P—K4	P—K4
2 P—KB4	P×P
3 Kt—KB3	Kt—KB3

A sounder defence than the immediate 3... P—Q4 4. P×P Kt—KB3 when White can regain his pawn with a good game by 5. B—Kt5 ch.! A game *Spassky-Sakharov, Russian Championship 1960*, continued 5... P—B3 6. P×P P×P 7. B—B4 Kt—Q4 8. Castles B—Q3 9. Kt—B3 B—K3 10. Kt—K4 B—K2 11. B—Kt3 Castles 12. P—Q4 Kt—Q2 13. Q—K2 P—Kt4 14. P—B4 Kt(4)—Kt3 15. P—KR4 P—KR3 16. P×P P×P 17. Kt(3)×P! B×Kt 18. B×P B—B3 19. QR—Q1 B—B4 20. B—K5 B×Kt 21. Q×B B×B 22. P×B Q—Kt4 23. R—B5 Q—Kt2 24. Q—KB4 KR—K1 25. R—Kt5 Resigns.

4 Kt—B3	P—Q4
5 Kt×P	Kt×Kt
6 P×Kt	B—K2
7 B—K2	

A strangely quiet move. It is not quite apparent why White does not make the opponent work for the queen's pawn.

7...   B—R5 ch.

Although the bishop will have to retreat later, it stops White from occupying the KB-file with a rook, always an important motif in the King's Gambit.

8 K—B1	Castles
9 P—Q4	B—B3
10 B×P	B—B4
11 B—Q3	

Milner-Barry, in the *British Chess Magazine*, calls this a fatal loss of time and suggests 11. Q—Q2 Q×P 12. B×P Kt—B3 13. K—B2 instead. This would allow White to unite his rooks in time to forestall Black's domination of the K-file.

11 ...	Q×P
12 B×P	Kt—B3
13 P—B3	QR—K1

It is better for the other rook to occupy the file first.

14 K—B2	R—K2
15 B—Kt3	

For White could now have played 15. B×B! because 15... Q×B 16. B—Q6 would have cost Black the exchange.

15 ...   KR—K1

16 R—K1

This loses to an elegant combination. White had to try 16. B×B Q×B 17. Q—Q2 R—K7 ch. 18. Q×R R×Q ch. 19. K×R Q—Kt4 ch. 20. K—K3 Q×P. Black would have had the superior game, but two rooks, unless permanently separated, always offer counterplay in the long run.

16 ...	R×R
17 Kt×R	Kt×P!

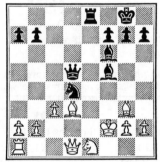

Winning by force. If now 17. B×B Q×B ch. 18. Kt—B3 Kt—B7 19. R—B1 Q—B4 ch.

18 P×Kt	Q×QP ch.
19 K—B1	R×Kt ch.!
20 K×R	B×B

This threatens 21... Q—K6 ch., which cannot be stopped by 21. Q—Q2 Q—Kt8 mate. If 21. B—B2 Q—K5 ch. 22. K—Q2 B—Kt4 ch. 23. K—B3 Q—B5 mate, and if 21. Q—B3 Q×P 22. Q×B Q×R ch. followed by Q×P ch.

21 B—B4   Q—K5 ch.

Resigns.

For if 22. K—Q2 Q×B ch. 23. K×B Q—Q5 ch. followed by Q×R.

155 White: Spassky—Black:
Bronstein

Russian Championship, 1960

1 P—K4	P—K4
2 P—KB4	P×P
3 Kt—KB3	P—Q4
4 P×P	B—Q3

Since the KBP cannot in the long run be held without the support of the KKtP, this move serves no real purpose. Exactly as in the game Spassky-Sakharov (see p. 136), the bishop only serves as a target for White's QKt and QBP.

5 Kt—B3	Kt—K2
6 P—Q4	Castles
7 B—Q3	Kt—Q2
8 Castles	P—KR3
9 Kt—K4	Kt×P

After this move the KBP will have to give way—whether by being captured or capturing itself is of no account. Thus Black has to play P—KKt4 after all if he wants to keep the KB-file closed.

10 P—B4	Kt—K6
11 B×Kt	P×B
12 P—B5	B—K2
13 B—B2	R—K1
14 Q—Q3	P—K7

So as to gain time for the defence of the king, but Spassky presses on regardless, investing a whole rook in a speculative attack.

15 Kt—Q6!	Kt—B1?

Excessive caution—or under-estimation of White's chances in the actual game? On 15... B×Kt 16. Q—R7 ch. K—B1 17. P×B Spassky himself gives 17... P×R(Q) ch. 18. R×Q P×P 19. Q—R8 ch. K—K2 20. R—K1 ch. Kt—K4 21. Q×KtP R—KKt1 22. Q×P Q—Kt3 23. K—R1 B—K3 24. P×Kt P—Q4. Since Black now threatens 25... Q—B7 one may doubt whether this is in any way advantageous for White. In practice, however, such attacks will always favour the aggressor: the time limit imposes a much more severe

strain on the defender whose single false step may lead to sudden death. Thus the ingenious 15th move fully deserves its exclamation mark.

16 Kt×KBP!

The real point of White's previous move: the rook remains to be taken.

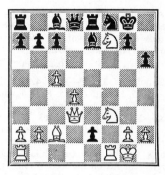

16 ...	P×R(Q) ch.
17 R×Q	B—B4

The knight is taboo, for if 17... K×Kt 18. Kt—K5 ch. K—Kt1 19. Q—R7 ch.! Kt×Q 20. B—Kt3 ch. and White mates in three more moves by Kt—Kt6. Since the text also loses in short order, 17... Q—Q4 18. B—Kt3 Q×Kt 19. B×Q ch. K×B has been suggested. Discovered checks now would not lead anywhere, but White wins by 20. Q—B4 ch.! K—Kt3 21. Q—Kt8, which stops the black king from getting back home.

18 Q×B	Q—Q2
19 Q—B4	B—B3
20 Kt(3)—K5	Q—K2
21 B—Kt3	B×Kt
22 Kt×B ch.	K—R2

If 22... K—R1 23. Q—Kt4 and Black has no defence against R×Kt ch. followed by Kt—Kt6 ch.

23 Q—K4 ch.!

Forcing the same position as in the previous note.

23 ...	Resigns.

A fantastic conception.

APPENDIX

SICILIAN DEFENCE

156 WHITE: PIETZSCH—BLACK:
O'KELLY

Madrid, 1960

1 P—K4	P—QB4
2 Kt—QB3	Kt—QB3
3 P—B4	

An unorthodox but quite playable method of meeting the Sicilian; White avoids the opening of the centre and hints at a later king's side-attack.

3 ...   P—KKt3

Simpler is 3... P—K3 4. Kt—B3 P—Q4 5. B—Kt5 (not 5. P—K5, when Black's KKt reaches a fine post at KB4) KKt—K2 6. P—Q3 P—QR3 7. B×Kt ch. Kt×B followed by ... B—K2. This formation looks more effective than a king's fianchetto since, while Black's KKtP remains on the second rank, the advance of White's KBP to B5 is less effective in breaking up the black king's defences.

4 Kt—B3	B—Kt2
5 B—Kt5	P—Q3

An interesting idea is Wade's suggestion of 5... Kt—Q5, trying to make White's last move pointless, e.g. 6. Kt×Kt P×Kt 7. Kt—K2 Kt—B3 8. P—K5 Kt—Q4 9. B—B4 Kt—Kt3 10. B—Kt3 P—Q3.

6 Castles	B—Q2
7 B×Kt	

White plans a king's side-attack with a firm pawn centre Q3/K4 as a bastion. In this scheme his white-squared bishop has no place, whereas the black knight can be active at Q5.

7 ...	B×B
8 P—Q3	Kt—B3

Around here Black has to decide how best to contest the centre. As he plays ... P—K3 and ... P—Q4 a few moves later, a more natural continuation here is 8... P—K3 9. Q—K1 Kt—K2 10. B—Q2 Castles 11. Q—R4 P—QKt4; with better counterplay than in the actual game.

9 Q—K1	P—Kt3

Obviously Black is hesitant about castling into a possible storm on the king's side, but a more definite idea is 9... Q—B2, preparing castling QR.

10 K—R1

Unnecessary; 10. B—Q2 immediately is simpler.

10 ...	Q—B2
11 B—Q2	P—K3

Opening the centre is hazardous with his king a potential target, but Black is already in a dilemma because of his previous inaccuracies. If 11... Castles KR 12. Q—R4 Kt—Q2 13. P—B5 (not 13. Q×P B—B3), followed by B—R6, Kt—KKt5, and R—B3—R3 with a tremendous attack, while after 11... Castles QR White also starts a pawn roller with 12. P—Q4, followed by P—QR4—5. In a higher sense, Black is already in *zugzwang*, and even a waiting policy would enable White to increase his control of the board by Q—R4, P—B5, and P—KKt4—5.

12 Q—R4

Threatening P—B5, followed by B—Kt5.

12 ...	P—Q4
13 P—B5	

A powerful thrust, which is far stronger than 13. P—K5 Kt—Kt1, followed by ... Kt—K2—B4. White intends P—K5 and P—B6, while if Black captures twice on his KB4, White can either regain the pawn at once by Q—Kt5 or continue the attack by B—R6. O'Kelly's reply is an attempt to keep the centre closed. If Black tries 13... QP×P 14. QP×P P—K4 with the same object, then White has the promising sacrifice 15. Kt×P! Q×Kt 16. B—B4 Q—K2 17. P—K5; while if 13... Castles KR 14. B—Kt5 is very strong.

13 ...   P—Q5

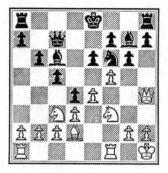

14 P×KP

The combinations begin. If 14... P×Kt 15. B×P Q—K2 16. P×P ch., followed by 17. Kt—K5, with an overwhelming attack. White had a possibly still better continuation here, however, with 14. B—B4, followed by 15. Kt—K2, keeping K5 as an accessible square for the white pieces.

14 ...	P×P
15 Kt—KKt5	

Another fine attacking move. The reply 14... P×Kt 15. Kt×KP Q—K2 16. Kt×B ch. Q×Kt 17. B×P leads to a decisive pin.

15 ...	Q—K2
16 P—K5	

The one flaw in White's attack; here 16. Kt—K2 is safer.

16 ...	P—KR3?

Overlooking his chance of defeating the combination by 16... P×Kt 17. P×Kt B×P 18. R×B P×P! (but not 18... Q×R 19. B×P P—K4 20. B×P!) 19. QR—KB1 Q×R! After 16... P×Kt 17. B×P Kt—Q4 18. R—B7 Q×R 19. Kt×Q K×Kt Black is also comfortable with three pieces for the queen.

17 Kt×P

Now the black king becomes hopelessly exposed. White can already afford to aim for higher stakes than the win of the exchange by 17. P×Kt RP×Kt 18. Q×R ch. B×Q 19. P×Q P×Kt 20. B×KtP.

17 ...	P×Kt
18 Kt×B ch.	Q×Kt
19 P×Kt	B×P ch.
20 K—Kt1	

Not 20. K×B Q—Kt2 ch. 21. K—Kt1 P×B with an unclear position; but after White's actual reply the black king is exposed to a crisp and decisive attack.

20 ...	Q—KB2
21 KR—K1 ch.	K—Q1
22 B×BP	B—B3
23 R—K7	Q—Q4
24 Q—Kt3	

Both preventing and threatening mate.

24 ...	R—QB1
25 QR—K1	P—KR4
26 R(K1)—K6	Resigns.

A game which shared the first brilliancy prize in the tournament.

CARO-KANN DEFENCE

157 WHITE: TAL—BLACK: SMYSLOV

Bled, 1959

1 P—K4	P—QB3
2 P—Q3	P—Q4
3 Kt—Q2	P—K4
4 KKt—B3	Kt—Q2
5 P—Q4!	

Seemingly all set to adopt a quiet King's Indian formation with colours reversed, White suddenly explodes the centre—and sacrifices a tempo to do so. Such a move is harder to think of than many a queen sacrifice.

5 ...	P×KP

Annotators all over the world have tried to improve on this and the next move, which merely goes to show how the impact of a sensational result tends to distort even the expert's judgment. The following opening of the game leaves Black without disadvantage, its only drawback being that it leaves the type of position Tal handles best. But this, surely, is no reason for going into such an inferior line as—to mention but one —that given by Barden in the *Manchester Guardian*: 5... B—Q3 6. P×QP BP×P 7. P×P B×P 8. Kt×B Kt×Kt 9. Kt—Kt3 Kt—KB3 10. B—KKt5, when White has the pair of bishops, the queen's side-pawn majority and control over the key square Q4—in short, all the ingredients of a winning advantage.

6 QKt×P	P×P
7 Q×P	KKt—B3
8 B—KKt5	B—K2
9 Castles	

9. Kt—Q6 ch. would leave White no advantage after 9... B×Kt 10. Q×B Kt—K5!

9...	Castles
10 Kt—Q6	Q—R4
11 B—QB4	P—Kt4?

An oversharp move played with a view to ultimately trapping the white KB, this is quite uncharacteristic of Smyslov, who must have had ideas of "punishing" White's unorthodox opening. 11... Kt—Kt3 would not only have been simple and strong, but also in Smyslov's style.

| 12 B—Q2 | Q—R3 |
| 13 Kt—B5 | B—Q1 |

Black must retain his support of the square KB3. Against 13... B—QB4? Trifunovic, in the *Neue Zürcher Zeitung*, gives the lovely variation 14. Q—R4 P×B 15. B—B3 Q×P 16. R×Kt! B×R 17. Kt-R6 ch. K—R1 18. Q×Kt! This line contains a great deal of what follows in the game.

14 Q—R4!

It is certainly surprising that even with KB3 firmly held by Black this sacrifice is possible.

| 14... | P×B |
| 15 Q—Kt5 | Kt—R4 |

Returning the piece, so as to gain time for his counter-attack against the QRP. After the game Smyslov described this move as the decisive mistake and recom-

mended 15... P—Kt3 instead. But the text is perfectly good—and the recommendation perfectly bad after 16. B—B3! Q×P 17. Kt—R6 ch. K—Kt2 18. Kt—Kt4 P—KR4 (best), when White has the choice between 19. Q—R6 ch. K—Kt1 20. Kt—Kt5 (threatening 21. Q—R7 ch. followed by Kt—R6 mate) P×Kt 21. R×Kt B—R4! 22. Kt—K6! Q—R8 ch. 23. K—Q2 Kt—K5 ch. 24. K—K2 Kt×B ch. 25. P×Kt and wins (Euwe) and 19. R×Kt P×Kt 20. R×B Q—R8 ch. 21. K—Q2 R×R ch. 22. K—K3 R—K1 ch. 23. K—B4 Q×R 24. B×Kt ch. K—Kt1 25. Q—R4! and wins (Barden).

| 16 Kt—R6 ch. | K—R1 |
| 17 Q×Kt | Q×P! |

Consistently following his defensive plan. Feeble would have been 17... P×Kt? 18. B—B3 ch. P—B3 (if 18... B—B3 19. B×B ch. Kt×B 20. Q×RP, etc.) 19. Q×P R—KKt1 20. Kt—Kt5! R—Kt2 21. Kt—K6 R—Kt3 22. R×Kt! B×R 23. Q—B8 ch. and mates in three.

18 B—B3

18... Kt—B3?

Only this loses. Admittedly 18... P—B3 would have allowed White to maintain his pressure after 19. KR—K1 (the Kt is still taboo!) but 18... B—B3! discovered by Barden, seems to put an end to the white attack. Best play for both sides would then lead to a repetition of moves after 19. B×B Kt×B 20. Q×P! Q—R8 ch. 21. K—Q2 Q—R4 ch. 22. K—B1 Q—R8 ch., etc. If White tries to avoid the draw by 22. K—K2, Black would reply 22... R×Q! (but not 22... R—K1 ch.? 23. K—B1 B—R3 24. Q—Kt8 ch.!) 23. R—Q8 ch. Q×R 24. Kt×R ch. K—Kt1 25. Kt×Q B—R3 26. Kt×P P—B6 ch. dis. ch.; if Black tries for more after 22. K—B1 R×Q? 23. R—Q8 ch. Q×R 24. Kt×R ch. K—Kt1 25. Kt×Q B—Q2 26. Kt—Kt7, the doubled pawns and bad bishop give him the inferior ending.

| 19 Q×P! | Q—R8 ch. |
| 20 K—Q2 | R×Q |

There is nothing better. Whatever checks Black resorts to are pointless because the black queen would always remain *en prise*.

21 Kt×R ch.	K—Kt1
22 R×Q	K×Kt
23 Kt—K5 ch.	K—K3
24 Kt×P(B6)	Kt—K5 ch.
25 K—K3	B—Kt3 ch.
26 B—Q4	Resigns.

Possibly the most discussed, disputed and analysed game of the last decade.

QUEEN'S GAMBIT ACCEPTED

158 WHITE: TAIMANOV—BLACK: POLUGAEVSKY

Russian Championship, 1960

1 P—Q4	P—Q4
2 P—QB4	P×P
3 Kt—KB3	Kt—KB3
4 Q—R4 ch.	QKt—Q2

Whenever Black plays this move he must take great care that the game is not suddenly opened. The move seriously retards the development of Black's queen side, which will be fatal if his king can be caught on the open centre files. The present game is a striking illustration of this theme.

5 Kt—B3	P—K3
6 P—K4	P—B4
7 P—Q5!	

With this and the next move, the opening of the centre files is accomplished.

| 7... | P×P |
| 8 P—K5 | P—Q5 |

The books used to recommend 8... P—QKt4 9. Q×KtP R—QKt1 10. Q—R4 P—Q5 11. P×Kt P×Kt 12. B×P R—Kt5, but this has been exploded by 13. Q—Q1! when the white attack gains too much momentum. Likewise, 12... P×KtP 13. B×P ch. K×B 14. Kt—Kt5 ch. has been found wanting for Black. With the text he loses

so much time that White can offer his queen in another four moves.

9 B×P	P×Kt
10 P×Kt	Q×P
11 B—KKt5	Q—B3
12 Castles (Q)!	

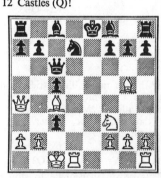

Startling at first glance, but you only have to look at Black's "development" not to be surprised. If now 12... Q×Q 13. KR—K1 ch. B—K2 14. R×B ch. K—B1 15. R×P ch. K—Kt1 16. R×Kt ch. Q×B 17. R—Q8 ch. K—B2 18. Kt—K5 ch., regaining the queen with a piece to the good.

12...	P×P ch.
13 K×P	B—K2
14 KR—K1	P—B3
15 B—Kt5	Q—Kt3
16 K—B1	

A quiet but deadly unpin.

16...	P×B
17 B×Kt ch.	K—B1
18 R×B!	K×R
19 Q—K4 ch.	K—Q1
20 B—B5 ch.	K—B2
21 Q—K5 ch.	K—B3

22 R—Q6 ch.	K—Kt4
23 Q—Kt2 ch.	Resigns.

Mate in three is unavoidable: 23... K—R4 24. Q—R3 ch. K—Kt4 25. Kt—Q4 ch. P×Kt (or K—B5) 26. B—Q3 mate. One of the most spectacular contemporary miniatures.

ALBIN COUNTER GAMBIT

159 WHITE: SPASSKY—BLACK: MIKENAS

Riga, 1959

1 P—Q4	P—Q4
2 P—QB4	P—K4
3 P×KP	P—Q5
4 P—K4	

A rarely-played line with which White abandons the attempt to "tickle" the QP, which is the main theme of most lines against the Albin.

4...	Kt—QB3
5 P—B4	P—KKt4
6 P—KB5	K×P
7 Kt—KB3	B—Kt5 ch.
8 QKt—Q2	Kt—QB3
9 B—Q3	P—Kt5

With this move Black tries to disorganize the white game—but White replies with the "Muzio" idea of giving up the knight for further gain in development.

10 Castles!	P×Kt
11 Kt×P	B—Q3

This proves inadequate to stop the threatened advance of the KP. Black has to try 11... P—B3 despite the obvious dangers on White's KR5—K8 diagonal.

12 P—K5!	Kt×P
13 R—K1	P—KB3
14 P—B5	B—K2

Hoping to gain time by the temporary obstruction of the K-file. After 14... B×QBP 15. Kt×Kt P×Kt 16. R×P ch., White has no problems.

15 Kt×Kt	P×Kt
16 R×P	Kt—B3

17 B—KKt5	Castles
18 Q—Kt3 ch.	K—R1

18... K—Kt2 would be answered with 19. QR—K1 R—K1 20. B—QB4, with the double threat of B—B7 and Q—KR3.

19 QR—K1

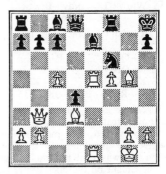

By the simplest means White recovers his piece, retaining a great positional advantage.

19...	KB×P
20 R×B	

White could have simplified to a probably winning ending by 20. R—K8 Q—Q3 21. Q—B7 Kt—Kt1 22. R×R Q×R 23. Q×Q B×Q 24. R—K8 K—Kt2 25. P—B6 ch., but his pieces are so much better placed than those of his opponent that a decisive material advantage is to be expected before long.

20...	Q—Q3
21 R(B)—K5	Kt—Kt5
22 B—KB4	B—Q2
23 B—Kt3	B—B3
24 R(5)—K4	Resigns.

142

GRÜNFELD DEFENCE

160 WHITE: GLIGORIC—BLACK:
UHLMANN

Hastings, 1959-60

1 P—Q4	Kt—KB3
2 P—QB4	P—KKt3
3 Kt—QB3	P—Q4
4 Kt—B3	B—Kt2
5 P—K3	Castles
6 B—K2	P—B3

One of the nuances of modern opening play is for White to transpose into black defences with a move in hand. Here, after the obvious 6... P—B4 7. Castles Kt—B3, White would be playing a Tarrasch Defence with colours reversed and hence a tempo extra.

7 Castles	B—B4

A bad error for a grandmaster; in many variations of the Queen's Gambit Black cannot develop his QB while White is in a position to attack the queen's side with Q—Kt3. Correct here s 7... P—K3; followed by ... P—Kt3 ... B—Kt2 and ... QKt—Q2.

8 P×P	Kt×P

Now White controls the centre, for if 8... P×P 9. Q—Kt3 P—Kt3 10. B—Q2 followed by KR—B1, when White occupies the QB file with his rooks and queen and eventually penetrates at QB7.

9 Q—Kt3	Kt—Kt3
10 R—Q1	QKt—Q2
11 P—K4	B—K3
12 Q—B2	B—Kt5

Another artificiality. Black should follow the golden rule of cramped positions and exchange bishops by 12... B—B5; although White retains the initiative by 13. P—QR4 or 13. B—K3.

13 B—KKt5	Q—K1
14 P—QR4	P—K4

Still hoping to obtain counterplay in the centre. If 14... P—QR4 15. Q—Kt3 P—K4 16. P×P and Black has to exchange his important fianchettoed bishop.

15 P—Q5

Otherwise Black's KB would jump into the game.

15 ...   P×P

Another mistake, and this time a decisive one. 15... P—QR4 is essential, even though White would retain a clear advantage by 16. Q—Kt3.

16 P—R5!	P—Q5

Black is betwixt the devil and the deep. If he accepts the sacrificed pawn, then after 16... P×P 17. Q×P B—B4 (17... B×Kt 18. Q×B Kt—B1 19. Q×P) 18. Q—QKt4 (but not 18. Q×KtP Kt—B4) Kt—B1 19. Kt—Q5, and the opening of the position leaves Black terribly cramped; White's pieces are dominating the board.

17 P×Kt	P×Kt
18 P×RP	P×P
19 Q×P	Kt—B4
20 Q—Kt4	Q—B3

20... Kt—K3 21. B—K7 also loses the exchange.

21 B—K7   KR—B1

Black could play on a while by sacrificing the exchange, but he would have no reasonable defence owing to the powerful pawn on QR7. Now, however, he loses a full rook.

22 B×Kt	Q×B
23 R—Q8 ch.	Resigns.

A drastic demonstration of the dangers of Black's developing the QB prematurely in a queen's side opening.

ANGLO-DUTCH OPENING

161 WHITE: GIUSTOLISI—BLACK: ZICHICHI

Lerici, 1959

1 P—QB4	P—K4
2 Kt—QB3	P—Q3
3 P—KKt3	P—KB4

This build-up, with the pawns on KB4, K4 and Q3, was a great favourite of the late grandmaster Nimzovitch, who tried to force it even against an early P—Q4 by White. In that case it is distinctly double-edged, whereas against P—QB4 followed by P—Q3 it offers Black excellent play.

4 B—Kt2	Kt—KB3
5 P—Q3	P—KKt3
6 R—Kt1	

L'Italia Scacchistica suggests 6. B—Q2, so as to provide cover for the knight and threaten an immediate advance by P—QKt4, and also retain the option on the manoeuvre Q—B1 followed by B—KR6.

6 ...	P—QR4
7 P—QR3	B—Kt2
8 Kt—B3	Castles
9 Castles	Kt—B3
10 P—QKt4	P×P
11 P×P	P—R3
12 Kt—K1	

Trying to contain the advance of Black's king side-pawns, but it soon becomes apparent that without an eventual P—Q4 White has no prospects of counterplay anywhere and has to wait passively for the king side-attack to mature.

12 ...	P—KKt4
13 P—K3	Kt—K2
14 P—B4	Kt—Kt3
15 P×KtP	

White wishes to stop the systematic continuation of Black's attack by P—Kt5 P—R4—R5, but in doing so may have overlooked the pawn sacrifice on move 18, which tears his position to bits.

15 ...	P×P
16 Kt—Q5	P—Kt5!
17 P—Kt5	Kt—R2
18 P—K4	P—B5!
19 P×P	P×P
20. Kt×KBP	

20. B×P? would allow 20... P—B3 21. P×P P P×P 22. Kt—Kt6 B—Q5 ch.

20 ...	B—Q5 ch.
21. K—R1	Q—R5!

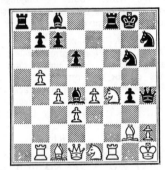

22. P—K5

For 22. Kt×Kt? R×R ch. 23. B×R Q—B7 would lead to mate.

| 22 ... | R—R7 |

Now even the queen's rook, freed from the burden of his *vis-à-vis* on the 6th move, takes a hand in the king side-attack. The end is elegant.

23 B—Q5 ch.	K—R1
24 Kt(1)—Kt2	P—Kt6!
25 Q—R5	R×Kt!

Resigns. He had three alternatives: 26. Q×Q R×R mate; 26. Kt×R R×P mate; and 26. R×R Q×Q.

INDEX
OF PLAYERS

The numbers refer to games

Adams	32	Canal	66, 92, 102a	
Ahlbach	65	Canisius College	37	
Ahman	84	Casas	82	
Alekseev	56a	Chesnauskas	139	
Alexander	5, 20	Christoffel	93	
Ambarian	58a	Christoffersen	88	
Andersen	73	Ciocaltea	21	
Andor	69a	Cipriani	36	
Angos	115	Clemenz	22	
Anokhin	90	Corte	1	
Asafov	111	Czerniak	77	
Averbakh	114a, 121			
		Darga	112, 113	
Baker	111a	Deutgen	135	
Balanel	123	Diemer	47, 101, 101a	
Balogh	78	Donner	105	
Barda	102	Dorrer	18	
Barendregt	39	Dreyer	9a	
Barnstedt	76	Dubinin	63a	
Barshauskas	139	Dubyna	125	
Bartsch	100	Dückstein	5a	
Bastrikov	122	Durao	3	
Behrenbruch	48d	Durasevic	134	
Behrensen	60	Dyckhoff	126	
Beni	137	Dyner	107	
Bennett	118a			
Bilek	70	Edgar	103	
Bisguier	14, 111a	Eisenschmidt	22	
Blau	23	Enevoldsen	13	
Bobotsov	121a	Eriksen	9a	
Boey	57	Espeli	73	
Bogolyubov	76	Euwe	5, 105	
Bolbochan, Jac.	1			
Bolbochan, Jul.	87			
Boleslavsky	51, 61, 67a	Fahnenschmidt	4	
Bonsdorff	42	Farré	11, 48	
Borisenko	85, 86, 86a	Feigin	132	
Botvinnik	116a, 128, 137a, 140	Feuerstein	118a	
Bouwmeester	141	Fichtl	41, 68	
Boxall	61a	Filip	137	
Bozic	116	Fischer	142	
Braun	145	Florian	131	
Bronstein	70, 106	Foltys	4a	
Brzozka	21	Foulds	46	
Buslaev	109	Franco	50	

Franklin	56	Kakabadze	74
Freeman	114	Kalkstein	51a
Fuchs	145	Kanayan	48a
Fuderer	6a	Karakhan	74
Fuller	101	Karaklaic	8, 81
Furman	91	Karl	29
		Keller	78a, 94
Galula	49	Keres	6, 20, 35, 58, 85,
Geller	54, 112a, 127		112a
Gereben	68, 83	Kiarner	117
Gerusel	130a	Kilyin	80
Giusti	36	Kinzel	5a
Gladkov	12	Kloss	101a
Gligoric	51a	Klovan	63
Goldin	58a	Kluger	31a, 59
Golombek	127	Koch	126
Gonzalez	129	Komarov	83
Gorfinkel	86a	Kondratjev	50a
Graf	95	Koranyi	67
Granitzky	69	Korchnoi	104, 117a, 134
Grau	97	Kunin	40
Gruber	116		
Grushevsky	141a		
Gudmundsson	48, 62a	Laaber	149
Gurgenidze	80	Lang	46
		Lange	72
		Lapiken	142
Haag	67	Larsen	144
Hanninen	31, 146	Leone	49
Harksen	88	Lepichin	24, 56a
Harnik	71	Liipola	42
Hearst	56	Lombardy	130a
Heidenfeld	2, 33	Lott	103
Herter	46a		
Herzog	9		
Högborg	149	Makarczyk	130
Honfi	31a	Malmgren	84
Horne	27	Mardle	7
Horowitz	66a	Marshall	30
Horseman	27, 108	Martin	23a
		Matanovic	15
Illig	47	Matchett	122a
Incutto	6	Matulovic	45
		Medina	99
		Mednis	114
Janosevic	15, 43	Menchik	95
Jaroslavtsev	86	Mertins	38
Jennen	100	Meyer	104a
Jezek	61	Mieses	71
Johansson	96	Milev	89
Joppen	48b	Milner-Barry	31
Junge	62	Miroshnichenko	90

Monticelli 132
Mora 72
Moran 50
Mühlberg 114a, 121a
Muth 136

Nagy 59
Najdorf 133, 137a
Navarovszky 131
Naylor 120
Ney 138
Nievergelt 46a
Nilsson 96

Ochsengoit 40
O'Kelly 57, 65, 122a
Olafsson 52, 62a, 64, 118, 143, 144
Opocensky 122b
Oren 107
Oxford University 37

Pachman 87
Padevsky 117a
Panno 94
Pedersen 78a
Penrose 23
Perez 55, 141
Perfors 44
Perrine 129
Piazzini 82
Pilnik 64
Pirc 79
Plater 105a
Podgorny 28
Pomar 11
Pompei 23a
Posch 18
Prins 3
Pritchard 98
Puiggros 19
Pukudruva 63

Rabar 45, 109a
Radulescu 79
Ravinsky 106
Rellstab 8
Reti 97
Rhodin 48c, 48d

Robatsch 81, 148
Rochlin 7a
Roiter 67a
Roizman 139a
Rojahn 77, 115
Rosenberg 96a
Rossetto 34, 60
Rossolimo 4a, 102
Rovner 50a
Rozhdestvensky 117
Rozman 25
Rubenchik 48a

Sämisch 26, 99
Sahlmann 62
Sajtar 58
Sandor 78
Sanguinetti 19
Scafarelli 66
Schmeil 38
Schmid 9, 13, 17, 104a, 120a, 135, 136
Schneider 48b
Scholtens 75
Schuster 29
Shaposhnikov 122, 138a
Shamkovich 138, 138a
Sherbakov 53, 140
Siegel 48c
Sliwa 130
Smollny 111
Smyslov 105a, 116a, 120a, 124
Söderborg 52
Sokolsky 139a, 150
Soultanbéieff 8a, 125
Spassky 6a
Stahlberg 34
Sterner 51
Stoltz 26
Strugatsch 150
Stulik 28
Stumpers 119
Suetin 63a
Szabo 118, 146
Szekely 92
Szukszta 110

Taimanov 53
Tal 10, 89, 110
Tarasov 24, 109

INDEX OF PLAYERS

Tartakower	69*a*, 96*a*, 119	Vidmar	93
Tchigorin	21*a*	Von Soldatenkov	30
Teschner	10		
Thal	69		
Timchenko	16	Wade	35, 61*a*, 113, 120
Tolush	91, 121	Wallis	108
Toran	14, 55, 102*a*, 112	Walther	147
Torre	32	Weghofer	148
Toth	133	Welz	17
		Winiwarter	41
		Wirtz	4
Ufimtsev	141*a*	Wolpert	33
Ugrinovic	43	Woolverton	98
Uhlmann	123, 124, 128	Wysowski	25
Van Oosterwijk		Zaitsev	7*a*, 16
Bruin	39, 75	Zietemann	2
Van Scheltinga	122*b*, 143	Zilber	104
Van Seters	44	Zimmermann	147
Varain	14*a*	Znosko-Borovsky	109*a*
Vatnikov	54	Zvorykina	12

INDEX OF PLAYERS IN THE APPENDIX

Achenbach	152	Pietzsch	156
Becher	152	Polugaevsky	158
Bronstein	155	Sakharov	154*a*
Gipslis	153	Smyslov	157
Giustolisi	161	Spassky	153, 154*a*, 155, 159
Gligoric	160	Taimanov	158
Haygarth	154	Tal	157
Mardle	151	Uhlmann	160
Mikenas	159	Wade	151
Milner-Barry	154	Zichichi	161
O'Kelly	156		